FRENCH INVASION ALGERIAN RESISTANCE (1830-1871)

S.E. Al-Djazairi

MSBN Books

S.E. Al-Djazairi: French Invasion - Algerian Resistance (1830-1871)
Published by MSBN Books
2017 edition
Website: msbnbooks.co.uk
Email: info@msbnbooks.co.uk
ISBN: 9781973148036

Design and Artwork: N. Kern

S.E. Al-Djazairi lectured and researched at the University of Constantine in Algeria for more than ten years. He also tutored at the Department of Geography of the University of Manchester, and worked as a research assistant at UMIST (Manchester) in the field of History of Science.

He has published many academic works. Publications in scientific journals include papers on environmental degradation and desertification as well as papers on politics and change in North Africa, and problems of economic and social development. He has also contributed historical entries to various encyclopaedias such as the Columbia Gazetteer, Encyclopaedia Britannica, Francophone Studies, and the Oxford Encyclopaedia of Philosophy, Science and Technology in Islam.

Other works by the same author: consult the internet.

CONTENTS

INTRODUCTION 1

1 FRENCH COLONISATION OF ALGERIA UNMUDDLED 11

2 THE CONQUEST OF ALGERIA 35

3 THE MILITARY CAMPAIGN IN THE EAST 58

4 EMIR ABD AL KADER 84

5 TOTAL WAR 104

6 ALGERIAN RESILIENCE 126

7 THE DESTRUCTION OF ALGERIAN SOCIETY 157

CONCLUDING WORDS 181

SELECT BIBLIOGRAPHY 182

Mediterranean

Skikda   Annaba
Bejaia
ALGIERS   Constantine
Oran
• Tlemcen

Morocco

Tunisia

• Touggourt

• Béchar

• Tindouf

• In-Amenas

Libya

Sahara

Tamanrasset
•

INTRODUCTION

Colonel Montagnac, one of the better known French officers of the Algerian colonial war (killed in combat, 23 September 1845), writing to his uncle on 31 March 1842, recounts:

> On 24 February we set off again at night. Snow is falling quite hard. We cannot see beyond ten paces. We are in a wooded area, and in front of us the Arabs are fleeing: horses dropping their loads, camels running in panic. Women and children caught in the sharp, thick bush, seeking to escape our charge. We kill; we slit throats; cries of pain and fear fill the air; the cries of the dying mixing with those of the animals, coming from all directions. It is hell, where instead of fire it is snow drowning us. The weather is atrocious, and it gives this scene an even darker character. Every soldier returns with a few wretched women or children whom he has chased like beasts running in front of him, or he holds by the neck a man who still tries to resist.
>
> Meanwhile another tribe, and the same scene, but there is a ravine, and the herds plunge down... There could only be heard the sounds of animals and children we have caught in the arms of their mothers dying of cold.
>
> The night is thick, and the faint and intermittent rays of the moon cut through the snow which has interposed itself between it and earth. The women and children are all huddled around, exposed to the horrid weather of this horrible night; the women press their bosoms against their children that cold had already made stiff; their groans mix with the moans of the little ones.
>
> We march back to the site where we passed the previous night, there, the ground is strewn with corpses of goats, sheep, dead from cold, men, women, and children, caught in the undergrowth, dead or dying.[1]

Montagnac's memoirs, just as those of other French officers, without a single exception, as to be amply seen in this work, are full of similar accounts. Perhaps hundreds, maybe even thousands of them, depict the systematic destruction of Algerian way of life and lives. Every officer saw his actions only as part of his duty, namely the removal of fanatical barbarians impeding the march of civilisation; a service rendered to his name and career, and most of all a service rendered to France and her grandeur. In return, France, to this very day celebrates the acts of these men, and the colonisation of Algeria is still regarded in France as a great deed of civilisation. On 23 February 2005 the French National Assembly passed a law which consecrated officially the civilising role of the French occupation of Algeria for over 132 years (1830-1962).

---

[1] De Montagnac: *Lettres d'un soldat*; Librairie Plon Paris; 1885; p. 215-218. Unless otherwise stated, passages quoted throughout this work have been translated by this author.

The action of 2005 was no mere act of political nature aiming at garnering some fledging conservative support, or a sudden flurry of populist/nationalistic/patriotic/religious or sentiments of similar nature. Rather, it was only the continuation of a view or impression that never deserted France, and that still permeates all levels of French elites and masses to this day: France's Grand Deeds Outremer. This view is systemically and systematically engrained in French culture. Of course, this annoys the historian such as this author, who is aware of French deeds in Algeria, and reports some of them in this work (only some of them, for to speak of all French crimes in Algeria would require a whole encyclopaedia.) But this author and maybe a couple of other Algerians aside, the rest, the elites in particular, regardless of their status, or functions, have hardly, if at all, been upset by the French National Assembly decision, or the French view/narrative of their colonial history in Algeria. From 1962, until this moment in 2017-18, with the rarest exceptions such as by D. Sari, Algerians have failed to give the picture of the French systemic destruction of Algerian lives and life (economic, social, cultural, and natural heritage.) From time to time some voices have spoken about France's crimes in Algeria, but on the whole, these sounds have been fleeting expressions, little whispers, or protests by a weak party in the direction of their bully. What's the cause or causes of this Algerian impotence, this author is not going into. Others are left to justify such impotence of theirs. Here we, first and foremost, try to explain, instead, the most fundamental issue: why did the French did what they did (slay so many Algerians and destroy so much in Algeria (as we shall depict in this work), and had they had the chance, they would have exterminated Algerians to the near last. We need to understand this because, after all they were not, and are not born monsters, and are for most of them lovely beings, and yet they did what they did. It is, indeed, only by understanding the cause of something evil that we can limit its re-occurrences, not by ignoring it, as Algerians do, for anything can happen again. History is a stupid beast that repeats itself.

Throughout the colonial period, and even today, the ideologues of the colonisation of Algeria found great support amongst French historians who echoed, when they did not legitimise, their ideology as well as their actions.

> Primitivism, writes one such historian, has remained written in the very genetic being of the Berber people. The Maghrebi, amongst the white races of the Mediterranean, represents the mentally deficient, left behind by everyone else; this race lacks positive attributes. The Maghrebis are therefore perpetually colonised because they have remained perpetually colonisable. As we go through the centuries of North African history, we understand that the region is marked by an innate incapacity to remain independent.[2]

---

[2] E.F. Gautheir: *Le Passe de l'Afrique du Nord; Les Siecles Obscurs*; Paris, Payot, 1939.

History, teaches us [says the famed archaeologist Stephane Gsell] that this part of the world is simply geared for barbarism... a strong military occupation of it is necessary in order to accomplish the removal of such barbarism. It is also important that civilisation (i.e colonisation) is backed by powerful settlements (of Europeans) who are committed to work the land and perform other tasks; this population of settlers will bring and spread the good example amongst the welcoming natives.[3]

In reality [says Louis Bertrand of the Academie Francaise], all these peoples, indisposed as they are by their traditions, customs and climates to live according to our social ideal, hate to endure the constraint of our police, of our administration-in a word, of any sort of regulated government, no matter how just and honest. Delivered from the most anarchic and vexatious of tyrannies, they remain in spirit more or less like our vagabonds... In vain do we point out to the Arabs of North Africa that, thanks to the protection of France, they are no longer pillaged by Turkish despots nor massacred and tortured by rival tribes... But it is not merely our municipal and administrative regulations which they find unsupportable; it is all our habits, taken en bloc- in a word, the order which regulates our civilised life.... What is certain is that these peoples do not yet understand what we mean by exactitude, and that the concept of a well regulated existence has not yet penetrated their heads.[4]

These views sum up the attitude of the colonisers (then and since backed by the largest sway of their historians) that a civilised nation had to assume the heavy burden of leading those Maghrebi people away from their lamentable state into progress and civilisation.[5] To this moment the same attitude permeates French policy except that it is expressed and implemented in other forms and by other means. Anyone doubting this only needs to click one or two keys on the internet.

In 1830, France, thus, took upon herself the burden to 'civilise' Algeria by the force of arms. It would subsequently do the same in Tunisia (in 1881) and Morocco (in 1912.) Algeria that the French had come to civilise was, however, far more civilised than France itself in many regards. There are descriptions of industries and workshops producing a diversity of goods, and even accounts of arsenals in Algiers, Jijel, and Cherchell, as well as construction industries all over the country.[6] Corporations, moreover, had brought together foundry workers, jewellers, metal construction and glass producers. Also, whilst at least 40% of the French were illiterate, in Algeria on the other hand, levels of instruction were quite appreciable, and in Algiers alone, there were more than a hundred Qur'anic schools where children learnt at the same time as religious education to read,

---

[3] Cited by J.C. Vatin: *L'Algerie Politique, Histoire et Societe;* Presses de la Fondation Nationale des Sciences Politiques; Paris; 1974; in H. Alleg et al: *La Guerre d'Algerie.* Temps Actuels, Paris, 1981, vol 1, p. 37.

[4] L. Bertrand: *Le Mirage Oriental*; Paris; 1910; pp. 441-2.

[5] H. Alleg et al: *La Guerre d'Algerie*; op cit, p. 37.

[6] Lacoste, Nouschi, Prenant, in H. Alleg: *La Guere d'Algerie*; op cit; p. 56.

write and calculate.[7] The thriving nature of Algerian towns and cities was caught by all accounts of the time. What impressed everyone most, not just the French, but also the many British, Germans, and others who accompanied them as soldiers, officers, scientists and scholars, curious minds, and the like, was the splendour of the towns and cities. Algiers, like other places impressed everyone thanks to her many beautiful houses, all in white contrasting with the blue of the sky and the sea, all gleaming with exquisite, nicely scented, gardens. Surrounding every town and city were green belts that fed and rested their dwellers. The French came across streams, rivers, and lakes full of wildlife, also forests in places denser than anywhere else; some places were dwelt by panthers and lions, and were filled with a rich fauna and flora, and to the south were verdoyant oases, caravans crisscrossing the vast stretches of the land, and everywhere rich bazars and market places. French accounts and those amongst Westerners who fought alongside them are full of the systematic destruction of all this as depicted in this work.

Of course, in the French or other Western literature of today, most such accounts of destruction cannot be found. This is the misery, the tragedy of modern scholarship which has done away with facts, and more seriously with sources of such facts dating from those times regardless if they were mostly French and some English and German. Modern scholarship has, throughout the decades, literally filtered knowledge in regard to colonial history, has kept for us what maintains an image of the civilised coloniser, and done away with the rest that paints an image that flatters not. Where the even greater tragedy resides is not in the ignoring of the past reality by the descendants of those who were nearly made extinct (i.e the Algerians), the real tragedy is in such descendants doing worse, even: they derive their knowledge of the colonial phase from such crooked version of history. Feeding on the crooked they feed the crooked, and consequently produce crooked minds and souls.

Now, how do you avoid reproducing the crooked and feeding it to the souls and minds? The first step is to avoid the crooked fodder, i.e the output by modern French scholarship and their sold out followers with native background. Instead you do the one thing that hardly anyone does: you rely on the actors. The only true history of the colonial phase is that which is found in the words of the actors, and in those of the witnesses who saw what they saw. It is, indeed, from amongst the latter, those marching by the side of the French army, the likes of the Germans, Moritz Wagner and Clemens Lamping, or the Englishman: Dawson Borrer. It is also from the French army officers that we get the most accurate accounts of what truly happened. They left us their memoirs and did not care massage their deeds. They spoke of their hatred of their Algerian enemies, and the destruction, which they carried out. It is indeed crucial to take note, that

---

[7] M.P. Rozet, 'Alger', in F. Hoefer *Algerie par Capitaines du Genie Rozet et Carette* ; Etats Tripolitains, Paris, 1846, p. 14.

unlike today's French opinion making, which seeks to present a humane or civilising story in Algeria, during the colonial war,

> The High Command (then) elevated the policy of general devastation to the level of a doctrine. They made no secret of burning the enemies' country in order to destroy their food supplies, nor did they try to justify the massacre of dissident tribes by humanitarian speeches. They took a pride in these achievements-whether Royalists, Republicans, or Bonapartists in politics.[8]

Indeed, to really know about that phase (1830-1871) it is precisely by letting those involved to tell us what they did, and why they did it. Only then we can have some of the truth of the history of colonisation. Also, it is not by putting words in their mouths but by letting them speak to us generously instead, using their own words, which we only need to translate into English, that we can have such a truth. This author has taken the bother to do most of the translation of such accounts from French into English directly rather than just summing them up in his own words.

When one delves into the sources and garner facts on the ground, one easily realises that contrary to what vastly cooked modern historians, whether French or others (including amongst Natives,) tell us, France never had any intention of civilising, or improving, or correcting anything in Algeria. France only wanted a land without the barbaric natives. We will see this plentifully. France never showed a shred of humanity towards Algerians. It is a challenge put by this author to any crooked mind or cretin, to give the name of one single Frenchman who opposed colonisation or who opposed the mass slaying of natives. The few voices of French humanity only came sometime later, a communist or two, or some priest of some sort, when it became clear that Algerians could not all be removed. There were even in the period 1954-1962, at the height of the war of independence, decent French army officers who did not slay Algerians when they could have (including officers who could have killed this author's father and mother, and maybe even this author himself as a child.) This author knows of many stories of such kind French officers. But to claim that colonisation was for a good aim, and that some French thinkers or religious persons opposed it, or were opposed to the eradication of native Algerians, is just a pile of turd. Also not to really appreciate or recognise the merit of those best amongst Algerians who fought the French from 1830 till 1962, and who sacrificed their lives so as Algeria survives, and not to publicise the scale of French crimes in Algeria, are the worst manifestations of today's Algerian impotence.

Algerian history by crooked French scholarship and their Algerian and other followers is an utter mess, a cesspit of fallacies. Briefly here, one can cite Algerian 'piracy,' the myth that has largely justified French colonisation. It is beyond count

---

[8] In Jane Soames Nickerson: *A Short History of North Africa*, Devin Adair and Co, New York; 1961; p. 102.

the times this author came across writings by Muslim 'intellectuals' (never mind the others) who kept repeating the same smut, talking of Algerian/Muslim piracy. There was no piracy; Algeria did not even have a fleet when the French arrived in 1830; there is no account of any attack by pirates in any literature of then. Algerian 'piracy,' in truth was an earlier (16th-17th centuries) reaction against Christian attacks. It was much less destructive and cruel than that of the French, the British, and that of other Christian nations. Anyone lending two hours of their attention to the statistics of attacks on sea, and to the accounts on the treatment of prisoners caught at sea or on the coastlines can easily see that.[9] Chapter one will tell us more on this.

The same chapter will also delve on the real aims of the colonisation of Algeria. It is only necessary here to mention briefly that it all had principally to do with the dismembering of the Ottoman Empire. It was this issue which made and unmade European policy from the start of the 19th century until the First World War (1914-1918.) It was the main cause of all major wars over that period, including that of Crimea, (1853-1856); the Balkans (1912-1913) and the First World War itself. The reason was simple: here was an agonising (Ottoman) realm with vast lands, and everyone rushed to take their share, and most often there was squabbling (quite bloody at times). It was the same as when a rich relative dies and everyone fights over the legacy, which then causes the worst in human nature to erupt in the open (hence the wars between Europeans themselves). And when all Ottoman Africa and Europe were shared out, the turn of Turkey herself arrived after the First World War except that she (Turkey) saved herself by a remarkable fight.[10] It was all this simple. Those who seek to explain French colonialism or any major event between 1806 (First Serb uprising against the Ottomans) and 1922 (the end of the Turkish War of Independence) in all the complex mire that historians invent are simply complicating their lives and confusing and muddling the minds of their audiences.

Of course, in the process of dismantling the Ottoman realm there arose the usual spiritual and other more immediate earthly wants and wishes. France, and most of its generals (Bugeaud, Montagnac, St Arnaud, Randon... all devout Christians),[11] were extremely keen to expand the boundaries of Christendom wherever there was somewhere to reach. The annexation of North Africa by France had already been agreed between European powers, and it even formed a secret article in a treaty with Russia.[12] France in undertaking that expedition

---

[9] See G. Fisher: *Barbary Legend*; Oxford; 1957.

[10] See S.E. Al Djazairi: *The Long War*; MSBN Books, 2015.

[11] Their accounts are full of references to the Lord, prayers and so on. M. Louis Veuillot said about Marshal Bugeaud the author of the war of devastation of Algeria: His house and home was the abode of simple sweet Christian virtues, all powerful over his soul. In Count H. Ideville: *Memoirs of Marshal Bugeaud from his Private Correspondence and Original Documents*; 2 vols; edited from French by C.M. Yonge; Hurst and Blackett; London, 1884; vol 2; p. 44.

[12] Baron de Testa: *Receuil des Traites de la Porte Ottomane*, t.1, p. 444; Paris; 1864.

agreed with her allies in regard to establishing a new order in the country, which was 'to the great advantage of Christianity, which would replace the by now defunct Muslim regime.'[13]

Algeria was also projected in French colonial circles to become a land of settlement for Europeans on the same model as America. Some leading figures proposed to make Algerians submit to the same fate as the American pioneers had reserved to the Indian Natives: their entire removal from earth.[14] V.A. Hain of the Societie Coloniale de l'Etat d'Alger considered the whole population of Algeria beyond redemption and only fit to be removed from the land.[15] The Minister of War, Girard, defending Duke de Rovigo, who massacred thousands of Algerians, held:

> We have to resign ourselves to push as far as possible (into the desert), in fact exterminating the native population. Devastation, burning away everything, ruin of their agriculture are perhaps the only ways to establish solidly our domination.[16]

Why we don't have today a native free Algeria, an America like land, was not due to French lousy action, or to their humanity. The French were neither lousy slayers, nor were they benevolent souls as crooked modern scholarship keeps telling us. In fact the French remain the champion mass slaughterers of history, and they showed their credentials wherever they went, and from the crusades onwards. It was only determined resistance by Algerians against what was in store for them that saved them.[17] Marshal Randon, who fought in the country and then became War Minister, and then governor of Algeria in the 1850s, was incensed by those who kept criticising the French army for not doing as well as was done in America, i.e cleansing away the native Algerians.

> In every direction you go, from behind every bush emerges a white burnous firing at you. They are people who love powder and love war. You cannot chase them away like the American Native by gunshots and buying them a bottle of liquor.[18]

In any part of the country the French set foot, as this work shows, and as the following chronological brief sums up, they found a resilient population unwilling to submit, rather prepared to fight to the last. In September 1833, a French armed corps, commanded by general Trezel, landed in Bejaia, on the eastern sea-coast, and with heavy canon fire flattened the city, yet without obtaining any surrender.[19] The inhabitants instead fought 'street by street, for every house,

---

[13] Ibid; p. 457.

[14] H. Alleg et al: *La Guerre d'Algerie;* op cit, p. 62.

[15] V.A. Hain: *A La Nation. Sur Alger*; Paris; 1832; pp. 31; 58 fwd.

[16] H. Alleg et al: *La Guerre d'Algerie*; op cit, p. 62.

[17] See accounts by French officers as in sources in this work.

[18] As translated and summed up from A. Rastoul: *Le Marechal Randon; D'apres ses Memoirs et Documents Inedits*; Firmin Didot; Paris; 1890; p. 184-186.

[19] H. Alleg: *La Guerre*; op cit; p. 62.

from every window, every step of the way.'[20] And after this, the surviving inhabitants took refuge in the mountains to continue the fight, and all the French could gain were empty ruins, in which 'nothing but corpses and gore had remained.'[21]

In Constantine in 1837, according to St Arnaud, future Marshall of France:

> Fierce artillery fire ceaselessly blasts the defence walls, and causes a breach. 25 men at the front rush into the breach... but instead of entering the city as thought, the first column is blocked by a second wall. All the walls, all the houses, all the windows are filled with defenders. It is a wall of fire that we have in front of us. The people of the city fight with the courage of despair. They fire at us, and we kill them... They are formidable soldiers; our bayonets kill them all. We take no prisoners... bullets shower us and fall all around us. We are held up by a formidable fire coming from a barricade made of everything: doors, planks, mattresses, anything. The population defends it with the most intense fire, and kills many amongst us....[22]

In the western parts of the country, from Oran to Mascara, Tlemcen, Saida, to Mostaganem, led by Emir Abd al-Kader, the Algerians fought with uncommon valour that bewilders whomsoever knows or discovers historical reality through the pages left to us by St Arnaud and Montagnac. Chapters four and five will show this.

And so, 'the saga continues,' notes the Comte d'Herisson. 'After the arrest of Hadj Ahmed, the defender of Constantine in 1848, we have the rising of Buzian in the (southern) Za'atcha in 1849, followed by a repression which 'struck terror in Saharan hearts and filled them with hatred, too.'[23] Then, in 1850 and 1851, it was Kabylia again, where Generals Camou and Bosquet burnt more than 300 villages, thirty of them in one day alone, cutting down olive trees and orchards, slaying villagers en masse, including those belonging to 'friendly tribes.'[24] Then, in 1852 it was Laghouat, which rose and 'we have to chastise a la Francaise,' and then it was the tribes on the Moroccan frontiers, always in 'perpetual rebellion,' which had to be dealt with.[25] In Laghouat, which was fiercely fought over, the painter and writer Eugene Fromentin, who visited the town soon after its fall to the French, ca 1852, wrote:

> Every house bore the trace fighting. Every stone is as if ripped off by bullets and canon fire. Men fought in every street, in every garden, in every house. When the time came to bury the Muslim dead, they were so many that in some streets they constituted as if barricades. Muslim corpses were

---

[20] X. Marmier: *Lettres sur l'Algerie*; Paris; 1847; in H. Alleg; *La Guerre*; op cit; p. 62.

[21] M. Wagner: *The Tricolor on the Atlas*, London; T. Nelson and Sons, 1854, p. 261.

[22] *Lettres du Marechal St Arnaud*; Michel Levy Frreres; Paris; 1855.

[23] Le Comte d'Herisson: *La Chasse a l'Homme, Guerre d'Algerie*; Paul Ollendorff; Paris; 1891; p. 346.

[24] Ibid.

[25] Ibid.

simply dragged en masse, and were thrown anywhere that could be found, in wells principally. One well alone was filled with 256 corpses.[26]

On no occasion did the French manage to pacify the country, nor were Algerians willing to accept French dictate. The general uprising of 1870-1 involved nearly a third of the Algerian total population, and despite its terrible outcomes in lives lost and destruction, more uprisings followed in the Oran south, in 1880, in the Sahara and the Aures, and as far as south in the Tuareg regions of the Hoggar in 1917.[27] Eventually Algerians rose in the final and decisive War of Independence, in 1954, and in one of the bloodiest colonial fights France was forced out of the country in 1962.[28]

It was this fight, this resilience, which the Algerians showed, which secured their survival. Unlike natives in other continents who eventually submitted to the incomers, as well as to the effects of alcoholic beverages and corrupting colonial practices, which in the end led them to be removed by the tens of millions,[29] Algerians did not, and thus did not just survive but also prevailed in the end.

The historian is left in awe at the Algerian spirit of resistance and the capacity of that nation to survive by far the most brutal colonial onslaught in history. Yet, as they were about to colonise Algeria, the French were particularly convinced that, as elsewhere, they would find a disunited population, ridden by ethnic warfare and divisions, whose conquest and subjugation would be a fairly easy task. The French view was:

> Too long oppressed by an avaricious and cruel militia, the Arab will see in us (the French) his liberators; he will implore our assistance. Reassured by our good faith, he will bring us the richness of his soil.[30]

The conquest 'of Algiers', it was stated, would lead to the civilisation of Africa.[31] And if the French respected Kabyle freedom they would be welcomed 'as liberators from their Turkish and Arab oppressors.'[32]

General De Bourmont, heading the expeditionary corps in 1830, exhorted the army to treat the Arabs kindly and honestly, as they were on the point of joining the French, and fighting 'their oppressors,' the Turks.[33] But a few days later this delusion was dispelled when on the 24th of June 1830 a new general attack was made on the French, both by Turks and Arabs.[34] Soon, from all around the

---

[26] P. Gaffarel *L'Algerie, Histoire, Conquete et Colonisation*, ed. Firmin Didot, 1883; pp. 79-80.

[27] H. Alleg: *La Guerre*; op cit, pp. 81-4.

[28] A. Horne: *A Savage War of Peace*, Macmillan; London; 1977. I. Courriere: *La Guere d'Algerie*, reedited, Fayard; Paris; 2001. See Le Monde and various French dailies, whether published in France or Algeria during the conflict to have a full measure of the brutality and violence of the war.

[29] For mass killing of natives in various continents see:

-Ward Churchill: *A Little Matter of Genocide*; City Lights Books; San Francisco; 1997.

-W. Howitt: *Colonisation and Christianity*: Longman; London; 1838.

D.E. Stannard: *American Holocaust; The Conquest of the New World;* Oxford University Press; 1992.

[30] In H. Alleg et al: *La Guerre d'Algerie*; op cit, pp. 28-9.

[31] F. Pananti, *Narrative of a Residence in Algiers*, Tr., E. Blaquière, London, 1818, p. 412.

[32] A. Thomson, *Barbary and Enlightenment*, Brill, Leiden, 1987; p. 109.

[33] M. Wagner: *The Tricolor on the Atlas*, London; T. Nelson and Sons, 1854, p. 230.

[34] Ibid.

country, Kabyles, Arabs, Turks, and Kuluglis (born of Algerian and Turkish parentage) joined in the fierce anti colonial fight. The resistance leader in central-western Algeria was Abd al-Kader, an Arab; the leader in the East was Hadj Ahmed, a Kulugli; the leaders of resistance elsewhere, whether al-Mokrani or others, were Berbers; Bu Zian was a man of the Sahara. And those who fought alongside each other were of diverse ethnic origins: Arabs, Turks, Kuluglis, Berbers, all united against the common foe, all united by one common bond: their Islamic faith.

> The book of Almighty God and the law of His Prophet [says Emir Abd al-Kader,] are the only rules of adjudication. Provisions for the support of our army abound, as well as men to fill the ranks. All this must be attributed to the blessing of God, obtained through your prayers and approbation. Otherwise, we should have been the weakest of men for such achievements.
>
> We did not come forward and assume the task of government from ambitious motives, or a desire for exaltation and power, or a love for the vanities of this world; but (and God knows the secrets of my heart) to fight the battles of the Lord, to prevent the fratricidal effusion of the blood of Muslims, to protect their properties, and to pacify the country, as zeal for the faith and patriotism require.[35]

Not only the Algerians were united by their faith, for which they fought, it was also that faith that played the ultimate part in saving them as a nation and as a people. As Wagner, the German scientist who accompanied the French expeditionary force against Constantine in 1836-7, remarked:

> The sober and frugal habits of that people, also an unchanged feature of their ancestors, is a great hindrance in the way of civilization; it makes their improvement as difficult as their expulsion or destruction. The North American red men were defeated and driven from the country of their fathers by the "fire-water;" wherever those savages tasted spirits, they were-enslaved by them, and lost both energy and freedom. But such means are of no avail with the Arabs.[36]

This is the story of great Algerian resistance and leadership, today disappeared from knowledge by the ex colonisers and their servants, a story that is also sunk in the vacuous, cretin, modern 'culture' of today, that the following revives.

---

[35] C.H. Churchill: *The Life of Abd Al Kader*, Chapman and Hall, London, 1867, p. 151.
[36] M. Wagner: *The Tricolor*, op cit, pp. 144-5.

One

FRENCH COLONISATION OF ALGERIA UNMUDDLED

Coloniser un pays c'est mettre en valeur son sol et exploiter son sous sol mieux que ne savent le faire les indigènes.[37]
(Colonising a country means fructifying its soil and exploiting its underground better than can the natives do.)

The Cries of Victory:

> According to me [said the French general, E. Pelissier,] this (the French colonisation of Algeria) is the second act (the independence of Greece being the first); this is the second act, I say, in the Mediterranean, of the inexorable absorption of the Muslim world by the Christians, a task being undertaken with great success by both the English and Russians in India and Central Asia.[38]

This sentiment of the moribund, and at last defeated, Muslim world being gradually absorbed by the now powerful and victorious Christian nation is also well expressed by the contemporary French historian, Rotalier. Writing in the mid 1840s, he held:

> Often, in the middle of my exhausting research for this book, and in view of the uncertainties that threaten our latest venture (the conquest of Algeria), I felt my courage dimming, and asked myself why should I trouble myself writing a book about a country France might never hold on to! But this sorrowful sentiment was soon replaced by the great hope that Algiers, child of 16th century piracy, will be born again to civilisation in this great movement which shakes the 19th century. Its era of barbarism is gone. France will erase the final traces of piracy, and will bring back to this, now so desolate, land, its old brilliance, and its immense fertility. Already we see the Cross standing again; its fall long ago (when the Muslims entered the country) had caused the desolation and misery which today sadden the eyes of the traveller. Pious missionaries now march with our soldiers, and whenever cannon holds its thunder up, whenever the screams of battle cease, these men walk to the vanquished Arabs, console them, and touch their hardened hearts, putting in front of their eyes the Cross, with the

---

[37] P. Bernard and F Redon: *Histoire, Colonisation, Geographie et Administration de l'Algerie*, Librairie Adolphe Jourdan; Algiers, 1906; p. 42.
[38] E.D. Pelissier: *Quelques mots sur la colonisation Militaire en Algerie;* Paris; 1847; in N. Daniel: *Islam; Europe; and Empire*, University Press, Edinburgh, 1966; p. 330.

picture of a god who had died for them. The Arab then kisses the hand of the wise, black robbed, missionary, and soon after his soul opens up to these pious words; he listens; he understands them... He will become Christian! If he did, the country would belong to us, the conquest would be complete.[39]

Decades later, writing at the height of Western colonial power, the leading Missionary, Samuel Zwemer, held:

Through incessant, spontaneous and almost fanatic parading, preaching, pushing of their faith by the mass of believers, and not solely by the power of the sword, Islam grew to its gigantic proportions. And if they used the sword, so also can we.... It is a bitter sword than theirs and slays to give Life Eternal. If they did so much with theirs, surely we can do more with ours. We can do it if we will. We have a better message, a more glorious faith, a higher motive, a richer reward, a more certain victory, a nobler inspiration, a better comradeship, and a Leader before Whose great white throne and great white life the mock majesty and the great whitewashed immorality of Mohammed shrink in abject terror. They did it for Mohammed. Shall we not do it for our Saviour in the spread of Christianity.[40]

1. Yet Another Crusade

Clemens Lamping was a German soldier who joined the French army in the 1840s and who left us some of the best accounts of the French operations in Kabylia and the environs of Algiers. In the preface of his work we read what motivated him to join the French:

The author of the first part of a work the little volume (Clemens Lamping), is a young lieutenant in the Oldenburg service, who, tired of the monotonous life of a garrison, resigned his commission in July, 1839, and went to Spain to win his spurs under Espartero. Unfortunately he was detained by contrary winds, and arrived just as the treaty of Bergara had put an end to the war. After spending six months at Madrid in abortive attempts to join the army in Aragon, then the seat of war, he resolved to go to Africa, and take part in the French crusade against the infidels. He accordingly went to Cadiz, encountering many adventures on his way through La Mancha and Andaluzia, and thence to Algiers, where he entered the foreign legion as a volunteer.[41]

Just like him, French troopers landing on Algerian soil were reminded of their crusading mission:

---

[39] C. De Rotalier: *Histoire d'Alger*; Chez Paulin, Paris; 1841; pp. xi-xii.
[40] S. Zwemer in M. Broomhall: *Islam in China;* Morgan and Scott Ltd; China Inland Mission; 1910; p. 38.
[41] Clemens Lamping: *The French in Algiers. Soldiers of the Foreign Legion; Prisoners of Abd el Kader;* tr. from German and French by Lady Duff Gordon, London; 1855; p. preface.

'You have renewed with the crusades' declared the French leading General de Bourmont to his soldiers in 1830.[42]

'Our war in Africa is a continuation of the Crusades,' said Minister Poujoulat to General Bugeaud in 1844.[43]

Early French historians of the campaign, then, unlike those of today, also saw it as a Crusade. For Nettement describing the military campaign as it began in June 1830:

The act that is now unfolding devours words and leaves them barely any time to fall on paper. The hand stiffens around the quill just as around a sword. Then, in the end, a reflection of the Crusading spirit erupts, preserved amidst the Christian family; it now comes to mingle with the rays of modern heroism. The letter begins with military joy and ends with a thought for God. To avenge the honour of France, this is the first feeling of the letter; but offering the victory to God is how it ends.[44]

The 19th century did consecrate what was then deemed to be the final victory of Christendom over Islam. This 'gigantic crusade', as the French historian, Driault, calls it, caught the spirit of the time, writers, artists, rulers and informed men, all stirring and sharing in the euphoria of this latest crusade, so much so, that all over the West, even children's histories and works of fiction were full of crusade ancestors and heroes.[45] This is indeed, the first time since the First Crusades (1095-1291), nearly ten centuries earlier, that the Christians are marching through the Muslim world in triumph. This deserved celebration, for the foe was at last subdued after so many centuries of trying.

Literary works reflected the mood. Chateaubriand expressed passionately his exultation for the old Crusader deeds not failing to lambast the too soft 18th century writers, who saw wrong in the Crusades. The nineteenth century, he found, however:

No longer represents these crusades under an odious form. I, amongst the first, claimed against this ignorance and this injustice.... It was not just necessary to free this Holy sepulchre, but also to know who was going to win on this land; whether a cult that was the enemy of civilisation, favourable to ignorance, despotism, slavery, or a religion which revives with the modern the genius of antiquity and abolished servitude. The spirit of Mohamedanism is persecution and conquest.[46]

---

[42] A. Surre-Garcia: l'Image du sarrasin dans les mentalites de la litterature Occitanes: *De Toulouse a Tripoli*, op cit; pp. 181-9; at p. 186.

[43] Ibid.

[44] M.A. Nettement: *Histoire de la Conquete d'Alger;* Jacques Lecoffre; Paris; 1856; p. 325.

[45] In E. Siberry: The New *Crusaders*; Ashgate: Aldershot; 2000; p. 160.

[46] Chateaubriand: Itineraire de Paris a Jerusalem; 1969 ed; pp. 1052-3; in C. Grossir: *l'Islam des Romantiques*; Maisonneuve; Larose; Paris, 1984; p. 41.

Islam, symbol of barbarism, justified in his eyes 'the grandiose movement of the crusades.'[47] Further justification for them, he saw, was that they 'preserved us from the Muslim yoke, without talking of other commercial benefits.'[48]

Chateaubriand's enthusiasm was further raised by his awareness of his crusading ancestor Geoffrey of Chateaubriand, who accompanied Louis IX to Egypt in 1248-1250. And he himself fulfilled his dream in 1806, when he travelled to Jerusalem, 'under the banner of the cross' and was made a knight of the Holy Sepulchre; and took pride in the achievements of his fellow countrymen in that land.[49]

In the wake of the successful landing in Algiers in 1830 and the progress of the French columns, the 'greatness' of the Crusades was revived in arts, expressing past French glories. Highly popular amongst artists were Louis IX's two crusades (1248-50; 1270), which symbolised successes of French history. Exhibitions of sculptures and paintings and tapestries of scenes from his life abounded. Thus was organised in the Salles des Croisades at Versailles a festival as part of King Louis Phillipe's (King 1830-1848) programme to turn the palace into a museum 'dedicated to the glories of France.' The five crusade rooms displayed each a key crusade events and individuals and the coats of arms of their participants. In total, there were 120 paintings of individual crusaders and scenes of battles and sieges in which French crusaders played a leading role.[50] Louis Philippe employed no less than fifty painters for such an enterprise. 'All in all' Siberry comments:

> The Salles des Croisades are the pictorial equivalent of a multi volume French history of the crusades, with, as has already been mentioned, a clear purpose, namely to emphasise the continuity of French history under Louis Philippe. And there seems to be a clear coincidence in timing between the commissioning of a number of the crusade paintings and the renewal of the crusades in Algeria.[51]

What gave the Crusade its historical legitimacy was the belief and claim that France was only resuming a Christian presence in a once Christian land. To the soldiers who were landing on Algerian soil, as to the settlers who would follow, it was repeated that all they were doing was returning to Christianity a former Christian land, a land that the Romans, two thousand years earlier, had brought out of Barbarism.[52] After a very long delay, France, at last, is now setting foot on this land, and was

> Throwing a bridge over the dark centuries so as to continue the interrupted great work of the great (Roman/Christian) ancestors.[53]

---

[47] Chateaubriand: Itinerary in H. Djait: *l'Europe et l'Islam*; University of California Press, 1992; p. 36.
[48] In D. Brahimi: *Arabes des Lumieres*; Editions le Sycomre, Paris; 1982; pp. 44-5.
[49] In E. Siberry: *The New*; op cit; pp. 51; and 68.
[50] In E. Siberry: *The New*; op cit; pp. 169-70.
[51] Ibid.
[52] H Alleg et al: *La Guerre d'Algerie*; op cit; p. 38.
[53] Ibid.

At the same time there was a revival of the old lyricism of the ancient Church of Africa. The Sunday that followed the landing at Sidi Ferruch (in June 1830), on the shore itself, God is praised 'for having allowed the return of the Christians.'

> Here was solemnised, for the first time since so many years, the Holy Day of the Lord. Catholicism has again taken over possession of a land where it once flourished. A renowned padre celebrated the Masse, and the soldiers, still stained with gun powder, and under the burning sun, stood in front of God 'who gave them victory in battle.' The Christian sacrifice now sanctioned the return of liberty and civilisation, daughters of the Bible, on this shore, where only a few days before, despotism and barbarism ruled over the desert.[54]

Subsequently, once the new churches were established, the stones for the altars were collected from the old chapels of Roman ruins.[55]

A crusading mind dressed in a modern form, to reform the Algerian personality, is here expressed by Antoine Salles about Cardinal Lavigerie:

> He sought for Algeria to escape the yoke of Islam, which for centuries, suffocated its rise and prosperity, but on condition that it placed itself under the protection of France once its freedom was secured. This is a remarkable programme to turn Christian and to turn French this land which was according to the Cardinal an extension of France.[56]

This line was sanctioned by subsequent historians. One of the most accomplished ideologues of colonialism of the 1930s, Louis Bertrand, wrote:

> In entering Africa, we have only recovered a province once lost by the Latin world. As the inheritors of Rome, we invoke rights which precede those of Islam.[57]

This is another manner of ascertaining that the real owners of the country were not the Algerians but the colonisers, who came in all legitimacy to reclaim what was their own land.[58]

The thought or claim that was also current then was that the original inhabitants of Algeria were only Muslim superficially, that their Islamisation was forced upon them by the Arabs, and now the time to liberate them had arrived. According to Dr Barth:

> A great part of the Berbers of the desert were once Christians, and that they afterwards changed their religion and adopted Islam.... that continual struggle which, always extending further and further, seems destined to

---

[54] Ibid. p. 39.

[55] Ibid.

[56] A. Salles: *Le Cardinal Lavigerie et l'Influence Francaise en Afrique*; Lyon; 1893; in N. Daniel: *Islam; Europe, and Empire*, Edinburgh University Press, 1966; p. 332.

[57] Louis Bertrand quoted in H. Alleg et al: *La Guerre d'Algerie*, op cit, p. 39.

[58] H. Alleg et al: *La Guerre d'Algerie*, op cit, p. 39.

overpower the nations at the very Equator if Christianity does not presently step in to dispute the ground with it.[59]
France would indeed dispute the terrain with the foe, and a vast policy was put to the effect. This will be examined in the final chapter of this work.

Further legitimacy to the French act 'of civilising Algeria,' it was claimed, was due to the fact that Islam was an obstacle to progress. This was amply expressed by the leading voices of the imperial era. J.D. Bate (1836-1923), a leading missionary, insists that it was Islam which was responsible for the state of 'degradation' of states where it had obtained 'its ascendancy;' as system of belief, it made any escaping such condition impossible, hindering not just social elevation, but also moral elevation, 'beyond a certain point, of even the most degraded people.'[60] Wherever Islam was in the ascendency, still according to Bate, progress was dealt 'the death knell' and stagnation had become the norm.[61]
 This view was shared by all, including Lord Baring (Lord Cromer,) the once ruler of Egypt (behind the façade of the Egyptian Khedive), who conceded that, true Islam improved the black African, but for others and as a social system, it was 'a complete failure,' because of its subjugation of women, the union of religion and law, its 'toleration of slavery and sectarianism.'[62]

Thus, here we have the general picture dressed: France, by her colonisation of Algeria was only removing a negative influence, which had intruded into the country, and had been imposed on a former Christian land by both Arabs and Turks. Now, as Alleg et al note, in colonial rhetoric, 'the brilliant Algerian Roman era aside,' Algeria had only resumed its existence from the moment General De Bourmont captured Algiers (in 1830).[63] Before this arrival, and down till the Christian Roman period, all that there was in Algeria were backward populations, scattered, submitting to the various conquerors, worst of whom were the Arabs and Turks.[64] Now, therefore, France was coming back with the Christian torch of civilisation,

> With the help of Divine providence, to give its rules and laws to the natives, who had never been able to create by themselves a state, to build institutions, administration, economic system, or a culture of any sort.. in brief, the French arrival helping terminate the state of savagery that had prevailed hitherto.[65]

---

[59] R.B. Smith: *Mohammed and Mohammedanism*; London, 1874, p. 49.
[60] J.D. Bate: *The Claims of Ishmael*; London; W. Allen; 1884; p. 301.
[61] Ibid.
[62] In N. Daniel: *Islam, Europe and Empire*, op cit; p. 470.
[63] H. Alleg et al: *La Guerre d'Algerie*, op cit, vol 1, p. 37.
[64] Ibid.
[65] Ibid.

2. The Civilising Mission

In 1906, Bernard and Redon, both holding high positions in the French educational system in Algeria, completed a pedagogical work, which on the first page stated:

(a l'usage des ecoles primaires, des ecoles Primaires Superieures, des Classes Elementaires, des Lycees et Colleges, des Cours d'Adultes,) etc.

Translating: A book for the usage of primary schools, elementary classes, lycees and colleges, and for adult courses, etc...

It stated amongst many other points, here one of the most repeated:

> L'Afrique, que les anciens Romains avaient si remarquablement colonisée, devenait chaque année plus inculte et plus misérable. La plupart des villes avaient disparu, les campagnes étaient envahies par les brousailles, les routes n'existaient plus; seuls, d'étroits sentiers serpentaient entre les herbes ou les ronces; les grands travaux d'autrefois: barrages, aqueducs, citernes avaient été abandonnés, les épidémies décimaient les populations, les disettes et les famines étaient fréquentes. Il appartenait à la France de faire cesser cet état de choses. En ouvrant le pays à la civilisation, la conquête française allait le régénérer.

Which translates:

> Africa, which the Ancient Romans had so remarkably colonised, became years after (after the Arab arrival) quite sterile and miserable. Most of the cities had disappeared, the countryside was invaded by thick undergrowth; only scarce, narrow paths could now be seen amidst the wild patches of undergrowth; the great works of old times: barrages, aqueducts, cisterns, have all been abandoned; epidemics now decimated the populations; hunger was constant. It thus belonged to France to put an end to this. In opening the country to civilisation, the French conquest was going to bring it to life again.[66]

Indeed, French rhetoric is full, crammed in fact, with pieces of writing on France's 'noble' task in Algeria as in other parts colonised by France. According to leading French voices, Algeria had indeed descended to the lowest levels of degradation under Arabo-Turkish rule. It had become a hotbed, in fact the hotbed of despotism and barbarism, a country, which according to Chevaliers D'Avrieux was inhabited by 'the dregs of the provinces of the Ottoman Empire,' without a doubt 'the most unworthy rabble in Africa and the country a lair of thieves.'[67] Algeria had become, according to Pananti, dwelt by the most degraded people,

---

[66] P. Bernard and F Redon: *Histoire, Colonisation, Geographie et Administration de l'Algerie*, Librairie Adolphe Jourdan; Algiers, 1906; p. 27.

[67] Chevallier d'Arvieux: *Memoires;* R. P. Labat; 6 Vols; Paris; 1735; vol V; pp. 288-9.

full of hatred for both Christianity and civilisation.[68] Barbarians, who, according to Abbe Raynal, had destroyed Christian civilisation in North Africa 'thanks to their genius for destruction and their fanaticism, and replaced it with slavery and tyranny.'[69] And so he, like the countless others, calls 'for Christian conquest to free Barbary from a handful of barbarians.'[70] It was the only road to betterment. This, Shaller (another proponent of colonisation) insists, could only be accomplished if the country was in the 'hands of Christian nations who would favour agriculture, industry and commerce and thus civilise the region.'[71] Pananti, for his part, insists that once Christians are:

> Masters of North Africa, the harem walls must fall and suffer the miserable inmates to regain their natural rights in society, rendering the most beautiful part of creation what it should be, the happiness and consolation of mankind…. Christians would convert those who are now scarcely superior to the brute creation into good men and industrious citizens…. The conquest of Algiers would lead to the civilisation of Africa.[72]

From the moment the French set foot in Algeria, in June 1830, it would seem, Algerians had not read the script, and had failed to appreciate the French noble mission. They mounted a stiff resistance against them. As a result the French inflicted on them what possibly was one of the harshest retributions in colonial history. So vast was French devastation that the whole Algerian population became at some point threatened with extinction. This was justified on the ground that it was a necessary step towards civilisation. General Pelissier in one of his many campaigns smoked to death whole tribes inside caves, which was justified by his superiors on the ground that:

> Rigorous methods had to be applied to submit the country, without which there would be no colonisation, administration, or civilisation.[73]

Even the supposedly liberals/lovers of the masses, such as Engels, agreed with the French firm hand. He wrote in 1848 in the Northern Star, that:

> The French victory over Emir Abd el Kader (in Algeria) was finally a good thing for the progress of civilisation, as the Bedouin are barbarous thieves preying on the sedentary populations, whose supposed noble liberty can only appear admirable from the distance.[74]

Everyone (including the military doing the killing and burning) was convinced, or convinced themselves that their work in Algeria was for a good cause, and that

---

[68] F. Pananti: *Narrative of a Residence in Algiers*; tr. E. Blaquiere: London; 1818; p 416.

[69] Abbe Raynal: *Histoire philosophique et politique des etablissements et du commerce des Europeans dans l'Afrique*; Paris; 1826; vol I; pp. 106 ff and 137.

[70] Ibid.

[71] W. Shaller: *Sketches of Algiers*; Boston; 1826; p.56.

[72] F. Pananti: *Narrative*; op cit; p. 415; p. 412; 416.

[73] H Alleg et al: *La Guerre d'Algerie;* op cit; vol 1; p. 69.

[74] Quoted by W. Bouzar: *Le Mouvement et la Pause*; (Algiers; 1983); vol 1; pp. 216-7.

they held the high moral ground. One of the noble duties they were performing was the liberation of Algeria's female population.

> The French soldier [Alleg et al. remark] had no doubt about his moral superiority, the noble nature of his task, when he read the short document handed to him just as he was about to get on board of the ship carrying him onto the conquest of Algeria. The women of Algeria, the document says, due to the laziness of their Arab husbands, indulge in all sorts of debauched acts. They practice so many abortions to avoid giving birth to children, children, who, until the age of 8, wander about naked, and sleep on dry leaves.[75]

The soldiers were also informed that the women had no religion, that many amongst them believed that their soul was mortal, and that their only role in this life was to procreate.[76]

This, of course, was incumbent on the French to correct. In correcting Algerian errors, the French at no time refrained from slaying and cutting off the limbs of Algerian women who had the 'bad habit' of wearing metal rings around their arms, ankles, and their ears. Every witness speaks of this:

> The narrow streets [says Dawson Borrer, an Englishman fighting amongst the French in Kabylia,] were soon crowded with French troops, ravishing, massacring, and plundering on all sides. Neither sex nor age was regarded; the sword fell upon all alike. From one house blood-stained soldiers, laden with spoil, passed forth as I entered it. Upon the floor of one of the chambers lay a little girl of twelve or fourteen years of age: there she lay, weltering in gore and in the agonies of death: an accursed ruffian thrust his bayonet into her.[77]

French thinkers of the moderate sort, likewise, could hardly fail to see in Algerians simple people who needed constantly French firm handling:

> Our natives (in North Africa) [says Mercier,] need to be governed. They are children, incapable of going alone. We should guide them firmly, stand no nonsense from them, and crush intrigues and agents of sedition. At the same time, we should protect them, direct them paternally, and especially obtain influence over them by the constant example of our moral superiority. Above all: no vain humanitarian illusions, both in the interest of France and of the natives themselves.[78]

The French had other reasons for correcting the Algerian ruffians.

---

[75] H. Alleg et al: *La Guerre d'Algerie;* op cit, p. 36.
[76] Ibid.
[77] Dawson Borrer: *Narrative of a campaign against the Kabailes of Algeria;* Spottiswoode and Shaw, London, 1848; pp. 92-104.
[78] E. Mercier: *La Question Indigene;* (Paris; 1901); p. 230.

3. Piracy

> At the end of nine centuries of Arab occupation the outcome of these advantages was a pirate state with its hand against every man and every man's hand against it. A state which had become so intolerable a nuisance that it was found necessary at last to stamp it out of existence, in the interests of society, as you might stamp upon an adder in the public highway.[79]

The view of the Barbary corsairs slaying countless thousands of Christians was a powerful call for action against the 'nest of pirates' (Algeria).[80] Algeria, allegedly, was conquered by France in order to remove 'Muslim piracy which infested the Mediterranean.'[81] The appeal made in 1858 by Monseignor Pavy, Bishop of Algiers, for the erection of the Cathedral de Notre Dame d'Afrique in Algiers dwelt on the horrors of 'la piraterie Musulmane' (Muslim piracy). Monseignor Pavy insisted that the conquest of 1830 of Algeria had brought 'these horrors to an end.'[82] In 1884, Sir Lambert Playfair, once a consul at Algiers, wrote a book entitled: *The Scourge of Christendom*, which highlighted the conventional view of the previous three centuries, of 'Barbary Corsairs' capturing Christian vessels and enslaving their seamen; and worse, even, the Regencies of the Barbary Coast were ruled by the 'Infidel Turk.'[83]

To this day, Muslim/Barbary piracy has remained the central issue, which according to the vast majority of scholarship, led to the French occupation of Algeria. Numberless are even the works by Muslim 'scholars,' including now, in 2017-18, which repeat the same claim and show the idiocy of their authors. It would seem, according to all literature, the arrival of the Ottomans in the region had triggered this vile piracy scourge. Even some Algerian and Turkish writers speak of Turkish and Barbary Coast Corsairs with the same tenor as their Western counterparts, once more highlighting their cretinism. Yet, this piracy business is one of the most farcical aberrations one could come across. So, there is a need to address it in order to help everyone regain their wits.

The Ottomans had from the late 15th century onwards become the protectors and suzerains of most of the declining Muslim world. This came as a result of the threats faced by both western and eastern Islam. In the west, which is of interest to us, in the late 15th and early 16th centuries, following their recapture of Grenada (in 1492), the Spaniards launched a series of military assaults against the Maghreb. After taking Melila in 1497, they captured Mers el-Kebir in 1505,

---

[79] L. March Phillips: *In the Desert, the Hinterlands of Algiers*; Edward Arnold; London; 1909; p. 13.
[80] A. Thomson: *Barbary and Enlightenment*; Brill; Leiden; 1987; p. 128.
[81] P. Earle: *Corsairs of Malta and Barbary;* London, 1970; p. 10.
[82] In *Revue Africaine*; vol 2 (1858); pp. 337-52.
[83] C. Lloyd: *English Corsairs on the Barbary Coast;* Collins; London; 1981; p. 18.

seen then as the first stage in the conquest of Greece, Turkey, Alexandria, and the Holy Land.[84] By then, the Portuguese had already captured much of coastal Morocco. This, of course, reflected the Christian ultimate ambition of conquering the whole world as was then known. A whole set policies and the ideological framework behind them for the destruction of the Muslim world, and the Christianisation of North Africa, as devised in the 14th century, in particular, exists, and can be consulted.[85] It shows how the Christians envisaged the conquest of North Africa, with the recapture of Grenada as only one step towards the big plan.[86] Following the previous successes, in 1509, Pedro Navarro led an expeditionary against Oran, described as 'the principal port of the trade of the Levant.'[87] The year after, Bejaia, Tenes, Dellys fell to the Spaniards, whilst Algiers came under threat, kept at canon range from their fortified place of the Penon a short distance into the sea.[88] As a result of such Spanish conquests, tens of thousands of Muslim men, women, and children were slain, kept captive in the presidios, or transported to the slave markets of the European mainland and from there to the trans-Atlantic imperial possessions, from Florida to Brazil.[89] The violence of the Spanish attacks and the terror inflicted on the conquered populations threatened the entire coastal areas.[90] This vast onslaught, as Bishko points out, represent the continuing thrust of the motives and objectives of the medieval re-conquest, the plan to acquire 'new Grenadas in the Maghrib.'[91] The conquest of the whole of North Africa, and its emptying of its Muslim population, was now a mere matter of time, except for the unexpected arrival on the scene of the so-called Barbarossa brothers.[92] Indeed, the sheikhs of Algeria had called the Barbarossa brothers, Arruj and Kheir Eddin, and with their alliance, the process of fighting the Spanish assault began. It was this conflict, which involved the Ottomans-North Africans on one side, and the armies of Christendom on the other, which was turned by Western historiography into Barbary Piracy.

In reality, there never was Barbary piracy as has been depicted in Western historiography and its inept Muslim following. Firstly, North African towns and cities, far from being dens of pirates, were places of commerce, where there took place much trade, including between European powers and Muslims. Far from being a den of sanguinary pirates, Algiers, for instance, was a recognised port of

---

[84] N. Housley: *The Later Crusades;* Oxford University Press, 1992; p. 306.

[85] N. Housley: *Documents on the Later Crusades; 1274-1580;* Macmillan Press Ltd; London; 1996. A.S. Atiya: *Crusade, Commerce and Culture;* Oxford University Press; London; 1962.

[86] C.H. Bishko: The Spanish and Portuguese Reconquest, 1095-1492, *in A History of the Crusades* Vol. 3: *The Fourteenth and Fifteenth Centuries,* ed., H.W. Hazard Madison: The University of Wisconsin Press, 1975.

[87] In G. Fisher: *Barbary Legend,* Oxford; 1957, p. 34.

[88] W. Spencer: *Algiers in the Age of the Corsairs;* University of Oklahoma Press; 1976; p. 16.

[89] N. Matar: Piracy and Captivity in the Early Modern Mediterranean: The Perspective from Barbary in C. Jowitt Editor: *Pirates? The Politics of Plunder,* 1550-1650; (Palgrave; Macmillan; 2007); pp. 56-73; p. 57.

[90] J.B. Wolf: *The Barbary Coast;* W.W. Norton & Company; New York, p. 5.

[91] C. J. Bishko: The Spanish and Portuguese Reconquest, 1095-1492, *in A History of the Crusades* Vol. 3: *The Fourteenth and Fifteenth Centuries,* ed., H.W. Hazard Madison: The University of Wisconsin Press, 1975; p. 455.

[92] J. Glubb: *A Short History of the Arab Peoples;* Hodder and Stoughton, 1969, p. 262.

call for European, including English shipping in the 16th century.[93] No less remarkable, Fisher points out, was the competition for permanent commercial concessions in the so called den of piracy.[94] Moreover, as Fisher,[95] referring to a number of contemporary sources, points out:

> Another conventional misconception, that the period of Turkish rule in Barbary was one of sterile stagnation, can be counteracted to some extent by the evidence of contemporary testimonials to the steady, and at one time startlingly rapid development of the city of Algiers during nearly three centuries from an obscure tributary of Spain to the capital of a strategically important state and even, for a brief moment, the centre of commerce in the Mediterranean, from which the French republican armies were in part fed and financed…[96]

Likewise, Bejaia, due to its great trading role, had a specially close connection with France.[97] France had a special presence in both Bonne and La Calle. In fact the whole of the North African coast was seen as a great mart, a place of exchanges that profited both sides.[98]

From the 16th century down to the colonial age of the 19th century, during the so-called reign of the Barbary Pirates, rather than Muslim piracy preying on Western shipping, it was Muslim North Africa that was devastated by Christian piracy.[99] As Matar points out, one of the recurrent motifs in early modern North African biographies, jurisprudential decisions, royal letters, and others, describes the danger of Euro-Christian invasions and the destructive impact of captivity on the region's stability, both political and social.[100] All coastlines were zones of great insecurity.[101] By the end of the 16th century, there were so many Muslim slaves in port cities from Genoa to Cadiz that they became a common theme in European painting and sculpture.[102] Muslim captives seized by European pirate and naval fleets belonged to various nationalities: Moroccans, Algerians, Tunisians, Turks and Arabs from Turkey and from Ottoman-ruled Egypt, Basra,

[93] In G. Fisher: *Barbary Legend*; op cit; pp. 123-4.

[94] Ibid.

[95] Ibid.

[96] H. De Grammont: *Histoire d'Alger Sous la Domination Turque*; Paris; 1887, p. 348; E. Plantet: *Correspondence des Deys d'Alger*; op cit; ii. 439-52; Add. MS. 34932, &C.

[97] G. Fisher: *Barbary Legend;* op cit; 23. V. Vitale: *Diplomatici e consoli della Republica di genoa; 1904-12;* Atti della Societa Ligure di Storia patria; vol lxiii; records Genoese consuls, &c., between 1492 and 1517. F.O. 77/3; 16 Feb. 1792; T. MacGill: *An Account of Tunis, its Government, etc.;* (Glasgow; 1811). J.L. M. Poiret, *Voyage en Barbarie;* 2 vols; (Paris; 1789).

[98] R. Tully: *Narrative of Ten Tears Residence at Tripoli in Africa (1783-93),* (London 1816); pp. 38 and 218. *Political History of England* (*Pol. Hist*); ed. W. Hunt and R. Poole; v. 120-1 and *Memorials of Henry VII* (ed, J. Gairdner, 1858), p. 263, both in 1505. James IV to Cardinal d'Amboise, 14 Oct. 1507, and to 'magnifico viro domino Philippo de Prates Cathalorum Alexandriae civitatis consuli sagaeissimo', same date, *Letters and Papers, Richard III and Henry VII* (ed. J. Gairdner, 1861-3), 252

[99] N. Barbour: *Morocco;* Thames and Hudson; 1965; p. 101.

[100] N. Matar: Piracy and Captivity in the Early Modern Mediterranean: The Perspective from Barbary in C. Jowitt Editor: *Pirates? The Politics of Plunder*, 1550-1650; (Palgrave; Macmillan; 2007); pp. 56-73; at p. 62.

[101] J. Mathiex: Trafic et Prix de l'Homme en Mediterranee au 17 et 18 Siecles; *ANNALES: Economies, Societes, Civilisations*: vol 9: pp. 157-64; pp. 163-4.

[102] N. Matar: Piracy and Captivity; op cit; p. 57.

and Hormuz, along with 'Muslim Indians,'[103] i.e native Americans who had been brought as slaves to Europe and had subsequently converted to Islam.[104] Algiers, in particular, was recurrently attacked, the greatest expedition against it being in 1541, led by Charles V, who aimed at emulating the Tunisian success of 1535, and ending Muslim rule in the country. Charles felt very sure of himself. Already master of Tunis, he saw himself adding the words "Emperor of Africa" to his title.[105] The Algerian stand in face of the invading force (helped by a huge storm,) destroyed the vast Christian armada.[106]

Attacks on the high seas against North African shipping were particularly vicious, and the Christian attackers made little difference between crew and unarmed passengers.[107] Pilgrims and merchant ships were constant prey of Christian Corsairs, most feared of whom being those armed by the Knights of Malta,[108] or flying the flag of the Two Sicilies. They harassed North African shipping and maintained a state of insecurity until the 18th century.[109] The religious crusading order of the Knights of St. John based in Malta[110] were dislodged by the Ottomans from Rhodes in 1522 but found refuge in Malta. From there, they swooped on and terrorised Muslim shipping, seizing hundreds of Muslim merchant ships from the 16th to the 18th century (204 ships in 1764 alone).[111] Also, every Western nation saw Muslim shipping as prey for attack. By the summer of 1600 British pirates terrorised the Mediterranean with their violence. They looked on Turkish and Algerian shipping as fair game, despite the fact that England was at peace with both states.[112] French pirates disputed them the sea, and shared the same lust for cruelty, making no difference between nationalities: all Muslims to them made good captives, regardless of their national origin and the state of affairs between the captive's country and France.[113] Throughout the early modern period, French pirates, along with the Maltese and the Italians, sailed under Majorcan or Portuguese flags (as Majorcans sailed under French flags, and Britons under Spanish flags), attacked Muslim shipping, and if they were at war with Algiers, every Muslim became an Algerian to justify enslavement.[114] North African coastlines and cities were ruined by Christian attacks, whilst Muslim Mediterranean shipping was literally decimated.

---

[103] Bu Sharab, *Wathaiq wa dirasat* (Rabat: Dar al-Aman, 1997), p.147; and Chapter 4 in *Maghariba fi al-Burtughal.*
[104] N. Matar: Piracy and Captivity; p. 60.
[105] G. Welch: *North African Prelude;* Greenwood Press Publishers; 1972; p. 400.
[106] Ibid; p. 401.
[107] W. Byron: *Cervantes: A Biography*; (New York; Paragon; 1988); p. 193.
[108] See E.W. Shermerhorn: *Malta of the Knights* (London; 1929).
[109] L. Valensi: *North Africa Before the French Conquest; 1790-1830*; tr., by K.J. Perkins; Africana Publishing Company; London; 1977; p. 47; and note 1; p. 54-5.
[110] J.B. Wolf: *The Barbary Coast,* op cit, p. 42.
[111] L. Valensi: *North Africa*; p. 47; and note 1; p. 54-5.
[112] P. Earle: *Corsairs of Malta and Barbary*; op cit, p. 38.
[113] N. Matar: Piracy and Captivity; op cit; p. 66.
[114] Ibid; p. 66-7.

If there was Barbary piracy, it came as a response to the piracy of which the Muslims were victims, and which had been going on for centuries.[115] Muslim piracy, moreover, was never as destructive and as cruel as the Christian, or as depicted in history. Barbary piracy, in fact, as demonstrated by Fisher, most particularly, remained one of the greatest myths of modern history to justify the colonisation of Algeria and North Africa.[116] This was a pattern established long before, the Portuguese conquest of Ceuta in 1415, for instance, was blamed on Muslim piracy, and similar justifications were used for Spanish attacks on Mers el-Kebir and Oran early in the following century.[117] More importantly, the French blaming piracy to justify the invasion of Algeria in 1830 rests on hardly any solid ground. Godechot notes how:

> While the Barbary danger had disappeared on the European coast for more than a hundred years the Christian danger existed on the African shores until the end of the eighteenth century.[118]

Algeria had no fleet left in the 19th century to justify the argument of piracy, this fleet having terminated its life in the 18th century.[119] When William Shaler, the new American ambassador arrived in Algiers, in 1815, all he could see of the Algerian fleet was four frigates, five corvettes, one brig, and a galley, a total of eleven vessels.[120] These were to suffer final annihilation by Lord Exmouth's famed bombardment of Algiers in 1816.[121] There was no fleet and there were barely any Christian captives, either. In 1830, when the French took Algiers, the number of Christian captives in the city was a mere hundred.[122]

Despite the fact that he country no longer had any vessel, the call rose for military invasion to put an end to 'the scourge of Muslim piracy.' James Grey Jackson thus held:

> The first principle of this barbarous and sanguinary government, according to the African adage, is 'to maintain the arm of power, by making streams of blood flow without intermission around the throne.' This government 'reflects disgrace on Christendom' and that the bombardment like that of Lord Exmouth in 1816 is insufficient punishment for 'the repeated insults offered by these ruffians to civilised Europe.[123]

And indeed, it was under such noble premise, of seeking to remove Islamic piracy that the French invasion in 1830 took place. Barbour notes how:

---

[115] H. Bresc: *Un Monde Mediterraneen: Economies et Societe en Sicile*, 1300-1450; 2 vols, Rome-Palermo, 1986.

H. Bresc: *Politique et Societe en Sicile; XII-XVem siecle*; Variorum; Aldershot; 1990.

A. Mieli: *La Science Arabe et son Influence sur l'eveil Mondial*; Leiden, Brill; 1939; p. 45.

[116] G. Fisher: *Barbary Legend*; op cit; L. Valensi: *North Africa*; op cit;

[117] G. Fisher: *Barbary Legend*; p. 24.

[118] Godechot: La Course Maltaise; Revue Africaine; 1952 in N. Barbour: *A Survey*; op cit; p. 38.

[119] See for instance: L. Valensi: *Le Maghreb Avant la Prise d'Alger*; (Paris; 1969). J. Mathiex: Trafic et prix de l'Homme en Mediterranee au 17 et 18 Siecles; *ANNALES: Economies, Societes, Civilisations*: vol 9; pp. 157-64.

[120] A. Hollingsworth Miller: One man's View: William Shaler and Algiers; in *Through Foreign Eyes*; (ed., A.A. Heggoy), op cit; pp. 7-55; at p. 18.

[121] C. Lloyd: *English Corsairs on the Barbary Coast*, op cit; pp. 163-4.

[122] N. Barbour: *A Survey*; op cit; p. 36.

[123] J. Grey Jackson: *An Account of Timbuctu and Hausa*; London; 1820; pp. 457-63.

In reality there is little doubt that the basic motive of the French Government was its desire to restore the tottering credit of the regime by a military success; and to win for the Restoration Government the credit which Napoleon had lost by the evacuation of Egypt. In the event Algiers was duly captured and the achievement inspired a number of laudatory poems throughout Europe including one in the dialect of Genoa.[124]

The bombardment of Algiers by Lord Exmouth in 1816 which entirely destroyed the Algerian fleet

The scramble for the lands formerly under Ottoman rule, the desire to spread Christianity, and others already noted, constituted good reasons for the French to invade. But there were few more reasons that justified the adventure. One of them, possibly the most important of all, was to found on the Algerian territory an important colony on the American model, following the removal of its 'inferior' natives and their replacement by superior people of European stock.[125] Native Algerians had to be driven into the desert; their elimination part of a natural law that stipulates the 'disappearance of backward peoples.'[126] Writing straight in the wake of the French capture of Algiers, the Paris daily *Le Constitutionnel* (11 July 1830):

> The seizure of Algiers begins a new era for world civilisation. If we arc able to exploit it, part of Africa in a few years will be blessed with a hard-working population, like America, and the Mediterranean will no longer be a mere lake.[127]

This belief was echoed throughout the period when emptying Algeria of its natives was both an aim and a possibility. As the mass eradication of Algerians

---

[124] *A Spedizion d'Arge*; (Genoa; 1834).
[125] M. Morsy: *North Africa 18001890*; Longman, London, 1984; pp. 287-8.
[126] Ibid.
[127] *Le Constitutionnel* (11 July 1830)

was proceeding, Marmier insisted in 1847 that Algeria was a land for a New France, to grow what the old France lacked, house the surplus population, expand industry and shipping, 'with no room for inferior natives.'[128] In 1832, the highly influential, V.A. Hain of the Societie Coloniale de l'Etat d'Alger, had condemned the whole population of Algeria to be 'beyond redemption and only fit to be removed from the earth.'[129]

There were many experts accompanying the French army, or landing soon after to make an inventory of all that was to be extracted from the country for the benefit of France, and many studies were made to that effect.[130] The priority was to turn Algeria into an outlet for French surplus population, and also a supplier of cheap materials and other produce.[131] Experimental farms were to be encouraged and promoted, and if they were successful, they would lead to a vast colonial effort.[132] The vast plains around Algiers, the Mitidja, could be taken over totally by pushing further south the indigenous populations 'that would refuse to submit.'[133] By this it was meant the tribes that would refuse to have their lands and whatever they owned taken away from them. France would yield produce now being imported from India and America, whilst Algeria would become another market for French mass manufactured products.[134] Duties on imported and exported goods would yield considerable revenues, which made it a high priority to capture all centres of commerce from the coast down to the desert.[135] The occupation of harbours would, besides, give control of every movement by people.[136]

James Grey Jackson, writing in 1820, foresaw what the conquest of Algeria (but by Britain) would bring: besides the 'civilisation of the Berbers' and their conversion to Christianity.[137] It would result in:

1. An incalculable demand for spices and East Indian manufactures of silk and cotton.

2. A similar demand for coffee and sugar manufactured and un-manufactured; as well as for other articles of West Indian produce.

3. An incalculable demand for all our various articles of manufacture. In addition, Britain would obtain from this fine country:

---

[128] X. Marmier: *Lettres sur l'Algerie*; Paris; 1847.

[129] V.A. Hain: *A La Nation. Sur Alger*; Paris; 1832; pp. 31; 58 ff.

[130] In P. Gaffarel: *Lectures Geographiques et Historiques sur l'Algerie et les Colonies Francaises*; Garniers Freres; Paris; 1886; 281.

[131] Ibid.

[132] Ibid.

[133] Ibid.

[134] Ibid.

[135] Rapport du doc de Rovigo au Ministre de la Guerre (1832) In P. Gaffarel: *Lectures Geographiques et Historiques sur l'Algerie et les Colonies Francaises*; Garniers Freres; Paris; 1886; 282.

[136] Ibid.

[137] J.G. Jackson: *An Account of Timbuctu and Hausa*; London; 1820; p. 463.

a. An immense supply of the finest wheat and other grain that the world produces.

b. Direct commerce with the interior of Africa.[138]

He pursued:

> The fertile and populous districts which lie contiguous to the Nile of Sudan, throughout the whole of the interior of Africa would become, in a few years, as closely connected to us, by mutual exchange of benefits as our own colonies; and such a stimulus would be imparted to British enterprises and industry, as would secure to us such a store of gold as would equal the riches of Solomon....[139]

A necessary means for the subjugation of the Muslim land has always remained the same and to this day, in 2017-18: associating some natives in the project. According to Duc de Rovigo, who would distinguish himself by large scale massacres of tribes, the idea was to use Arab chiefs at first to serve France.[140] He elaborates on his plan: the persons selected should be from amongst the most influential, and to be doubly sure of their collaboration, members of their families should be kept as hostages, and this would secure the entire control of the country.[141] If these chiefs did not collaborate colonisation would fail. So, their interests should coincide with those of France, and they should be protected from rivals.[142] These people should be made to collect taxes on 'our' behalf, and they should receive their share; as France's strength on the ground increases she could always add new conditions on these people. This way, colonisation should expand fast.[143] Then, he concludes:

> We must create two rival factions one temporal exerted by the great sheikhs, and another spiritual exerted by the marabouts. These two influences will share out an ignorant population on roughly equal line. Our aim is to fight one with the other.[144]

By colonising Algeria at a time when its stature in Europe was wobbling, France sought to regain a position of respect, strengthen the feeling of national pride, and make up for the loss of lands to the English. There was no room for defeat.

> Ejected from North America by Great Britain, absent from Latin America, France was seeking a colonial empire to remake her image and to reaffirm her power in Europe. Describing Algeria in a tourist guide book at the end

---

[138] In A. Thomson: *Barbary*; op cit; p. 136; 50; etc.

[139] J.G. Jackson: *An Account;* op cit; p 463.

[140] Rapport du doc de Rovigo, in Gaffarel; op cit; p. 282.

[141] Ibid.

[142] Ibid.

[143] Ibid.

[144] Ibid.

of the Century, one author wrote: 'Losing America, we have regained Africa, to which Algeria is the gateway.'[145]

5. Dealing with Natives

Throughout the long years of colonisation, Alleg et al remark, French education in Algeria has exaggerated the differences and

> Hereditary hatreds that experts have 'discovered' existed between Berbers and Arabs. It had become traditional to oppose the descendants of the Arab conquerors with those of the conquered Berbers as if they were two people fundamentally different from each other, and always at war with each other.[146]
>
> There is nothing fortuitous or innocent in this presentation of history, by flattering and exaggerating ancients prejudices, the aim was to prevent a coalition of the colonised against their coloniser... and for this reason the opposition to the Arab 'invaders' has been greatly exaggerated. The role of the Berber woman leader, Al-Kahina, and her 'heroic' death fighting against those same 'invaders' has left the memory of Berber resistance against the soldiers of Islam, whilst in truth, despite some sporadic opposition to Islam, the most important fact was the welcome offered by the local population to the conquering Muslims.[147]

This was one side of the issue, to which it will be returned at some length in chapter 7. There was another side to it. It was the creation of yet another sharp divide this time between Arabs and Turks. Thus, according to the colonialist Rozet:

> The Bloody Despotic Turkish Dey (ruling on behalf of the Sultan) exercised arbitrarily the right of life or death over his Algerian subjects until he was inevitably assassinated during one of the numerous revolts by his rag tag gang of army, whence blood flowed.[148]
>
> The meanest Turk rejects with infinite disdain all equality of a native with him; and the proposition which had been inculcated during a succession of ages, that Turks are born to command and the natives of Algiers to obey.... Has long been received here as political axiom [says the American consul in Algiers, Shaler, on the eve of the French occupation.][149]

---

[145] L. Addi: Colonia Mythologies: Algeria in the French Imagination: HAL; at https://halshs.archives-ouvertes.fr/halshs-00397835 Submitted on 23 Jun 2009
[146] H. Alleg et al: *La Guerre d'Algerie*, op cit; vol 1, p. 46.
[147] Ibid.
[148] M.P. Rozet, 'Alger', in F. Hoefer *Algerie par Capitaines du Genie Rozet et Carette* Etats Tripolitains, Paris, 1846, p. 14.
[149] W. Shaler: *Sketches of Algiers, Political, Historical and Civil*; Boston; Cummings; 1826, pp. 28-9.

In 1830, on entering Algeria, the French proclaimed to the population that their intention was

> To secure, and for eternity, the happiness of the people whose arms have freed from a humiliating yoke... and that France was not seeking to abandon you (Algerians) to the vengeance of your former oppressors from whom we have freed you.[150]

French scholarship to this moment highlights the benevolent role of France. Fleury,[151] Julien,[152] Mantran and others depict for us the atrocities supposedly inflicted on each other by Arabs, Berbers, Turks, and Kuluglis, a visceral hatred, bloodier than all civil wars in history. Mantran, in particular,[153] discovers a unique enmity between Turks and Arabs. In all, whether in colonialist discourse, or in scholarly writing, French benevolence saved the persecuted Algerians. The following chapters will show us, indeed, this benevolent act on the part of France.

Here, though, let's look at some claims of the sort just seen, and what sort of anomaly they present.

Moritz Wagner, a German scientist who accompanied the French expeditionary force against Constantine writes:

> Ahmed (Hadj Ahmed Bey, the governor of the eastern province of Constantine) (a Kulugli; i.e of Turkish-Algerian descent) now increased his regular force, principally by Kabyles, of whom he was peculiarly fond. They did not pay more than a nominal tribute, and their Marabuts received even presents from him, while he held the Arabs of his province in a state of complete oppression.[154]

> Ahmed received them (the Turks) very kindly, but afterwards had them nearly all beheaded, one after the other, under various pretexts. He was a Kurugli, jealous of the thorough-bred Turks, and favouring the half-breed Kuruglis; all his officers belonged to that denomination.[155]

These and similar claims are however contradicted by facts. Hadj Ahmed, a Kulughli, described as an anti Turk, was in fact the most pro-Ottoman of all Algerian leaders.[156] His links with the Sublime Porte are well documented by a series of archival documents, which show how far the links went and how strong the bonds were.[157] In fact, the reason Hadj Ahmed's role in Algerian resistance was totally disregarded by French historiography, Morsy remarks, was his pro-Ottoman stand.[158] Colonial historiography, as Temimi notes, has deliberately

---

[150] G. Fleury: *Comment l'Algerie Devint Francaise*; Perrin, Paris, 2004, p. 122.

[151] Ibid, p. 121.

[152] C.A. Julien: *History of North Africa;* tr., from French by J. Petrie; Routledge & Kegan Paul; London; 1970.

[153] R. Mantran: North Africa in the Sixteenth and Seventeenth Centuries; in *The Cambridge History of Islam;* edited by P.M. Holt; A.K. Lambton; B. Lewis; Cambridge University Press; 1970; vol 2a; pp. 238-65; at p. 250 ff in particular.

[154] M. Wagner: *The Tricolor on the Atlas*, op cit, p. 243.

[155] Ibid.

[156] M. Morsy: *North Africa 1800-1900;* Longman; London; 1984; p. 137.

[157] A. Temimi: *Le Beylik de Constantine et Hadj Ahmed Bey (1830-1837), Revue d'Histoire Maghrebine*, Vol 1, Tunis, 1978, appendixes.

[158] M. Morsy: *North Africa*; op cit; p. 137.

chosen to exploit and to inflate the role of some historical figures and some events, as well as some phases of history which suit its ideology but have inflicted terrible damage to the history of the Maghrib.[159] In regard to Algeria, Temimi adds, both Abd al-Kader and Hadj Ahmed dominated the period between 1830 and 1840, however, in colonial works, Abd al-Kader has been unjustly given preference over Hadj Ahmed who has been deliberately neglected.[160]

Churchill, who wrote by far the most personal account of Abd al-Kader, in the 1860s, went to extremes in highlighting the supposed hostility between Arabs and Turks:

> Abdel Kader arrived at Constantinople, January 7, 1853 On landing he went directly to the grand mosque of Tophane, filled with joy and gratitude at finding himself once more in a temple of the Prophet. The French ambassador gave a grand entertainment in his honour, to which the principal personages of the Frank society were invited. This act of hospitality closed the social relations of Abdel Kader with the civilised world. During his passage through it, his worth, his genius, his honour, had been magnanimously recognised in one long ovation. He was now in a capital where (Turkish) barbarism is harlequinised into a constrained semblance of European civilisation.[161]
> He visited the Turkish ministers. They received him with ill-feigned demonstrations of civility and respect. Policy alone made them outwardly courteous. Such is the eradicable arrogance and self-sufficiency of the Turks, that they despise all races alike but their own. Utter strangers to noble sentiments, and scorning to admit the possibility of there being anything in the world more important than themselves, they regarded the attentions paid to Abdel Kader (despite his glorious struggles for their common faith) with jealousy and even derision. His fame oppressed them. An Arab hero was, in their minds, an incongruity, an impertinence.[162]

It is of course difficult to understand or explain why if Abd Al-Kader was so hated by the Turks he chose to settle in the city of Bursa until the massive earthquake of 1855 forced him to leave for Syria. Churchill himself was in Turkey, and wrote:

> I was at Constantinople in the month of September, 1853. Abd al Kader was living, an exile, at Broussa. To have been within such an easy distance of one who had for so many years been invested in my mind with all the attributes of heroic greatness.[163]

---

[159] A. Temimi: Le Beylik de Constantine et Hadj Ahmed Bey, op cit; p. 9.
[160] Ibid.
[161] C.H. Churchill: *The Life of Abd Al Kader*, Chapman and Hall, London, 1867, p. 299.
[162] Ibid, p. 300.
[163] Ibid, preface viii.

In 1840, whilst he was still fighting the French, Abd al-Kader himself made efforts to enlist support for his movement from the Sublime Porte.[164] To him as to Hadj Ahmed little help came, for the Ottoman realm itself was on the collapse.

Whilst Ottoman weakness in the 19th century played the major part in the lack of support for Algerian resistance, modern Western historiography tends, of course, to dismiss the fact that had it not been for the 16th century and subsequent Algerian-Turkish alliance, it is difficult to see how Algeria (just as the rest of North Africa) could have survived in times of Christian onslaught and conquest. Had, indeed, the Spanish conquest of Algeria succeeded in the 16th century, the Algerians would have faced the same fate as did the natives of the Americas who were colonised at the same time: mass extinction.

Regarding the Algerian population, rather than it being formed of distinct groups, it was, instead, very difficult to break it into separate entities, for it was and remains a symbiosis of inter-ethnic relations. A large portion of the Algerian population was and is a result of inter-marriage between Turks and local women or between Arabs and Berbers. Moreover, when they occupied Algiers, the French, Alleg et al. remark, the country's inhabitants, whether Arabs, Kabyles, or Koulouglis, did not welcome at all their 'liberators from Turkish oppression.'[165] Whatever their differences in fortune or the situation they were in, and despite economic and other differences and even some tribal feuding, all these groups were conscious of their belonging to one community, profoundly marked by Islam and Muslim civilisation.[166] The following chapters will show that from the moment the French set foot in Algeria, they were fought by all. Turkish and Kabyle infantry worked with Arab cavalry; armed units were constituted of all ethnic groups who fought and died together. Apart from some individuals from all groups who for whatever reasons sided with the French, no entity failed to resist the French, and pay the heavy price for it. In a letter from Abd al-Kader to Qaid Ibrahim, a Turk, on 2 April 1833, we read:

> It is my duty to rally you to my banner, for only unity means power, division produces weakness. Let us therefore efface the racial differences among the true Muslims. Let us see Arabs, Turks, Kulughlis, and Moors live as brothers, all worshiping the true God, and let us altogether have one armed hand raised against the enemy.[167]

---

[164] M. Morsy: *North Africa*; op cit, p. 138.
[165] H. Alleg et al: *La Guerre d'Algerie*, op cit, vol 1, p. 58.
[166] Ibid.
[167] Translation attached to: General Boyer to Minister of war, Oran, 3 April, 1833, AHG: H20.

6. Colonisation in Western Narrative

Note has been made above of the work by Bernard and Redon aimed for schools of all levels. Here are picked some of the instances of how such a work interprets and conveys Algerian history, and what sort of impact this has.

-Regarding the causes of the French expedition, it says: France in 1830 had no intention of conquering Algeria. It only undertook that long and difficult action in response to the provocations and the insolence of the Turks.[168] France had two main complaints: Damages caused by Algerian piracy to its trade and that of European powers for three centuries, and the outrage caused by the Dey to the French consul Deval and the French flag.[169]

-Battle of Staoueli, which took place in the wake of the French landing: The Great Battle was engaged on the Plateau of Staoueli. The Turks and their Allies: Arabs, Kabyles, and Negroes rushed onto our infantry trying to encircle the men in small numbers and 'then massacre them.' French troops sustained the shock and resisted. Reinforcements arrived; artillery caused great havoc in enemy ranks, and then the infantry took the offensive. With Bayonets and daggers it threw down the Turks and entered their camp.[170]

-Algiers which was entered by the French on 5 July 1830 did not present any sad aspect whereby a victory had allowed in an enemy. The shops were closed, but the merchants were tranquilly seated in front of their doors, waiting for the opening time. The resignation to the will of God so deeply ingrained in the Muslim spirit, the awareness of the power of France, her generosity well known, were all reasons which spread confidence, and so it was. This trust in France was justified by the behaviour of the conquerors, the first days were marked by a scrupulous respect for agreements. Persons, private property, mosques, everything was respected.[171]

-The expedition against Constantine 1836-1837: The city was under the rule of an energetic 'and cruel old man,' Bey Ahmed.[172]

Then this:

> Les Arabes, qui guettaient les colons et leurs établissements, profitaient de toutes les occasions pour voler ou assassiner.

Which translates:

> The Arabs kept a watch on the colons and their farms, then took advantage of every opportunity to steal and murder.[173]

---

[168] P. Bernard and F Redon: *Histoire, Colonisation, Geographie et Administration de l'Algerie*, Librairie Adolphe Jourdan; Algiers, 1906; p. 29.
[169] Ibid.
[170] Ibid; p. 31.
[171] Ibid; p. 34.
[172] Ibid; p. 38.
[173] Ibid; p. 43.

And the following: Expeditions were carried out in both Kabylies (Greater and Lesser Kabylia) against the Agitator Bou Barla, 'whose fanatical preaching' had stirred many tribes of the Djurdjura region into rebellion.[174]

Throughout, the picture is that of: French gallantry, fair treatment of the natives, and Turkish-Arab and Kabyle bloodlust and cruel deeds. As facts on the ground and accounts by French officers would reveal to us in the subsequent chapters, it was entirely the reverse of everything the two authors claim. However, one takes note of how the reshaping of facts could through the educational system entirely shape the view of whole generations.

Should it be thought that the situation would improve amidst the better informed or higher scholarship, this would be entirely mistaken. This scholarship entirely reshapes French colonial history in every single aspect. Let us briefly quote a few views.

First on the causes of French occupation, piracy, primarily. Mantran, for instance, says:

> Everywhere (in the Maghrib) there had arisen small autonomous states. The ports had also made themselves independent, and local governments had turned them into bases for corsairs who raided merchant ships and at the same time carried on the war against the infidels.[175]

Charles Andre Julien claims:

> From Djerba (Gerba, Jerba) to Morocco each of the ports constituted a sort of republic organised for piracy: Tunis, Bizerta, Bougie (Bejaia and other spellings), Algiers, Oran, Honein, each at its expense fitted out galleys which scoured the Mediterranean. The corsairs of the 14th and 15th centuries were not pure robbers, as the Turks were to become.[176]

Hiskett goes even further:

> Muslim preying on Christian shipping in the Mediterranean had begun almost as soon as the Muslims had become established in North Africa. It was inseparable from the whole theocratic, Koranic perception of the Muslims which left them with the unshakable belief that to attack the infidel as and where he was to be found was consistent with the Will of Allah. As in the case of enslavement, so also in that of piracy, there was no moral restraint on Muslim behaviour, only the constraints of expediency. Agreements to restrain privateering were not honoured... Under such circumstances the eventual occupation of the area by one of the European powers seems, in hindsight, to have been both inevitable and understandable. The alternative was to cease trading in the Mediterranean.[177]

---

[174] Ibid; p. 59.

[175] R. Mantran: North Africa in the Sixteenth and Seventeenth Centuries; in *The Cambridge History of Islam;* edited by P.M. Holt; A.K. Lambton; B. Lewis; Cambridge University Press; 1970; vol 2a; pp. 238-65; at p. 248.

[176] C.A. Julien: *History of North Africa;* tr., f rom French by J. Petrie; Routledge & Kegan Paul; London; 1970; p. 274.

[177] M. Hiskett: *The Course of Islam in Africa;* Edinburgh University Press; 1994; p. 27.

This narrative has two effects:

1. It is the sort of crooked history that has been studied by many Algerians (and other Muslims), and they becoming its victims, believing it, just as this author did once upon a time until he went back to the sources, including accounts by French officers who sought the eradication of Algerians, and who proudly described their deeds in their memoirs.

2. When putting all explanations in Western narrative together, that the French had come to Algeria to civilise, to quell pirates, to remove the Turkish despot, and to fight a fanaticised, murderous, mob, it makes their acts acceptable. So, whatever was inflicted on such Algerian society, including the slaying of millions, was only for the good, and was hence justified. This is precisely the argument that has for centuries to this very day justified Western violence on Islamic society, just as on other societies in the Americas, Africa and Oceania.[178]

French colonial officers in Algeria, a product of such an ideology, thus, saw themselves absolutely legitimised in their deeds:

> According to me [says Montagnac,] This is how war should be made to the Arabs: Kill all men over the age of 15; take all women and children, fill boats, and send them to the Marquise Islands or elsewhere. In a word eradicate everything that does not crawl at our feet like dogs.[179]

---

[178] D. E. Stannard: *American Holocaust; The Conquest of the New World;* Oxford University Press; 1992.
W. Howitt: *Colonisation and Christianity*: Longman; London; 1838.
J. Fontana: *The Distorted Past*, Blackwell, 1995.
W. Churchill: *A Little Matter of Genocide*; City Lights Books; San Francisco; 1997.
E.R. Wolf: *Europe and the People Without History*; University of California Press; Berkeley; 1982.
[179] Letter to de Leuglay; sent from Philipeville (Skikda) on 24 January 1843; Colonel L. Francois de Montagnac: *Lettres d'un Soldat*; Paris; 1885; p. 334.

Two

THE CONQUEST OF ALGERIA
(1830-1836)

It is not too much to say [Lane Poole observes,] that from the moment when the French, having merely taken the city of Algiers, began the work of subduing the tribes of the interior in 1830, to the day when they at last set up civil, instead of military, government, after the lessons of the Franco-German war in 1870, the history of Algeria is one long record of stupidly brutal camp-rule, repudiation of sacred engagements, inhuman massacres of unoffending natives of both sexes and all ages, violence without judgment, and severity without reason. One French general after another was sent out to bring the rebellious Arabs and Kabyles into subjection, only to display his own incompetence for the inhuman task, and to return baffled and brutalized by the disgraceful work he thought himself bound to carry out. There is no more humiliating record in the annals of annexation than this miserable conquest of Algiers. It is the old story of trying to govern what the conquerors call "niggers," without attempting to understand the people first. Temper, justice, insight, and conciliation would have done more in four years than martial intolerance and drum tyranny accomplished in forty.[180]

General Pellissier, famed for his smoking of Algerians, says:

Let us be convinced that cruelty in war is not foreign to any race, and that the most civilized nations are, in this respect, often more barbarous than the savages.[181]

Extreme, bloody, brutality defined French colonial history of Algeria, a story which began three years before the French entry in 1830. In April 1827, the Dey of Algiers (the ruler of Algeria on behalf of the Ottoman sultan) angrily struck the French Consul, Deval, with a fly whisk; the reason: the French envoy's insolence over a disputed unpaid debt incurred by France.[182] It was the excuse used by France to invade the country.[183] The background to the fly-whisk was this: Hussein Dey, on assuming power in 1818, inherited a financial problem dating back to the Napoleonic era.[184] When Napoleon began his rise to power, between 1793 and 1798, Algerian wheat was bought for the French army through two

---

[180] S. Lane Poole: *Barbary Corsairs*; Fisher & Unwin, 1890; pp. 303-4.

[181] M. Wagner: *The Tricolor on the Atlas*, op cit, p. 149.

[182] C.A. Julien: *Histoire de l'Algerie Contemporaine, 1827-1871*; Presses Universitaires de France, 1964; pp. 21; 33.

[183] R. Ageron: *Histoire de l'Algerie Contemporaine;* Presses Universitaires de France, Paris, 1964. For details on causes that led to the French invasion, see H Alleg et al: *La Guerre d'Algerie*: op cit; vol 1.

[184] J.M. Abun-Nasr: *A History of the Maghrib*, Cambridge University Press, 1971, p. 236.

Algerian Jewish merchant families, Bakri and Bushnaq (Busnach).[185] The arrears in the payment for this wheat amounted in 1798 to about eight million francs, which the Jewish merchants claimed they could not pay until they themselves had been paid by the French.[186] By 1801, the amount of the debt had doubled from what it was, but after lengthy negotiations, agreement was reached that the amount to be paid to Algeria was 7 million francs.[187] However by 1827, nothing had been paid yet, and the Dey's letters of protest had remained ignored.[188] The Dey then requested the extradition of Bushnaq from France but was told this was impossible because the latter had been granted French citizenship, whilst Bakri was now residing in Livourne, in Italy, and had no wish to return to Algiers.[189] Deval, appointed consul in Algiers in 1815, did not seem capable of, or interested in, solving the dispute to a conclusion, especially since the Dey suspected him of collaborating with Jacob Bakri to the detriment of Algeria's interests.[190] The Dey's anger at Deval got worse when he was informed that the latter's nephew, Alexandre Deval, the French vice-consul in Bona (eastern Algeria, today Annaba) since 1825, in contravention of the agreements under which the French merchants operated in the Regency, had the French factories in Bone and La Calle fortified and armed with canons.[191] This amounted to a serious infringement, setting a state within a state. The argument between the Dey and Pierre Deval on 29 April 1827 was thus the culmination of a long period of frictions, and on that occasion the Dey was especially angered by the consul's statement that his government would not bother with his letters relating to the debts.[192] Deval's answer was in fact: 'The King had other things to do than replying to someone of your kind.'[193] Angered by this insolence, the Dey struck the consul on the face.

The Fly Whisk Incident

[185] Ibid.
[186] Ibid.
[187] H. Alleg et al: *La Guerre d'Algerie*; op cit, p. 22.
[188] Ibid.
[189] Ibid.
[190] J.M. Abun-Nasr: *A History of the Maghrib*, op cit, p. 236.
[191] Ibid.
[192] Ibid.
[193] H. Alleg et al: *La Guerre d'Algerie*; op cit, p. 24.

Two or so centuries earlier, France would have just bowed to the fact; in fact two or so centuries earlier the problem would have never arisen, for France out of fear of an Algerian retribution would have paid the debt on the spot. By 1827, however, these were the days of Ottoman decline, and it was the Turks and Algerians who were meant to accept every sort of ignominy. So, the Dey was promptly summoned by the French to make reparations for 'the insult' by a gun salute to the French flag when hoisted at the Kasbah of Algiers. When the Dey refused to comply, the French government ordered a blockade of Algerian ports on 16 June 1827.[194] Three years after, in June 1830, the conquest of Algeria began.

1. The Conquest Begins

In April 1830, Minister Polignac wrote to the French ambassador in Vienna, informing him of the various scenarios for the French conquest. According to one such scenario, Algeria would be shared out amongst European powers as follows: Austria would gain Bone; Sardaigna: Phillipeville (Skikda), Toscany: Djidjeli/Jijel; Naples: Bougie/Bejaia; France: Algiers; Portugal: Tenes; England: Arzew; and Spain: Oran.[195] Very possibly, as was then current, all powers had agreed their shares in various parts of the vast Ottoman domain, and so France was left with Algeria, undisputed.

Early in the Summer of 1830, an impressive French armada sailed out of the southern port of Toulon. Admiral Duperre was in command, and the land-forces on board numbered thirty-seven thousand foot, besides cavalry and artillery.[196] Delayed by bad weather, the fleet was not sighted off Algiers till June 13th, when it anchored in the Bay of Sidi Ferruj, on the western outskirts of Algiers.[197] The French army landed there on the next day, with little opposition, and began to throw up entrenchments.[198]

The plan of campaign had been based upon the secret report made by a French agent—a man named Boutin—in 1808. Algiers, strongly protected from the sea, was known to be relatively weakly defended on the land side, and De Bourmont proposed to disembark his army near the peninsula of Sidi Ferruch and to attack the city from the west.[199] Fort L'Empereur, a castle on the outskirts of Algiers on the site of Charles V's encampment, back in 1541, presented the only serious

[194] J.M. Abun-Nasr: *A History of the Maghrib*, op cit, p. 237.
[195] P. Gaffarel: *Lectures Geographiques et Historiques sur l'Algerie et les Colonies Francaises*; Garniers Freres; Paris; 1886; p. 168.
[196] S. Lane Poole: *Barbary Corsairs*; op cit; p. 302.
[197] Ibid.
[198] Ibid.
[199] W. Blunt: *Desert Hawk*; Methuen & Co. Ltd; London; 1947, p. 11.

obstacle to the operation. The leading Algerian officer, Ibrahim, whose spies had kept him informed of the intention of the French, decided to let the invaders land, and then throw them back into the sea. His decision proved to be a strategic error.[200] The French once landed, could not be repulsed. They had a much stronger force than the Algerians could muster, and more importantly, they had a very powerful artillery, which once in operation could sweep Algerians away at will.

The French attack had been expected by the Dey Hussein for some time already. He had since his coming to power understood the threat that 'Christian countries represented for the land of Islam.'[201] He prepared the country for such an attack, and sought military support from Turkey, most particularly from Khusru Pasha, Minister of the Ottoman Navy, the sending of battle-ships, and the recruitment of janissaries in Anatolia so as to reinforce the military potential of the Regency, now threatened by both England and France.[202] The reply from Ottoman Turkey was rather subdued at best. The Dey kept insisting, asking the Sultan repeatedly to help him set up strong defences and a strong army.[203] Little there was in response, maybe other than some kind words. The reason was simple: the Ottoman realm was then agonising, fighting for its own survival. Ottoman Turkey was no longer the power it had been two or three centuries earlier. To make matters worse, incompetent ministers and personnel who, as nearly always happens, occupied strategic positions, whilst various groups were also plotting against the central authority from within.[204] In fact, much worse, the dismemberment of the Ottoman realm had now become the focus of Western powers. The Treaty of Bucarest, signed on 28 May 1812, that is nearly two decades before the French invasion, was considered the departing point of such dismemberment.[205] This plan became achievable following the destruction of the Ottoman navy at Navarino on 20 October 1827 by the combined fleets of Christian powers. Profiting from this situation Russia declared war on the Ottomans in 1829, which led her army to cross the Balkans, whilst the Russian fleet landed troops at Anhialov, Mesevria and Thrace. Adrianople was captured on 19 August of the same year, and so was Erzurum, and now the Russian armies were marching on Trebizond.[206] Ottoman power was being further undermined by uprisings in Greece, Serbia, and other places, and Mohammed Ali of Egypt chose that very moment to launch a large offensive against Turkey itself. His army had captured Damascus, Aleppo, Antioch, Tripoli, and had now penetrated into

[200] Ibid.

[201] A. Temimi: Le Beylik de Constantine et Hadj Ahmed Bey (1830-1837), *Revue d'Histoire Maghrebine*, vol 1, Tunis, 1978, p. 34.

[202] A. Devoulx: *Registre de Tachrifat*, Algiers, 1852, p. 78.

[203] A. Temimi: Le Beylik de Constantine, op cit, p. 36.

[204] Ibid; p. 37.

[205] Lamouche: *Histoire de la Turquie;* nouvelle Edition; Paris, 1953; p. 249.

[206] M.S. Anderson: *The Eastern Question*, London, 1966, pp. 53-87.

Anatolia, shattering the Ottoman army.[207] In such conditions, Turkey could just about worry about her own survival, let alone help the Regency of Algiers. And when the Sultan ordered some of his representatives elsewhere to come to Algerian help, the French were quick to raise the spectre of massive retribution which calmed everyone's religious or patriotic zeal in seeking to provide assistance to fellow Muslims.[208] The Bey of Tunis was also given similar warning, that should he give assistance to the Dey Hussein, he would suffer the same fate.[209] Prince Polignac in fact wrote to the Pasha of Tunis:

> The expedition which is being prepared in Toulon, is directed against the Dey of Algiers. The other Muslim countries of the African coast are not concerned by this, and their role should be to stick to perfect neutrality; if they have the impudence to divert from this line and seek to give assistance to our enemies, they will, not before long, attract the same power of France against them.[210]

The Regency of Tunis was also in 1830 going through a serious financial crisis, being also heavily indebted to French commerce, and could not afford aggrieving its French partner.[211]

Much weaker militarily than the French and standing alone, the defenders of Algiers still resolved to fight, and put up as bitter opposition to the invaders as much as their strength and courage permitted. The colonial legend, Alleg et al. note, has sought to spread the belief that the French army only met insignificant resistance, and that the advance from Sidi Ferruch to Algiers was a simple walk.[212] (In fact, it was precisely that which this author himself was taught at school and college.) In truth the losses caused to the French army according to French accounts of the time were many times worse than acknowledged in later historical narrative. According to reports by chiefs of staff (who always minimise losses), three months after the landing, 6,000 men had been put out of action, which corresponds to one fifth of the total force.[213] The French found in front of them opponents who fought, and fought well, despite their inferiority in armament, especially in regard to artillery. In many of the accounts, it is even admitted the French showed much admiration for people whom they hitherto regarded only a savages and cowards.[214]

> The day before yesterday, [wrote Captain Matterer (dated 19 June 1830)] we saw a Bedouin walking from amongst the enemy.[215] We shot at him, but

---

[207] E. Creasy: *History of the Ottoman Turks*; Beirut; 1968; p. 522.

[208] ANT Dossier 386 bis, carton 223, document No 1.

[209] Ibid. ANT No1.

[210] Letter dated 13 April 1830; in A. Temimi: Le Beylik de Constantine; op cit; p. 81.

[211] M. Cherif: Expansion Europeene et Difficultes Tunisiennes de 1815 a 1830; in *Annales Economies Societes, Civilisations*, May-Juin, 1970.

[212] H. Alleg et al: *La Guerre d'Algerie;* op cit, p. 32.

[213] Ibid.

[214] Ibid.

[215] Ibid.

he continued to walk fearlessly towards us; bullets flew by his side but he was not disturbed in any way. Then the firing stopped as he was unarmed except with a stick.[216] He greeted us in a stern manner, then looked at our brilliant army... This man was taken to general Berthezene, who asked him the following:

-Why have you come here?

-In order to see you, said the man.

-What do you think of what is in front of you?

-Well impressive but it does not frighten us.

-You are our prisoner.

-Grace be to Allah.

-As you cut off the arms and legs of our men, we are going to do the same to you.

-Grace be to Allah.

This man (pursued Captain Matterer) had a dignity and calm that most men in our courts do not have. His eyes were full of life and pride. Then he speaks:

-Why have you come here?

-To free you from your Turkish oppressors, replied the general.

-Have we complained to you that we are under Turkish yoke?

-No, but the whole universe knows it.

-How many of you are here?

-40,000, and we are expecting the arrival of another 40,000.

The Bedouin raised his eyes towards the sky, and in a stern voice said:

-We are in our land, what gives you the right to come to destroy and take our cities?

-Because your Dey has showed lack of respect for the King of France.

-How can you take arms against a whole population because our Dey had a dispute with your consul, a man who is insolent, turbulent, and a merchant? This is not right!

All the people attending the scene looked at each other, and admired the judicious answers given by the man.

The Bedouin then returned to his camp, and despite orders, some men fired at him. He gave no attention to their shooting, and instead continued towards the group of Arabs who were waiting for him to inform them of what had taken place.

Matterer noted in his journal that the Bedouin in question was a chief who disguised himself as a shepherd, and who sought by himself to know what the French wanted.[217]

---

[216] Ibid.

[217] Ibid. p. 33.

'It is all obvious now that the Arabs are going to side by us, and that we will only fight the Turks,' was the belief amongst the French.[218] The expedition had been accompanied by propaganda to the effect that the French were coming 'to liberate the Algerians from their Turkish tyrants:'

> We French, your friends [said one document], are leaving for Algiers. We are going to drive out your tyrants, the Turks who persecute you, who steal your goods, and never cease menacing your lives . . . our presence on your territory is not to make war on you but only on the person of your Pasha. Abandon your Pasha; follow our advice; it is good advice and can only make you happy.[219]

Soon came the answer. From all sides there fell on the French Turks, Arabs, Berbers, Kuluglis, and in all parts of the country, beginning in Algiers and its surroundings.

An assembly of Algerian military leaders took place under Ibrahim Agha, the Dey's son in law. Present in the assembly was Hadj Ahmed, who had marched with his men from his eastern, Constantine, Regency. He advised Ibrahim not to throw all his forces at once against the French, French overwhelming power, especially artillery, would decimate them at once, but instead, to mount repeated attacks against their flanks and rear-guard.[220] The purpose of that was to break the French progress towards Algiers by causing them the greatest losses possible, maybe even force them into retreat. Hadj Ahmed spoke optimistically that France would experience the same failure as had previous invaders.[221] This was the tactics Algerians adopted from the beginning. From Sidi Ferruch to the outskirts of the city the French were attacked by Arab and Kabyle horsemen who swept down from the mountains, and who continued to harass the troops almost to the gates of Algiers.[222]

Battle of Sidi Ferruch

---

[218] Ibid, p. 29.

[219] Baudicourt: *La Guerre et le Gouvernement de l'Algerie*; (Paris; 1853); p. 160.

[220] M. Emerit: Les Memoires d'Ahmed Bey de Constantine; in *Revue Africaine,* 1er et 2em trimester, 1949, pp. 71-125; p. 71 ff.

[221] Ibid; p. 72.

[222] W. Blunt: *Desert Hawk*; Methuen & Co. Ltd; London; 1947, p. 30.

From the onset, the fighting was fierce and costly. We lack information from the Algerian side, but accounts abound on the French side, and they do, indeed, highlight the bitterness of the fighting. The corpses of Arabs and Turks, Nettement informs us, were strewn everywhere, marking the spots where they fought and fell. 'We found the bodies of five Turks who had thrust themselves inside our line and got themselves killed together as if they had vowed to do so.'[223] One of them was a young man with 'a very attractive face,' and his expression in death was so soft that he would seem to be sleeping, which contrasted with the expression of the oldest, a very strong man, with a white beard, whose face expressed anger and all the passion of fighting.[224] Those who witnessed the fighting said that they saw this 'old lion,' wounded in the hip, the arm, and thigh, about to fall in French hands, gathering all his strength and thrusting a dagger into his heart.[225] Captain Matterer on a similar incident says that two young Turkish fighters, who, when wounded, knowing they were about to fall into French hands were found with daggers in their right hands, plunged deep into their chests 'with bravery and rage encrusted onto their faces.'[226] The first Frenchman to fall, Nettement also tells us, was a sailor, named Francois Marie Guillevin; he was a first class sailor from Quiberon. He was a Breton, a Morbihanais; he was hit 'by the first bullet in this first French and Christian expedition.'[227]

Hadj Ahmed had decided to organise resistance at Staoueli and to lead it in person. The contingents led by himself and seconded by the Beys of Oran and Tittery positioned themselves two leagues off Staoueli and on the right of Sidi Ferruch, and thus could control the movements of the French army.[228] The vigour of the attacks of the Constantine contingent immobilised the invaders for four days.[229] On one occasion, Hadj Ahmed, leading his troops, managed to break through the left flank of the French and caused them severe losses.[230] Other Algerian units, following fierce fighting, managed to breach into, and plant their standards in, the French camp.[231] French artillery fire, on every occasion,

---

[223] M.A. Nettement: *Histoire de la Conquete d'Alger;* Jacques Lecoffre; Paris; 1856; p. 357.
[224] Ibid.
[225] Ibid.
[226] H. Alleg et al: *La Guerre d'Algerie*, op cit, p. 33.
[227] M.A. Nettement: *Histoire de la Conquete d'Alger;* op cit; note; p. 331.
[228] P. Grandchamp: La Chute D'Alger, d'Apres une Relation du Consul Sardes; in *Revue Tunisienne*; 1935; p. 239.
[229] AMG, H3, rapport du general de Bourmont au Ministre de la Guerre en date des 14, 17 et 19 Juin, 1830.
[230] Ch. L. Ferraud: Notices sur le Ouled Abdel Nour, *Receuil des Notices et Memoires de la Societe Archeologique de Constantine* (RSAC) 1864, p. 178.
[231] P. Gaffarel: *Lectures Geographiques et Historiques sur l'Algerie et les Colonies Francaises*; Garniers Freres; Paris; 1886; p. 170.

ultimately repulsed the attackers, with so heavy losses as to force them out of the field.[232] Nettement writes:

> The following day after the victory at Staoueli was a Sunday. We celebrated mass on an improvised set at Sidi Ferruch... This ceremony seemed to sanction the return of civilisation to this beach.[233]

The Algerians severely defeated on the 19th, with the loss of their camp and provisions, allowed the French to slowly push their way towards the city.[234] Algerian resolve was soon evident. At dawn on the 20th, 'we could see thousands of men proclaiming as they came out of Algiers 'We are ready to die for the sake of Allah!'[235] Troops of Kabyles and Arabs joined with them that same morning, forming in the end an army of 18 to 20,000 men. They were for many under the command of Mustafa, Bey of the Tittery, who seeking to avoid a frontal attack (due to French artillery fire), understandably, harassed French flanks on all sides, and night and day.[236] The fighting lasted days without interruption. The worst day of fighting would seem to be the 24th, and once more, French superiority in artillery, despite all Algerian precautions, caused immense havoc in their ranks. The vast gap in technological warfare was now obvious, and it would show on multiple occasions throughout the colonial war. It was also precisely in these first days that became obvious the other means of French warfare that would eventually starve out Algerian resistance: plundering their means of sustenance; it began with the seizure of 400 cattle heads.[237] This tactic of seizing livestock or destroying it (millions of heads by 1871), besides destroying crops, emptying silos, and cutting olive trees and orchards, would eventually kill Algerians in their hundreds of thousands at least.[238] This means of defeating native resistance and also destroying native life at the same time finds parallel with the widespread destruction of the Bison flocks in North America which ended eventually in the starving of millions of Native Indians there.

France in those days, it ought to be remembered, was the first or second world military power, and its expeditionary corps was not only superior in armament to anything the Algerians could muster, it was also superior in organisation to the men fighting it in dispersed order. Everywhere, though, the defenders fought bitterly, but the odds were overwhelming, and the only wonder was that so

---

[232] Ch. L. Feraud: *La Prise d'Alger en 1830 d'Apres un Ecrivain Musulman*, in *Receuil des Notices et Memoires de la Societe Archeologique de Constantine*; (RSAC), 1865, p. 73.
[233] M.A. Nettement: *Histoire de la Conquete d'Alger;* op cit; p. 360.
[234] S. Lane Poole: *Barbary Corsairs*; Fisher & Unwin, 1890; p. 302.
[235] M.A. Nettement: *Histoire de la Conquete d'Alger*; op cit; p. 365.
[236] Ibid.
[237] Ibid; p. 377.
[238] See Jo Melia: *The Triste sort des Indigenes d'Algerie;* D. Sari: *La Depossession des Fellahs 1830-1962;* Algiers; SNED; 1978. H. Alleg et al: *La Guerre d'Algerie*; op cit, p. 80. L. Blin: *l'Algerie du Sahara au Sahel;* l'Harmatan, Paris, 2000, p. 68. M. Lacheraf, in L. Blin: *L'Algerie*; op cit; note 3; p. 112. M. Morsy: *North Africa*; op cit; p. 9; pp. 287-8.

overpowering invading force, both by sea and land, should have shown so much caution and lack of confidence in its own immense superiority.[239] 25-26-27 and 28 June were spent in continuous fighting; the French holding in defensive positions as they were being attacked from all sides by bands of Turks, Arabs and Kabyles.[240] Nettement describes some such encounters: on the 26th, Arab horsemen came down from the higher grounds, and poured their fire on the French advanced positions, then soon after came another line which did the same. Then, behind every group of Arab cavaliers followed Kabyle infantry, reaching close to French positions, ambushing themselves, and by midday there were between 1500 and 2000 men ambushed just over 100 paces from French positions.[241] Then came the Arab cavalry, again, allowing the Kabyles to fire heavily, easing the way for the Arab cavalry push forward.[242] Under this dense fire the Arabs penetrated 'our lines,' cutting with swords the French infantry. It took the forceful intervention of reserve units to save the situation yet losses were considerable.[243] On the 28th of June Algerian columns surprised a battalion of the 4th light-infantry regiment, just in the act of cleaning their muskets, and killed considerable numbers.[244] The French could make but slow progress towards Algiers, and now began to value their foe much more highly.[245] It was a foe who when beaten preferred to die rather than surrender.[246]

On the 29th, when the French army came in view of Algiers, straight all Western ambassadors assembled in the American consulate then sent word that they offered their services to the French army; and in a simultaneous move all abdicated their functions towards a government (of Algeria) 'now about to die.'[247]

Fort L'Empereur, which protected Algiers, constituted the main obstacle in front of the French advance.[248] Fierce fighting took place there. The French assault was overwhelming with power, but the place was defended by Turks, who fought hard, even if behind their broken defences they were easy targets for French fire.[249]

> They are replacing their dead and wounded with more men, unmovable, unmoved, even if the ground was covered with corpses. Shells fall on them; our fire hit them from all sides.[250]

---

[239] S. Lane Poole: *Barbary Corsairs*; op cit; p. 302.
[240] M.A. Nettement: *Histoire de la Conquete d'Alger;* op cit; p. 389.
[241] Ibid.
[242] Ibid.
[243] Ibid.
[244] M. Wagner: *The Tricolor on the Atlas*, op cit, p. 230.
[245] S. D'Estry: *Histoire d'Alger*….Tours, A. Mame 1843.
[246] H. Alleg et al: *La Guerre d'Algerie*, op cit, p. 33.
[247] M.A. Nettement: *Histoire de la Conquete d'Alger;* op cit; p. 405.
[248] C.R. Ageron: *Modern Algeria*, op cit, p. 6.
[249] P. Gaffarel: *Lectures Geographiques et Historiques sur l'Algerie et les Colonies Francaises*; Garniers Freres; Paris; 1886; p. 173.
[250] Ibid.

The impressive French artillery is in particular evidence again, Fort L'Empereur being blasted from about every direction with high calibre guns that would bring down any wall or defences.[251] The Algerians did surely not lack courage but as Nettement noted, they did lack military science.[252] If they had just a little military experience, he remarks, they would have reinforced their positions on the higher ground which dominated Fort l'Empereur.[253] Instead, now, from these dominant positions French artillery could sweep Algiers and blast away any troop concentrations coming from any direction. So the Algerians could only act in small units, so somehow in the same manner as in 1541 when the Spaniards landed. Warfare means and techniques had evolved in Europe but not so much in Algeria. Nonetheless the French suffered heavily around 200 men were lost every day.[254] Again and again Algerians made sorties, as in the night of 3 to 4 July when they invested French positions, and became involved in hand to hand combat, before they were repulsed by superior fire-power.[255]

Fort l'Empereur itself was only captured after four days of atrocious fighting. On 4 July its pounding began early, and remained relentless, crushing Turkish artillery counter fire, which also came from the Casbah and Bab Azzoun. The defenders at first stood their ground bravely, no sooner one died, another took his place.[256] In the end the place was abandoned by its remaining defenders before it was blown up.[257]

The loss of the fort now decided the fate of the city. Realising he had nothing to put in face of the French, that he even risked the total destruction of Algiers, on the 4th of July, the Dey asked for terms of surrender.[258] Promised safety of person and property for himself and for the inhabitants of the city by the French commander, the Dey gave in, and on this condition the enemy occupied Algiers on the following day, July 5th.[259] On that same day, the Dey affixed his seal to the agreement to surrender Algiers and the *casbah* (citadel).[260]

Algiers had fallen for the first time in its history. The last time its defences were breached was when Lord Exmouth in 1816 effected his bombardment but only through deception, coming close to the city under parliament pavilion.[261] Now, the French were in control.

---

[251] M.A. Nettement: *Histoire de la Conquete d'Alger;* op cit; p. 412.

[252] Ibid; p. 410.

[253] Ibid.

[254] Ibid; p. 415.

[255] Ibid; p. 410 ff.

[256] Ibid; p. 430.

[257] H. Alleg et al: *La Guerre d'Algerie*, op cit, p. 33.

[258] S. Lane Poole: *Barbary Corsairs*; op cit; p. 302.

[259] Ibid.

[260] C.R. Ageron: *Modern Algeria*, op cit, p. 6.

[261] M.A. Nettement: *Histoire de la Conquete d'Alger;* op cit; p. 418.

Entering the city in a triumphal procession, the French commander De Bourmont guaranteed to the 'inhabitants of all classes respect for their liberty, their religion, their property, their trade and their women.'[262] A proclamation written in Arabic and diffused at the arrival of the troops asserted that the French had not come to take possession of the city.[263] General De Bourmont had drawn up a proclamation even before his departure from France, to 'the *Koulouglis,* the Arabs and the inhabitants of Algiers', declaring that the French army had come 'to drive out the Turks, your tyrants', and that they would reign as before as independent masters of their native land,' and thus had no intention of ceding the city to the Ottomans now that it was won.[264] On 8 June, the French government, having indicated to De Bourmont its disapproval of an attack on 'the Turks in general, with whom France has remained at peace', seized all copies of this proclamation, which hardly corresponded with its policy.[265] The general was ordered 'to say nothing which might prejudge our eventual intentions in the matter of Algiers,' and a second proclamation was drawn up speaking only of war upon the Dey.[266] After announcing that the whole of the regency would be conquered within a fortnight, he declared first that 'the Moors and Arabs looked on us as liberators,' then that he was busy 'rebuilding a government with educated and intelligent Moors,' and finally that, having compromised them in this way, he was unable 'to allow them to fall back under the rule of the Turks.'[267] The operation was presented as 'a temporary occupation, simply aiming at expelling the despotic Turks, and then to return the country to the Arabs, its legitimate masters.'[268]

> Which anticipated with some genius, but not without duplicity, the promises of Louis Bonaparte to Abd al-Kader (1855) and those of Lawrence of Arabia to the Shereef of Makkah in 1916, [say Courbage and Fargues.][269]

---

[262] C.R. Ageron: *Modern Algeria*, op cit; p. 6.
[263] Y. Courbage, P. Fargues: *Chretiens et Juifs*; op cit; pp. 108-9.
[264] C.R. Ageron: *Modern Algeria*; op cit, p. 7.
[265] Ibid.
[266] Ibid.
[267] Ibid.
[268] Y. Courbage, P. Fargues: *Chretiens et Juifs*; op cit; pp. 108-9.
[269] Ibid. 108-9.

*****

Kabyle Song Mourning the Capture of Algiers

From the day when the Consul left Algiers,
The powerful French have gathered their hosts:
Now the Turks have gone, without hope of return,
Algiers the beautiful is wrested from them.
"Unhappy Isle that they built in the desert,
With vaults of limestone and brick;
The celestial guardian who over them watched has withdrawn.
Who can resist the power of God?
"The forts that surround Algiers like stars,
Are bereft of their masters;
The baptized ones have entered.
The Christian religion now is triumphant,
O my eyes, weep tears of blood, weep evermore!
"They are beasts of burden without cruppers,
Their backs are loaded,
Under a bushel their unkempt heads are hidden,
They speak a *patois* unintelligible,
You can understand nothing they say.
"The combat with these gloomy invaders
Is like the first ploughing of a virgin soil,
To which the harrowing implements
Are rude and painful;
Their attack is terrible.
"They drag their cannons with them,
And know how to use them, the impious ones;
When they fire, the smoke forms in thick clouds:
They are charged with shrapnel,
Which falls like the hail of approaching spring.
Unfortunate queen of cities--
City of noble ramparts,
Algiers, column of Islam,
Thou art like the habitation of the dead,
The banner of France envelops thee all."[270]

---

[270] A. Hanoteau, *Poésies Populaires de la Kabylie du Jurjura*, Paris, 1867, 8vo. pp. 2, 3, 5, 7, 9, 11.

*****

The French Take Over of the Algerian Treasury

Dey Husseyn left Algiers but not before he granted access to the treasury, which was estimated at 50 millions.[271] The value today is certainly in the billions.

Nettement tells us how the French, most certainly following the agreement not to blast the city in exchange of the treasury, were conducted to the treasury rooms.

The first room was cut by a small wall of 3 feet dividing it into two compartments full of Algerian currencies. Once the door of this room was locked up, the official in charge led the French group and opened the second door, which led to another part, and there opened a third door leading into a room of about 20 metres in length, which contained three large boxes full of gold bullion and silver ingots. Then three doors equally spaced from each other were opened, each of the rooms contained wooden compartments. The middle room contained golden coins of all origins, including the *roboasoltani* of 3fr 80 and the Mexican quadruple of 168 frcs in gold. Then many more currencies of diverse origins were inventoried. The commission after making certain there was no other entry to the treasury, from whatever side, locked up all the doors scrupulously, putting seals on each of them, then placed there a post of Gendarmes commanded by an officer.[272]

*****

The French Proclamation to the Algerian People

'People of Algiers, the powerful king of France, Louis Philippe I, has entrusted me (de Bourmont) with this army which now occupies the regency and has placed the government of the provinces under its sway. The intention of the King of France is to secure, and till the end of times, the happiness of the people. His arms have freed you from a humiliating yoke. We will impose justice and the rule of law, and will protect the good and severely punish those who do evil, regardless of the class they belong to. Some ill intentioned minds have spread evil rumours about the French character, accusing us of being unjust and favouring some sections of the population. Do not listen to these perfidious calumnies. I promise you in all good faith your security and protection; however I expect from you your entire trust, and also your support in helping me secure peace and order.

People of Algiers, your religion, your customs, your values, will all be respected. I will listen to your grievances, and I am expecting to only praise you for your attitude, and that you will never put me in the situation whereby I have to prove to you my keenness to quell trouble whether in or outside the capital. I have already ordered the exemplary punishment of some men who have spread evil words aimed at spreading doubt and fear, and had malevolently accused us of seeking to abandon you to the vengeance of your former oppressors from whom we have freed you.'[273]

---

[271] P. Gaffarel: *Lectures Geographiques et Historiques sur l'Algerie*; op cit; p. 42.

[272] M.A. Nettement: *Histoire de la Conquete d'Alger*; op cit; pp. 443-4.

[273] G. Fleury: *Comment l'Algerie Devint Francaise*; Perrin, Paris, 2004, p. 122.

2. Colonial Vi[...]ase

To make colo[...] Bourmont proceeded to expel those Turks who were set[...]e country.[274] Hussein Dey, himself, having signed a conve[...]t giving France sovereignty over the whole of the Ottoma[...]eft the country and settled in Naples.[275] He was able to [...]0,000 golden sequins, a small part of his immense pers[...]ted that one hundred million francs reached France from [...]ed from the Dey's captured treasures and looting of pri[...] about half this sum reached the treasury, roughly equiv[...]expedition. The rest was pocketed by officers and other per[...] the invasion.[277]

To the Frenc[...] they were told, was a land abandoned to sterility and [...] 'the laziness of the native.'[278] The soldiers, instead, disc[...]ked after: magnificent orchards and orange groves. The [...] Algiers, said to be disease ridden marshland proved to be [...] Everywhere could be seen beautiful country villas, surrou[...]t on the hills; thick vegetation, 'everywhere streams of w[...]growing in abundance,' wrote an officer of the expeditionar[...]r of aqueducts was staggering, generously supplying th[...]here were also underground tunnels, built in concrete, co[...]ng distances.[281] Bugeaud himself admitted his surprise to [...]re civilised and more prosperous than he believed. 'In [...] Algeria in 1836 and 1837, I conceived that the historians of [...]n they claimed that Africa was the granary of Rome... Alge[...]re than that; it is a rich country; everywhere land is farm[...]t numbers of livestock ...and the population quite numer[...]

The French [...]dged civilisation for the country; 'a moral justifications[...]say Alleg et al.[283] Now came the act. Those who backed colon[...]nufacturers, tradesmen who sought to enlarge their market[...]hareholders in large shipping companies, arm

---

[274] C.R. Ageron: *Mo*[...]

[275] J.M. Abun-Nasr: *A History of the Magh*[...], p. 238.

[276] Ibid.

[277] Ibid.

[278] H. Alleg et al: *La Guerre d'Algerie;* op cit, p. 61.

[279] *La Campagne d'Afrique par an Officier de l'Armee Expeditionaire*; Paris; 1831.

[280] Ibid.

[281] Cdt Claude Antoine Rozet: *Voyage Sous la Regence d'Alger, ou Description du Pays Occupe par l'Armee Francaise en Afrique*; A Bertrand; Paris; 1833.

[282] H. Alleg et al: *La Guerre d'Algerie*; op cit, p. 61.

[283] Ibid.

suppliers, high officers who were after promotion and wealth, and an avalanche of adventurers.[284] Now all these fell on the country.

> A true swarm of speculators fell on Algiers, buying at low prices from the natives in order to resell very quickly, first the buildings in the city, then in the countryside later.[285]

Together with the army in place, they unleashed an orgy of looting and destruction with which that of Iraq in 2003 pales into insignificance. It began with the luxuriant gardens and handsome villas in the first three weeks of July (1830).[286] The officers were indifferent when the first palms and orange-trees were felled by the axes of the soldiers, to be used for camp-fires. Gangs of Frenchmen broke into the villas, deserted by their frightened inhabitants, and destroyed even the walls in the hope of finding hidden treasures.[287] The traces of this vandalism took years to be removed, especially on the Buzarea, where, Wagner says, 'we often suddenly fall in with modern ruins in the midst of the finest gardens.'[288]

Such destruction was not confined to the encamped army. Soldiers and officers fought amongst each others in the narrow streets of the Kasbah over the loot, overloaded with silks, women clothes, luxury footwear with golden decorations… their pockets overflowing with jewellery of all sorts, precious objects soon to be peddled in the streets of Paris.[289] Even greater crimes were committed by the superior officers who were quartered in the public buildings of the city: they stole all precious collections and treasures of the country.[290] The splendid vases, the rich arms, buried in the vaults of the Kasbah, were stolen; and the rich plate, of considerable artistic value, was melted and coined. It is believed in Algiers that many superior officers, generals, and the military household of Marshal de Bourmont, had taken part in these embezzlements. Inquest was afterwards made into the matter by a commission, but the report was never published.[291]

When they finished with the looting of Algiers, the French took their civilising act to other levels and other parts. In the very month of July following their capture of Algiers, the French executed publicly, primarily by hanging, tens of citizens of Algiers suspected of being 'conspirators.'[292] The gesture, obviously, as in Egypt decades before in 1798, when notables and leading figures in Cairo were publicly executed, was to install a climate of fear of the French.[293]

---

[284] Larcher: *Traite Elementaire de Legislation Algerienne*. A Rousseau; Paris; 1911.
[285] Ibid.
[286] M. Wagner: *The Tricolor on the Atlas*, op cit, p. 232.
[287] Ibid.
[288] Ibid, p. 233.
[289] H. Alleg et al: *La Guerre d'Algerie*, op cit, p. 34.
[290] M. Wagner: *The Tricolor on the Atlas*, op cit, p. 233.
[291] Ibid.
[292] H. Alleg: *La Guerre d'Algerie*, op cit, vol 1, p. 36.
[293] M. Morsy: *North Africa*; op cit; p. 80.

As they began to advance out of Algiers the French crossed the difficult defile of Teniah, on the 21st of November, 1830, not without a serious struggle with an alliance of remaining Turks and local mountaineers, who were dislodged from their positions only after a severe fight.[294] The French lost here 220 men; and General Clauzel, from the heights of the defile, made a euphoric proclamation, telling his soldiers that "they had fought like giants."[295]

Meeting with greater resistance as the days and weeks passed, the French decided for 'appropriate' measures. Sébastiani, the Minister of Foreign Affairs, appointed the husband of his own mistress, General Savary, Duc de Rovigo, governor of Algeria from December 1831 to April 1833.[296] No sooner he took charge of the country, Duc de Rovigo, who could not show his manliness in his private life, compensated for it in his new position by exhibiting a brutality little seen before. He ordered and went himself on a campaign of killing and destruction, showing no quarters to even the few friends France found in the country; and even tribal leaders, who were lured to Algiers by promises of safe conducts were slain.[297] On the night of 6 April 1832, a military detachment left Algiers and surprised the tribe of Uffiya who, disarmed, camped in their tents. The general leading the troops ordered the tribe, falsely accused of anti French sedition, to be exterminated to the last man, woman, and child.[298]

> Old men silently awaiting the death-blow, women crying for mercy, and children, who did not know what was to befall them, were unmercifully slain by the sabre and the bayonet.[299]

Witnesses speak of 12,000 dead.[300] Only a few individuals escaped by being taken under the protection of some more humane French officers.[301] The soldiers returned with rich booty, carrying in triumph gory heads on the tops of their lances and bayonets to the camp, where Rovigo ordered a firework display in celebration.[302] Rovigo ordered the shopkeepers in Algiers to light up the streets and remain open so that the soldiers could trade their loot.[303] A contemporary Algerian observer, Hamdan ben 'Uthman Khudja, in his personal account, *Aperçu Historique et Statistique Sur La Regence d'Alger,* published in Paris in 1833, states that bloody ear-rings and bracelets with remains of severed wrists were sold.[304] It was subsequently proved that the Uffiya had not been responsible for what they had been accused of, and the insurrection which this incident provoked, was

---

[294] M. Wagner: *The Tricolor on the Atlas*, op cit, p. 238.
[295] Ibid..
[296] C.R. Ageron: *Modern Algeria*, op cit, p. 11.
[297] Ibid.
[298] M. Morsy: *North Africa*; op cit; p. 134.
[299] W. Blunt: *Desert Hawk*; Methuen & Co. Ltd; London; 1947, p. 31.
[300] H. Alleg et al: La Guerre *d'Algerie*: p. 64. P. Christian: *L'Afrique Francaise*....; Paris 1845-46.
[301] M. Morsy: *North Africa*; op cit; p. 134.
[302] W. Blunt: *Desert Hawk*; op cit, p. 31.
[303] M. Morsy: *North Africa*; op cit; p. 134.
[304] Ibid.

put down by further wholesale massacres and pillage, and huge fines which only served to increase the resentment and fire of revolt.[305]

Late in April 1832, a detachment of the Foreign Legion, commanded by Lieutenant Cham, a Swiss, was surprised near 'Maison Carree,' and cut down by the tribe of the Issers, who dwelt east of Cape Matifu. Only one soldier, a German, was spared, because he uttered the name Mohammed at the moment when the yatagan was raised against him.[306] The Algerians carried him away as prisoner, but he succeeded in escaping, and returned to the army. It so happened that nearly all the soldiers slain belonged to the companies which had participated in the massacre of the Uffiya, and that their heads fell close to the spot where, three weeks before, they had killed the many thousands.[307]

The war of conquest soon descended into a pandemonium of reprisals and massacres. On capturing the town of Blida, west of Algiers, the French razed it to the ground; the devastated streets were filled with corpses of old people, women, children and Jews.[308]

> Heads! Bring heads, heads, block burst water mains with the head of the first Bedouin you meet, [ordered the Duc of Rovigo] to his officers.[309]
>
> The Duke, [Wagner remarks,] was accustomed, as a police-minister, never to be restrained from harsh and arbitrary measures by regard to justice and equity. Every means, even the most cruel, was welcome to him, if it answered the purpose he had to carry, namely, to extend the sway of France all over the old dominion of the Dey, and to subdue the tribes unconditionally. But that system failed altogether; hearts were hardened by mutual misdeeds; every drop of blood spilt cried for revenge; and any sincere accord between the conquerors and the natives became impossible when the passions of national and religious hatred were let loose. It was, in a great measure, the influence of the Duke which gave to the war between the Arabs and French that savage and terrible character which it maintained as long as it lasted.[310]

Terror, massacres, sacks, constituted the daily acts of the strategy of conquest. The French path was to be littered with masses of corpses, burnt hamlets, devastated lands, and ruin everywhere; it was, in words, a war of extermination.

> Everything must be taken, sacked, without distinction for age or sex. Grass should not grow anywhere the French army sets foot. In a word eradicate everything that does not crawl at our feet like dogs, [would Montagnac sum it up years later.][311]

---

[305] W. Blunt: *Desert Hawk*; op cit, p. 31.
[306] M. Wagner: *The Tricolor on the Atlas*, op cit, p. 254.
[307] Ibid.
[308] C.A. Julien: *Histoire de l'Algerie*; op cit; p. 67.
[309] P. Christian: *L'Afrique Francaise;* Paris 1845-1846; Cited by H Alleg et al: *La Guerre*; op cit; vol 1; p. 64.
[310] M. Wagner: *The Tricolor on the Atlas*, op cit, pp. 250-1.
[311] Colonel L. Francois de Montagnac: *Lettres d'un Soldat;*

The same Montagnac who admitted that

> To chase away dark thoughts that besiege me, sometimes I have heads cut off.[312]

According to another serving officer:

> We bring barrels of ears which had been harvested in pairs... No prisoners are taken.[313]

For Montagnac, any officer who brought an Arab alive was punished with a blow of the sabre.[314]

Facing the French might, the Algerians could find no ally, whether in the Tunisians, the Moroccans, or the Ottomans.[315] None could do anything. The Tunisians had received sufficient warnings, and their military capacity could hardly dent the might of France. The Moroccan kingdom, likewise, was extremely powerless, its military strength insignificant as to be proved later at the Battle of Isly when they sought to support Emir Abd al-Kader. The king of Morocco, Mulay 'Abd al-Rahman, had, in fact, from the start shown his unwillingness to become involved in an international conflict, and had resisted popular pressure both in Morocco and Algeria to assist his neighbours and fellow Muslims.[316] France, in fact, blocked any move the Sovereign might make by dispatching the Earl of Mornay to Morocco in 1832 to warn the sovereign against helping the Algerians.[317] As for the Ottomans, not only they were distant, they were themselves embroiled in fighting for the survival of their own realm.

From the early stages the French authorities sought to gain the alliance of the feudal lords who were at the service of the Turks; chiefs of various tribes around Algiers and Oran, seeking to rally them to their cause so as to divide Algerian opposition against them; but this failed.[318] Those leaders who were tempted to join the French or collaborate so as to preserve their privileges could not ignore the popular opposition to colonisation. Thus the Bey of Titteri, who had accepted to submit was forced by people's pressure in Medea to renegade his promise to the French and so refused alliance with them.[319] The need to organise collective resistance was the main subject that preoccupied Algerians. Popular leaders or holy men came to the fore, attracting large audiences as they made impassioned pleas for the defence of Islam.[320]

---

[312] Y. Lacoste, A. Noushi, and A. Prennant: *L'Algerie: Passe, Present*; Editions Sociales; Paris; 1960; p. 306.

[313] Extracts from the journal of an officer, cited by Maurice d'Herisson dans: *La Chasse a l'Homme, Guerres d'Algerie*; P. Ollendorf, Paris, 1891.

[314] Colonel L. Francois de Montagnac: *Lettres d'un Soldat*; Paris; 1885.

[315] M. Morsy: *North Africa*; op cit; p. 138.

[316] Ibid.

[317] Ibid.

[318] H. Alleg et al: *La Guerre d'Algerie*, op cit, p. 59.

[319] Ibid.

[320] M. Morsy: *North Africa*; op cit; p. 134.

Despite the great military inferiority of the Algerians, and the disorganised nature of their ranks, there was a high spirit of resistance amongst the population. The fight for the city of Bougie (Bejaia) in 1833 highlights such a spirit. The French expedition against Bougie was fitted out at Toulon, and left that port the 22nd September, 1833; the fleet consisting of a frigate, numerous corvettes and brigs, and fifteen transports, carrying two battalions all under the command of General Trezel.[321] The troops landed on the 29th, after they had quelled the fire of the forts and of the citadel by cannon fire.[322] General Trezel was greatly mistaken when, at his departure from Toulon, he said to the officers of the expedition,

> Our troops are not destined for a very warlike expedition; they will have to wield rather the spade and the axe, than the sabre and the bayonet.[323]

These expectations were cruelly disappointed by the opposition which the expedition experienced from the Arab-Berber population. The resistance of the inhabitants was nowhere so gallant and so obstinate as at Bejaia, observes Wagner.[324] Outside the city, every foot of ground was contested by the Algerians concealed amongst the groves of fruit-trees, from where a determined fire was kept up.[325] Every garden was garrisoned with 'desperadoes,' who held out to the last moment; then, retreating into the ravines which intersect the place, they fortified themselves in the holes and crannies of the rocks, blocking any French advance during day and then sallying forth during the darkness of night, scattering themselves under any cover, before falling upon the foe from every side.[326] From the eminences upon which the town itself is scattered, a heavy fire was continually directed against the French.[327] It was at considerable cost that they managed to make their entry into the city. But once inside, there took place another fierce fight. The inhabitants of the city fought 'street by street, for every house, from every window, every step of the way,' says Marmier.

> It was another siege of Zaragossa, a siege made all the more difficult that, all the dwellings were scattered on the hills, in the ravines, and that the army had to attack them one by one.[328]

House by house was fought over, and height after height; until at last, driven out by superior strength, after seven days' desperate fighting, the inhabitants retired to the summit of Mount Gouraya, which commanded the town, and from there without a respite hit the invaders.[329] The fighters there

> Accepted neither peace, nor cease-fire, and from all sides surrounded us, and every hour mounted one assault after another against us.[330]

---

[321] Dawson Borrer: *Narrative of a campaign against the Kabailes of Algeria;* Spottiswoode and Shaw, London, 1848; p. 168. M. Wagner: *The Tricolor on the Atlas*, op cit, p. 261.
[322] M. Wagner: *The Tricolor on the Atlas*, op cit, p. 261. Dawson Borrer: *Narrative of a campaign;* p. 168.
[323] M. Wagner; 261.
[324] Ibid; 261.
[325] Dawson Borrer: *Narrative of a campaign;* op cit; p. 168.
[326] Ibid.
[327] Ibid.
[328] Marmier in H. Alleg et al. *La Guerre;* op cit; p. 62.
[329] Dawson Borrer: *Narrative of a campaign;* op cit; p. 168.
[330] Marmier in H. Alleg et al. *La Guerre;* op cit; p. 62.

On the 12th of October this almost inaccessible position was gallantly attacked, and taken at the point of the bayonet by the French.[331] Even when victory was seemingly secured, Duvivier, chief of battalion, was appointed Commander of Bejaia, and earned much honour there by his frequent fights with the local people, without achieving any important result.[332] The local population, supported by the Bey of Constantine, made a desperate attack on the town and the block-houses erected in the neighbourhood.[333] Some time afterwards, news spread that nearly the whole garrison was weakened by the fighting, the tribes gathered together, resolving to make one more onslaught on the town.[334]

> The Kabyles of the vicinity of Bejaia, [says Wagner] belong to the most warlike and unruly tribes of Barbary; they are so deeply imbued with religious fanaticism and love of independence, that in spite of all material advantages and promises, they could not be induced to enter into peaceful communication with the French.[335]

The French capture of Bejaia

Six thousand tribesmen marched upon Bejaia during the night; their women and their children following in their rear.[336] Within the town itself it was generally believed that the last moment of the French dominion there was at hand, and the civilians sought refuge in the ships in the port. The Bejaia sharp-shooters covered the heights of Gouraya, pouring a ceaseless shower of bullets upon every open space in the town below.[337] During this time the bulk of the Algerians fell with fury on an isolated blockhouse some distance from the town. The French defence

---

[331] Dawson Borrer: *Narrative of a campaign*; op cit; p. 168.

[332] M. Wagner: *The Tricolor on the Atlas*, op cit, p. 261.

[333] Dawson Borrer: *Narrative of a campaign;* op cit; p. 168.

[334] Ibid.

[335] M Wagner: *The Tricolor*; op cit; 261.

[336] Dawson Borrer: *Narrative of a campaign*; op cit; p. 168.

[337] Ibid.

was itself resilient, and, once more had that element in its favour: superior fire power, especially artillery.[338] After six hours of bitter fight, the Algerians suffered heavily and had to retire, without failing to make even more attacks but without any lasting results.[339] It was a setback for the resistance, but it did not defeat their belief in ultimate victory.

******

The Algerian and Death

The Arab is great and admirable at the hour of death. I have seen many Arabs die, but never did I see one beg for his life or utter any unmanly complaint.[340]

Whoever has watched the Arab in the fight — how his eyes sparkle — how his imposing person rises erect on the saddle of the war-horse with barbarous majesty — how the fiery battle- inspiration shines forth from every feature of his expressive countenance — how his battle-cry or his songs, which praise the whistling of the bullets as his dearest music, resound over the plain, — whoever, indeed, has observed the demeanour of the Arab in the field, will be convinced that this is a people born to war.[341]

And when he is about to face his death at the hands of the Frenchman:

Altogether [says Wagner,] the Arab is never embarrassed by human power and greatness, nor cowed into subjection. He never loses his proud carriage, and does not cast down his eyes, either before the splendour of the throne, or the yatagan of the executioner. The words which he puts in the mouth of Allah:

"My slave, why dost thou fear my slave?

Is this life not as much in my hands as thine?"

Express beautifully and forcibly this feeling of human dignity with the Arab. He maintains the same sentiment when a prisoner before his enemy or his judge. I saw in May, 1837, at Blida, prisoners advancing to the presence of General Damremont and his staff, who were not at all overawed by his splendid military retinue, and who answered his questions with a haughtiness which, under similar circumstances, very few Europeans would display.'[342]

Respect for the dead is mentioned as one of the virtues of the Arab people, but it is common to all the Mohammedan nations. From the eye-witnesses of the Circassian war with the Russians, we may hear of nearly the same feats as happen at every encounter between French and Arabs. The latter always make the greatest efforts to save their dead from the hands of the enemy, and many of them become the victims of such efforts. It was often seen that Arab horsemen galloped off with one or two corpses on their horses, and did not drop them even when the French chasseurs were

---

[338] Ibid; p. 169.

[339] Ibid.

[340] Clemens Lamping: *The French in Algiers. Soldiers of the Foreign Legion; Prisoners of Abd el Kader;* tr. from German and French by Lady Duff Gordon, London; 1855; p. 5.

[341] M. Wagner: *The Tricolor on the Atlas,* op cit; p. 155.

[342] Ibid, p. 140.

on their heels; or if the dead remained in the hands of the French, the Arabs never failed to re-appear on the battlefield, in order to get possession, if possible, of the remains of their countrymen. They carefully bury them, and cover the resting-place with broad slabs or masonry, that the wild beasts may not dig them up. The careless manner in which the French bury their dead contrasts much to their disadvantage with the pious respect paid by the barbarians to the corpses of their beloved. The French throw their killed soldiers into the next ditch or trench, and cover it so superficially, that the jackals and hyenas gather around in crowds at night to feast upon them. Wherever Arab laws are in force, the violator of the grave is punished by death. The Arabs generally select the finest scenery of the neighbourhood for their cemeteries; and plant them with palms.[343]

---

[343] Ibid, p. 144.

Three

THE MILITARY CAMPAIGN IN THE EAST
(1836-1837)

In 1833, the eastern province of Constantine, had not as yet been conquered. Its local administration had been set up by the former Ottoman government and had at its head a *Bey*, Hadj Ahmed. The province was wealthy and prior to the French invasion had supplied Algiers with cereals and timber for shipbuilding.[344] It was also well populated (two-fifths of the total population of the Regency).[345] The province was made of three different regions: that of the Lesser Kabylie mountains to the north, the western agricultural zone, and in the south a desert area inhabited by nomad Arab tribes.[346] The port of Bone was its window open to the rest of the external world; it was here that were concentrated all commercial activities with foreign powers, and in particular with Marseilles.[347] The Bey who ruled the province from 1826 onwards, Hadj Ahmed, belonged to a local family. His father and grandfather before him had occupied posts in the local Ottoman administration.[348] Hadj Ahmed Bey was himself a *kulughli,* born ca 1784 of an Ottoman father and Algerian mother, his Algerian mother being the daughter of one of the major hereditary tribal chiefs of the south, the Ben Gana.[349] He received first class education in a madrasa and gained high qualifications.[350] He showed his defining characteristics: utter trust in the Ottoman Sultan, and above all great belief in the Islamic faith.[351] Hadj Ahmed was a formidable fighter who played a great part in the resistance for Algiers when the French landed, and, unlike Abd al-Kader, who could show extreme qualities of soft character, Hadj Ahmed could be fierce in his deeds, and severe in his retributions.[352]

Following his unsuccessful intervention in fighting the French who had landed in Algiers, Hadj Ahmed retreated towards his capital having suffered considerable loss of men, including some of his best fighters.[353] He left the capital accompanied by a considerable number of refugees, but also including many Arab chiefs who

---

[344] A. Noushi: *Enquete sur le Niveau de Vie des Populations Rurales Constantinoises de la Conquete jusqu'a 1919*; Tunis, 1961, p. 130.
[345] M. Morsy: *North Africa*; op cit; p. 135.
[346] Ibid.
[347] A. Temimi: Le Beylik de Constantine et Hadj Ahmed Bey, op cit, p. 52.
[348] M. Morsy: *North Africa*; op cit; p. 135.
[349] Ibid.
[350] AMG., H 226. Rapport presente par Rousseau a M. Blondel, directeur des Finances a Alger, 29 Septembre 1838.
[351] A. Temimi: Le Beylik de Constantine et Hadj Ahmed Bey, op cit, p. 60.
[352] Ibid, p. 61.
[353] Ch. L. Ferraud: La Prise d'Alger; in *RSAC* 1865; pp. 76-7

joined his ranks.[354] Ahmed Bey was intent on building the strength of Constantine and the province, fully aware that the French would soon turn their arms east.

Ahmed Bey had been officially deposed by the French in 1830; but from his mountain fortress he continued to rule over some two million subjects.[355] His authority was unchallenged throughout most of eastern Algeria, and he received support, however more discreetly, from Turkey and provisions from Tunis.[356] Another remarkable man was his second-in-command, Ben Aissa, himself a Kabyle, who had reorganized the *beylik* and who could be relied upon in moments of crisis.[357] Ahmed-Bey's greatest support lay likewise among the Kabyles, among the tribes south of Bejaia, between the Rivers Wad Ajebbi and Summam.[358] It was to Hadj Ahmed that the population of Bejaia appealed for support against French occupation.[359] He was, they were convinced, the only man with enough clout, belief, courage and ability to vanquish them and throw them out of Algeria.[360]

The French likewise recognised that in Hadj Ahmed they had the only formidable adversary to their colonial enterprise. The French consul in Tunis de Lesseps, had already on the eve of the landing in Algiers contacted Hadj Ahmed informing him that rather than supporting Hussein Dey, he should instead take advantage of the new situation, and become independent, i.e set up an independent kingdom in the east of the country.[361] Rather than being tempted by the offer that could have easily broken Algerian territorial unity for good, Hadj Ahmed, instead, lent all his support to the defence of Algiers and only had to retreat back to Constantine once his army was greatly depleted. Following the capture of the Kasbah of Algiers, De Bourmont himself asked Hadj Ahmed to submit to France, and in return he would keep his Beylik.[362] Again, the Bey categorically refused. Still, General Damrémont opened negotiations with Ahmed Bey, offering him independent rule over his realm, with only the surrender of the immediate area of Bône and La Calle as French possessions, and an annual tribute of 100,000 francs.[363] Ahmed Bey refused.

In 1832, the Duke of Rovigo, now in charge, declared that the occupation of Constantine had become a necessity. Instructing the Duke of Raimbert in January of the same year, he asked him to keep him informed of all that was of importance occurring in the province, and most of all, to undermine Hadj Ahmed's authority

---

[354] A. Temimi: Trois letters de Hadj Ahmed Bey de Constantine a la Sublime Porte, in *ROMM*; No 3; Aix, 1968; pp. 132-55; p. 144.
[355] W. Blunt: *Desert Hawk*; op cit, p. 86
[356] Ibid.
[357] Ibid; p. 87.
[358] M. Wagner: *The Tricolor on the Atlas*, op cit, p. 282.
[359] G. Esquer: *Correspondence du general Voirol*; Voirol au MG., 14 September 1833; Paris, 1924; p. 227.
[360] *Correspondence du general Voirol*, 26 October 1833; p. 279.
[361] A. Temimi: Le Beylik de Constantine; p. 91.
[362] Archives des Affaires Etrangers (A.E.) Tunis, 1. De Lesseps au MAE.16 August 1830.
[363] C.R. Ageron: *Modern Algeria;* op cit, p. 15.

as much as to cripple his policies and decisions.[364] At the same time he was pursuing these policies, the Duke kept the hope of still making Hadj Ahmed accept French rule in the country.[365]

The first French attack on the Eastern Province was made when the harbour of Bone was taken briefly in 1830, and permanently in 1832; this with the capture of Bejaia cut off the province's communications with the outside world by sea.[366] Hadj Ahmed could no longer receive help by sea and this was quite damaging as the French also put pressure on Tunisia to block the overland route.[367] The situation in Bone itself took a turn for the worse following the appointment as commanding officer of Yusuf, a man raised at the court of the Dey of Tunis as a Muslim, and whose subsequent deeds in the colonial war would render him by far the most despicable character of all, despised by the French, and hated by the Muslims. General Monck d'Uzer felt:

> Disgusted by the intrigues of Yusuf... who is devoured by ambition. He wants at all costs to become Bey of Constantine. It is indispensable that the Governor remove him from Bone and place him under the orders of Colonel Marcy who will keep him in check.[368]

Hadj Ahmed realised he could not throw the French out of Bone, and he could not risk launching an attack that might finish his army, fully aware that quite soon the French would be marching against his capital.[369] Already in 1830, he was well aware that the French officers were negotiating with the Tunisians with a view to conquering Constantine. De Bourmont's successor, General Clauzel relied on the usual policy of establishing French rule by using Muslim chiefs as French agents.[370] Following a plan suggested by de Lesseps, the French consul at Tunis, he proposed to install Tunisian princes as *beys* at Oran and Constantine, and to this end signed two treaties with the ruling family of Tunis.[371] In the first, he secretly granted the Tunisians the *beylik* of Constantine in full sovereignty.[372] (There were two versions of this *treaty.* One was in French, unknown to the Tunisians, which contained a clause added by Clauzel placing the *bey* of Constantine under the authority of France.)[373] In the second, he obtained the promise of a *bey* for Oran under French protection. The *bey* of Oran, overwhelmed by tribal revolt, had been effectively eliminated, while the sultan of Morocco took

---

[364] G. Esquer: *Correspondence du Duc de Rovigo, 1831-1833*; t1. Algiers, 1914; T2. Algiers, 1920; T3: Algiers, 1921; t.4 Algiers, 1924. T.1; p. 43; 1ˢᵗ January 1832.
[365] G. Esquer: *Correspondence du Duc de Rovigo*, 29 January 1832; t.1; p. 151.
[366] M. Morsy: *North Africa*; op cit; p. 136.
[367] Ibid.
[368] Ibid.
[369] W. Blunt: *Desert Hawk*; op cit, p. 87.
[370] C.R. Ageron: *Modern Algeria*, op cit, p. 11.
[371] Ibid.
[372] Ibid.
[373] Ibid.

possession of Tlemcen.[374] Happy with these arrangements, the Bey of Tunis asked for the redaction of a proclamation to the people of Constantine. In it he informed them that henceforth, they were under his rule. The proclamation said:

> Following the French arrival, the country has fallen prey to chaos, and you don't have the strength to fight the French army, your duty, therefore, is to unite and to stop fighting them.[375]

The Bey also sent a letter to Ferhat Ben Said, a powerful foe of Hadj Ahmed, asking him to join his party.[376]

Whilst all this was taking place, Ahmed Bey kept strengthening Constantine's defences. He began by reorganising the troops. This involved the disbanding of the *janissary* corps and the recruitment of 2000 regulars, generally men of tribal origins. Moreover, he could depend on civilian support, contemporaries estimating them at 30 000 fighting men.[377] At the same time as he armed the population, he made alliances with influential families and tribal chiefs.[378] He erected speedily new military barracks to accommodate his increased army, made primarily of Arabs and Berbers. 'I have [he wrote to the Ottoman Sultan Mahmud II] raised new troops and cavalry, which cost me all my available revenues.'[379] He also set up strong defences, reinforcing the city walls where they were vulnerable, and prepared a powerful artillery stock.[380]

Hadj Ahmed also kept a watchful eye on goings on in Algiers and in Paris where the Moorish Committee had appealed to public and parliamentary opinion. His chief political agent was his father-in-law, Hamdan ben 'Uthman Khudja, whose reports throughout this period were unrealistically optimistic.[381] Hadj Ahmed again renewed appeals to the Sultan and sent this same Hamdan to Istanbul to ask for military reinforcements. Appeals also went to the Ottoman Governor of Tripoli.[382] Hadj Ahmed's letters were increasingly insistent:

> We have endured difficulties and sufferings too great to be imagined, all this to safeguard religion and we declare ourselves to be Ottoman subjects.... We can only resist with your help. You are our only hope.'[383]

In Istanbul, political circles, themselves in disarray, hardly in control of a crumbling realm, were divided as to the course of action to be followed, which led to inaction.[384]

---

[374] Ibid.
[375] A. Temimi: Le Beylik; op cit; p. 89; G. Esquer: *Correspondence du Duc de Rovigo*, t. 1. p. 369.
[376] Ibid.
[377] M. Morsy: *North Africa*; op cit; p. 135.
[378] Ibid; p. 136.
[379] A. Temimi: Trois Lettres; op cit; p. 144.
[380] A. Temimi: Le Beylik de Constantine; op cit; 63.
[381] M. Morsy: *North Africa*; op cit; p. 136.
[382] Ibid.
[383] Ibid.
[384] Ibid;

Even European public opinion was called upon and, in 1834, a petition signed by 2307 persons was sent to the British parliament which, as the signatories put it, was 'well-known for its defence of human rights.'[385] It pointed to acts of injustice being committed in Algeria and asked for support. Obviously in the international context of the 1830s, no help could come from outside.[386]

Hadj Ahmed was, Morsy points out, realistic enough to know this as can be seen from his efforts both to fortify the region and to enlist popular support. He consulted the *diwan* on every move and kept it informed of French attempts to negotiate with him.[387] He would point out that he was for peace but could not accept French offers for religious and political reasons, especially in view of the bad faith of the French who had shown total disregard for Muslims and agreements made when Algiers had capitulated.[388] Hadj Ahmed wrote to all the chiefs in Blida, Medea and the tribes that they should prepare to fight on the first signal.[389] He invited them to declare Jihad and take up arms, and he vowed terrible vengeance on those who failed to heed the appeal.[390] He called for the uprising of all the people to march against the French by his side, and should they fail to do so,

> He would abandon them to the shame which would one day be their fate under the French.[391]

To put his words into effect, and speedily, he marched with as large force as he could muster to the north-west. As he closed on Medea, taking place simultaneously, agitation gripped the mountain tribes, whilst in Medea itself, Turks and Kulughlis, numbering between 300 and 400,[392] tried to loot the powder magazine, rejecting French rule, and declaring themselves instead to be subjects of Hadj Ahmed.[393] The combined effects of his presence, agitation and rebellion from inside, helped his cause. Hadj Ahmed entered the city, and according to the Englishman St John, English consul in Algiers, in a letter to the Foreign office, dated 22 November 1833, and then another dated 28 January 1834:

> Hadj Ahmed is in quiet possession of Medea with a large force…. The Bey of Constantine is now in possession of the whole regency except Bona, Bejaia, Algiers and Oran.[394]

Meanwhile in Bone, having already been appointed Bey of Constantine by the French in replacement of Hadj Ahmed, Colonel Yusuf exerted his reign of terror

---

[385] Ibid.

[386] Ibid.

[387] Ibid.

[388] Ibid.

[389] A. Temimi: Le Beylik de Constantine; op cit; p. 131.

[390] G. Esquer: *Correspondence du general Voirol; Voirol to MG* 15 June 1833; p. 100.

[391] G. Esquer: *Correspondence, Voirol;* letter dated 30 August; 1833; p. 208.

[392] G. Esquer: *Correspondence du General Drouet d'Erlon*, 1834-1835; Paris; 1926; Drouet d'Erlon to MG; p. 241; 9 January 1835.

[393] A. Temimi: Le Beylik de Constantine; op cit; p. 132.

[394] F.O., 3/35; St John to Stanley, 22 Nov, 1833; F.O. 3/36; St John to Hay; 28 January 1834.

upon 'uncooperative' tribes.[395] He earned a great notoriety for his decapitating Arabs and Berbers, especially the local elites, and in beating locals to death.[396] Relentlessly Yusuf urged Marshal Clauzel to march against Constantine, promising him a high degree of native support, and declared firmly that the city would surrender at the mere sight of a French soldiers.[397] The French listened to Yusuf but only up to a point, and only decided to march on the city when the conditions were right, in the Autumn of 1836.

1. The First Assault Against Constantine, Autumn 1836

Constantine was a third smaller in extent than Algiers, had a population of about 25,000 most certainly increased by the great numbers of refugees from Algiers, Bone, Bejaia and other places captured by the French. It had four gates: Bab-el-Kantarah, or the "Bridge-Gate," leading over the Roman bridge across the Ruramel to the plateau El-Mansurah; Bab-el-Rahbah, or the Market-Gate, and the two smaller gates, El-Jedid, (New-Gate,) and El-Wad, or the Water-Gate, leading to the Kudiat-Ati.
Its citadel was built on the highest rock in the city, and is surrounded by walls, composed of the ruins of old Cirta. Westwards from the citadel, a steep rock overhangs the valley of the River Rummel, just where the river forms a foaming cascade. The river disappears in places and reappears again beneath the citadel, where it forms a threefold thundering cascade of about 300 feet.[398]

After a long stay at Paris, Marshal Clauzel returned to Algiers towards the end of August 1836. He had laid a complete plan of conquest before his government, according to which all the cities and all strategic points of the interior were to be occupied by French troops, whilst flying columns were to maintain the communications between them.[399] Such a system aimed at curtailing the power of both leaders of the Algerian resistance: the Emir of Mascara, Abd al-Kader, and the Bey of Constantine, Hadj Ahmed. The two leaders would be stopped from building magazines and powder-mills, and both would lose the possibility of concentrating troops.[400] This plan was in many ways similar to the one advised by other high officers, and so, the expedition against Constantine was deemed of 'the highest importance.'[401] For Clauzel, a limited occupation of the country made no sense; what was necessary was the conquest of the whole of Algeria, then strong immigration into the country by European settlers would plant:

---

[395] W. Blunt: *Desert Hawk*; op cit, p. 87.
[396] *Archives des Affaires Etrangeres*, Tunis 2; *Depeche du MAE au Consul Deval*, 20 Avril 1836.
[397] W. Blunt: *Desert Hawk*; op cit, p. 87.
[398] M. Wagner: *The Tricolor on the Atlas*, op cit, pp. 97-101.
[399] Ibid; p. 283.
[400] Ibid.
[401] G. Esquer: *Correspondende Drouet d'Erlon;* p. 196; letter addressed to M.G. 13 December 1834.

> Deep roots... and with great perseverance a new population would arise, and this new population would grow and grow even faster than that which did in North America less than a century ago.[402]

By transferring troops from Algiers and Oran, Clauzel managed to gather a strong army at Bone, the point from which the attack was to be launched. It was felt that the participation of native Algerians was necessary for the success of the operation. 1,300 native soldiers out of the thousands promised by Yusuf were gathered, whilst of the thousands of horsemen promised by Ferhat ben Sai'd, only a few hundred Saharians appeared.[403] The tribes in the vicinity of Bone went over to Hadj Ahmed; of the rest, some had altogether refused to join the French; and the remainder had faded away again into the mountains.[404] But it was generally said, more in hope than in belief, that the latter would put in an appearance as soon as 'the army began its triumphal march.'[405]

Hadj Ahmed tactics consisted in giving the defence of the city to his general Ben Aissa who headed an army of 1400 experienced men reinforced by thousands of citizens bearing arms, who were allocated different sectors and responsibilities in the defence of the city.[406] Hadj Ahmed for his part headed the cavalry outside the city, with his usual tactic of harassing French flanks, advanced and rear-guards, in words preventing a French entry into the city.[407]

In Constantine itself, the Kasbah, served as the main stronghold, and was defended by 8 pieces of artillery. It dominated the rock mounts which surround the city, and which are in places 100 metres high.[408]

On the 8th of November, the French army left Bone, with one single objective: capturing Constantine. Marshal Clauzel took the command in person. Yusuf, who was appointed Bey of Constantine in the place of Ahmed Bey, led the Spahis and Arab auxiliaries.[409]

At Dréan, about a dozen miles south of Bone, Clauzel built a fortified camp, which soon received raiding parties from Constantine.[410] Optimism was still the defining element of the operation. The gates of Constantine seemed in Clauzel's imagination to be already half open, and the army carried a quantity of pamphlets, which opened optimistically with the words: *'Aujourd'hui le corps éxpeditionnaire entrera dans Constantine.'* 'Today the expeditionary Corps will

---

[402] G. Esquer: *Correspondence du Marechal Clauzel*; t1; Paris, Larose; 1948; p. 29.

[403] M. Wagner: *The Tricolor on the Atlas*, op cit, p. 284.

[404] W. Blunt: *Desert Hawk*; op cit, p. 87. M. Wagner: *The Tricolor*; op cit; p. 284.

[405] W. Blunt: *Desert Hawk*; op cit, p. 87.

[406] *Archives du Ministere de la Guerre*, Vincennes, Paris, (AMG), H.235.

[407] M. Emerit: Les Memoires d'Ahmed Bey de Constantine, *Revue Africaine*; 1er et 2em trimester; 1949; pp. 71-125; p. 93.

[408] AMG., H40; Expedition de Constantine; notes de Memoires Presentees par le Capitaine St.Hypolite au Gouverneur General en Date du Mois d'Aout 1836.

[409] M. Wagner: *The Tricolor on the Atlas*, op cit, p. 284.

[410] W. Blunt: *Desert Hawk*; op cit; 88.

enter Constantine.'[411] Clauzel was convinced he was going to crush Bey Ahmed.[412] The signs were not favourable, though. Attacks by Algerian cavalry had multiplied, and tens of men were shot down by snipers; many more were killed by daggers.[413]

Led by Yusuf's men who guided them through the unknown territory, the French vanguard, at last, came in view of Constantine on the evening of 20 November 1836.[414] At dawn the sky cleared, and for a few moments sunlight provided the first glimpse of the old fortress. It hung suspended above the valley mist, whilst silhouetted against the western horizon could be seen: Hadj Ahmed's cavalry.[415] When at last the city was in sight from the plateau of Al-Mansurah, 'every one of the weary soldiers,' says Wagner, 'selected with his eyes the house which he was to occupy, and was glad to have the prospect of a dry bed after eight wet and severely cold nights in the mountains.'[416]

The opinion prevailed that Constantine would not offer much resistance.[417] Clauzel, with his staff and a small escort, now rode on ahead towards the city to receive, so he was convinced, the deputation which would come out to him with the keys of the city.[418] In fact, Clauzel was so convinced of this, and the success of his military operation, he had already appointed Trezel as military governor of Constantine.[419] But suddenly the red flag was raised on the "gate of the bridge," and the batteries of the citadel opened their fire.[420]
'Didn't I tell you,' shouted Clauzel towards the Duke of Nemours 'that we would be welcome by a salvo of honour?'[421]
The officers approved their chief's remark. But their optimism soon left way to great disappointment when a second explosion, much more powerful than the first, resounded, and a canon ball fell in their midst forcing the whole group to seek shelter behind the rocks.[422] Clauzel was completely surprised by the response, and now realised the true intentions of the population of the city, as from everywhere he could hear the echoes and sounds of fierce fighting at Coudiat Aty, where the two regiments had advanced.[423] Then, to his amazement he could see hundreds of Muslim horsemen attacking his advanced men, whilst the citizens, amongst them women, stirred by the calls of muezzins from the

---

[411] Ibid.
[412] G. Fleury: *Comment l'Algerie Devint Francaise*; Perrin, Paris, 2004, p. 186.
[413] Ibid.
[414] Ibid.
[415] W. Blunt: *Desert Hawk*; op cit, p. 90.
[416] M. Wagner: *The Tricolor on the Atlas*, op cit, p. 284.
[417] Ibid.
[418] W. Blunt: *Desert Hawk*; op cit, p. 90.
[419] G. Fleury: *Comment l'Algerie Devint Francaise*; op cit; 187.
[420] M. Wagner: *The Tricolor on the Atlas*, op cit, p. 284.
[421] G. Fleury: *Comment l'Algerie Devint Francaise*; op cit, p. 187.
[422] Ibid.
[423] Ibid.

minarets, launched in fierce assault against the French troops.[424] The engagement was violent and blood ran thick on the ground. French heads were soon seen impaled upon the ramparts. Shrill cries from the women greeted these first trophies and urged their warriors to yet greater efforts.[425] The roles of besieged and besiegers were now reversed: while the besieged were free to sally from the town as often as they wished, the besiegers found themselves virtually blockaded, and to make things even worse for the French Ahmed Bey's cavalry was on them from all sides.[426] On the Mansourah, no sooner had Clauzel erected his battery than it was overturned by Algerian fire. With his men utterly exhausted and most of his horses killed, he did not even attempt to place a battery upon the Coudiat-Aty.[427]

The following day, the French launched the assault which was followed by ferocious fighting in front of the city.[428] At last a French artillery battery was successfully placed in position on the side of the Mansourah less than a quarter of a mile from the El-Kantara; and in spite of the smallness of its cannon it managed to do some damage to the outer gate of the double gateway.[429] The assault proved unsuccessful.

Another day passed-a day during which the Constantine cavalry made repeated attacks from all directions harassing with great damage the French rear.[430] At nightfall another attack took place. All the men carrying the scaling-ladders were killed, and so were those carrying the explosives.[431] General Trézel, the conqueror of Bejaia, was himself shot in the neck. Colonel Hecquet, who had taken over the command, saw that only one course was left open to him: retreat.[432]

When Clauzel marched to the edge of the Plateau of al-Mansurah he saw the pitiful condition of his great army. From Coudiat Aty, he could see the units of the vanguard streaming out, fleeing disorderly, pursued by the horsemen of Constantine, causing terrible havoc amongst them.[433] The French managed to gather many of their wounded as they now pushed further away from the city, and leaving countless numbers of their dead or dying on the ground.[434] Marshal Clauzel was now convinced that success was impossible, and resolved to retreat; leading the remains of his shattered army back to Bone.[435] In the darkness of the

---

[424] Ibid.
[425] W. Blunt: *Desert Hawk*; op cit, p. 91.
[426] Ibid.
[427] Ibid.
[428] G. Fleury: *Comment l'Algerie Devint Francaise*; op cit; 188.
[429] Ibid; W. Blunt: *Desert Hawk*; op cit; p. 92.
[430] Ibid.
[431] Ibid.
[432] Ibid; 93.
[433] G. Fleury: *Comment l'Algerie Devint Francaise*; op cit, p. 189.
[434] Ibid.
[435] M. Wagner: *The Tricolor on the Atlas*, op cit, p. 285.

night from everywhere resounded the sounds of the Muezzins, praising Allah for the victory, accompanied by the shrills of the thousands of women.[436]

Sick, hungry, disillusioned men, exposed constantly to the attacks of a triumphant adversary whose fire they could hardly afford to return, had to be marched across more than a hundred miles of difficult country.[437] Yet, the decision was and had to be taken; and the retreat began as orderly as possible to avoid drawing Algerian attention. To little effect. No sooner was it certain that the French were retreating, than the whole population of Constantine, men and women, surged out of the gates. The French were surprised, yet again. The destruction of materials which could not be carried back was interrupted.[438] The flight was general. Even some of the wounded, for whom no place could be found upon the remaining wagons, had to be left behind where they lay, and here they met their death 'at the hands of the pitiless amazons of Constantine.'[439]

Retreat from Constantine

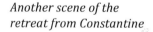

Another scene of the retreat from Constantine

[436] G. Fleury: *Comment l'Algerie Devint Francaise*; op cit, p. 189.
[437] W. Blunt: *Desert Hawk*; op cit, p. 93.
[438] Ibid.
[439] Ibid.

2. Preparing the Next Round

While Ahmed Bey was pinning to his breast the order of *Nitcham Iftihat* conferred upon him by the Ottoman Sultan in reward for his signal services against 'the infidels,' Clauzel was on his way to Paris to give an account of his failed operation.[440] He never returned to Algeria. In fact the Marshal was soon after summoned to defend his strategy in the Chambers.[441] On the 12th of February 1837, the *Moniteur* announced his dismissal.[442] In the same month, General Damrémont was appointed to succeed him as Commander-in-Chief of the French forces in Africa.[443] Abd al-Kader, whom the Marshal had several times officially declared to have fled to the desert to hide his shame, was now blockading the French garrisons in Tlemcen and in the camp on the Tafna, and his horsemen scoured the country up to the gates of Oran.[444] In the meantime, Yusuf, who prior to the defeat was nicknamed the 'Arab Eater,' had now become simply 'the Arab,' even accused of having ruined the French treasury and for 'having sullied the good name of France by his wanton massacre of Algerian natives.'[445]

Abd al Kader was making the best possible use of the opportunities which the French had placed in his hands.[446] He stirred up the Hajuts to lay waste the country surrounding Algiers; he organised revolts in the west and negotiated a highly favourable agreement with General Brossard, who now commanded at Oran, by which he received arms and ammunition from the French in exchange for corn.[447]

The successor of Marshal Clauzel, Lieutenant-General Count Denys de Damremont, had in 1830 commanded a brigade under De Bourmont, and taken active part in all the fights against Algerians up to the surrender of Algiers.[448] The French were by now determined to avenge the affront of the 1836 defeat at Constantine.[449] That defeat had taught them that in Hadj Ahmed they had a great enemy who was much more intransigent than Abd al-Kader, and with whom they had to finish regardless of the means to be used.[450] 'French honour was at stake here.' This honour was going to be regained either by a sparkling action or through an arrangement of the sort.[451]

The latter was adopted. In order to avenge Constantine, France needed the assurance of peace in the west of the country. It thus became crucial to secure

---

[440] W. Blunt: *Desert Hawk*; op cit, p. 94.
[441] M. Wagner: *The Tricolor on the Atlas*, op cit, p. 285.
[442] Ibid.
[443] W. Blunt: *Desert Hawk*; op cit, p. 94.
[444] M. Wagner: *The Tricolor on the Atlas*, op cit, p. 285
[445] G. Fleury: *Comment l'Algerie Devint Francaise*; op cit, p. 192.
[446] W. Blunt: *Desert Hawk*; op cit, p. 95.
[447] Ibid.
[448] M. Wagner: *The Tricolor on the Atlas*, op cit, p. 286.
[449] M. Morsy: *North Africa*; op cit; p. 136.
[450] A. Temimi: Le Beylik de Constantine; op cit; p. 184.
[451] G. Iver: *Documents Relatifs au Traite de la Tafna (1837)*; Alger, Bastide-Jourdan, 1924; p. 150.

peace with Abd al-Kader as soon as possible in order to have all the forces stationed in the west available against Ahmed Bey.[452] According to the British consul in Algiers, St John:

> It is the intention of the French government to assemble a strong force at Oran, and then offer terms to Abd al-Kader. In case he refused he was to be attacked. I have also heard that he had acceded to all of the propositions lately made to him, till they called on him to join them in an attack on the Bey of Constantine, on which, it seems, that he broke off all further relations with them.[453]

It was at this juncture that Bugeaud volunteered to approach Abd al Kader and to attempt to negotiate a treaty.[454] After negotiations, on the 30th of May 1837, the Treaty of the Tafna was signed by the two parties (for details on treaty see following chapter).

General Damremont was informed of the treaty at the Tafna, just when he had proceeded with a column against the Hajuts. He immediately held off the operation, and all hostilities were suspended. The French could now turn all their forces against the Bey of Constantine.[455] Soon there began the formation of the largest force in men, equipment and flower of French generalship, of the colonial war.

3. The Second Battle and Fall of Constantine (October 1837)

In 1837, with 20,400 men and a strong force of artillery, Damremont marched towards the capital of the Eastern Province.[456] Last efforts were made by the French to get Hadj Ahmed to negotiate, but these proved worthless.[457] On one occasion, a Moroccan emissary, Al-Harishi, and also Ben Badjou, a Jew at the service of Hadj Ahmed, were sent to ask the latter to submit to France, but he refused.[458] Another Jewish emissary, Busnach, sent by Damremont asked the Bey to desist from fighting France, and amongst others, that he recognised the French suzerainty over Algeria, and that the French flag should fly twice a year in Constantine, that he paid a tribute of two millions; that he accepts a French garrison in Constantine, and that in exchange he would receive the title of Pasha,

---

[452] M. Wagner: *The Tricolor on the Atlas*, op cit, p. 290. A. Temimi: *Le Beylik de Constantine*; op cit; p. 185.
[453] F.O., 3/40; St John to Palmerston, 13 March 1837.
[454] W. Blunt: *Desert Hawk*; op cit, p. 95.
[455] M. Wagner: *The Tricolor on the Atlas*, op cit, p. 299.
[456] M. Morsy: *North Africa*; op cit; p. 137.
[457] Ibid.
[458] A. Temimi: *Le Beylik de Constantine*; op cit; p. 191.

and that he would be allowed to rule the Beylik of Constantine beyond M'jaz Ammar.[459] Hadj Ahmed rejected the offer outright.

In the meantime, Hadj Ahmed had not been inactive. Aware of the French movement, he had sent a message to Istanbul, again, seeking support from Sultan Mahmud II, and also sent messengers to the Dey of Tunis, Mustapha ben Mahmud, and also to the Ottoman Pasha ruling in Tripoli.[460] The response from both Tunis and Istanbul could not be other than kindly words due to the reasons already cited. The Pasha of Tripoli was more forthcoming, though. However, no sooner he heard of the moves that Tripoli was sending ships to Tunis in response, the French King, Louis Philippe, sent a large fleet from Toulon to counter their progress.[461] Once more Hadj Ahmed had to rely on his resources, however limited. He spent considerable amounts acquiring armament on the black market from Tunisia, including powder, canons, and guns, costing up to ten times their real value.[462] Much of the armament was for the population, which was extremely eager to fight and repulse the invader.[463] Hadj Ahmed also wrote to all the local tribes inviting them to join him for the common cause, and to declare the Holy War against the French:

> You are good Muslims [he wrote,] you don't want to surrender your children to the Infidels, come alongside me, let's defend our country and the law of the Prophet, or let us all die together.[464]

Proclamations to this effect were read in all mosques at the hours of prayers in order to stir the zeal of the people and bring them to unite against the French.[465] France had also done its work to call upon its local allies to discourage such moves. In total, according to some estimates, the defenders of Constantine reached 5000 cavalry men and 2000 foot besides soldiers at the service of Hadj Ahmed.[466] There were also thousands of citizens bearing arms ready for the ultimate fight. In the army's composition, there were besides the Kabyles from southern Bejaia, considerable numbers of local Arabs, and also, as the German Wagner notes, 2,000 Kuluglis and Turkish fighters, many of whom had left Algiers at its fall to continue the fight in Constantine.[467] Seeking to reinforce the city's defence, Hadj Ahmed had some houses cleared, and replaced with strong battlements; besides mining parts of the city.[468] He himself, as in the first

---

[459] See the peace project in G. Iver: *Correspondence du General Damremont, Gouverneur General….*; Paris; Champion, 1927.; pp. 278-9. See also M. Emerit: *Les Memoires de Hadj Ahmed;* pp. 102-3.
[460] G. Fleury: *Comment l'Algerie Devint Francaise*; op cit, p. 200.
[461] Ibid.
[462] G. Iver: *Correspondence du General Damremont*; pp. 210-11; Letter dated 22 June 1837.
[463] AMG., H235; Notes de Bin Aissa sur le Beylik de Constantine.
[464] G. Iver: *Correspondence du General Damremont*; p. 336.
[465] A. Temimi: Le Beylik de Constantine; op cit; p. 196.
[466] M. Emerit: *Les Memoires*; op cit; p. 105.
[467] M. Wagner: *The Tricolor on the Atlas*, op cit, p. 325.
[468] A. Temimi: Le Beylik de Constantine; op cit; p. 197.

campaign, took command of the vanguard that was to attack the French as they advanced towards the city.[469]

Quite importantly, in the French camp there was the presence of one of the leading figures of French colonial history: Lamoricière. He was a colonel, in command of the Zouaves which he had made the finest regiment in the French army. He studied African warfare with great success, and was just as clever in devising a plan of operations as in carrying it out on the battlefield. Lamoriciere was one of the few French officers who had soon learned Arabic.[470]

On the 1st of October, 1837, long before sunrise, the roll of the drums and the flourish of the trumpets were heard. Clouds covered the sky when the vanguard began to move; the bulk of the army followed rather heavily, as the soldiers had, besides their heavy sacks, to carry a supply of wood for several days on their backs.[471]

On the evening of the 5th of October, hostilities began. Until now no fighter from Constantine had shown himself. However on the way, the straw-huts once inhabited by the locals, and all villages from Ras-al-Akbah down to Constantine were in flames before the French arrived.[472] This fact did not show a peaceful disposition, and was striking as, during the first expedition of Marshal Clauzel, the inhabitants of these very same villages had remained quietly in their huts, allowing their herds to graze under the very eye of the army.[473]

The French army which had progressed without any hindrance so far, as it began slowly descending down to the valley of the Ruramel towards Constantine, was suddenly attacked on its left flank by hundreds of horsemen. This was meant to disrupt and break the French army, and make it easier to crush separate elements.[474] Apart from causing some loss and disruption, the attack did not succeed as French troops remained compact and solid. They continued their advance and at about one hour from Constantine, the camp was formed. Dusk had already set in, and although the number of Muslim attackers was now increasing incessantly, it was ultimately ineffectual as they could not disrupt the French compactness and draw them into combat.[475]

On the 6th of October, the army encamped close before Constantine. The vanguard slowly approached the plateau of Al-Mansurah.[476] The baggage, the field-hospital, and the rear of the army, encamped on a small plain at the foot of the mountain of

---

[469] Ibid.

[470] M. Wagner: *The Tricolor on the Atlas*, op cit, p. 306.

[471] Ibid. 312.

[472] Ibid. 318.

[473] Ibid.

[474] Ibid.

[475] Ibid.

[476] Ibid, p. 319.

al-Mansurah, whilst the suite of General Damremont took its quarters in an old house of the Marabut Sidi Mabruk.[477]

As soon as the French arrived on the al-Mansurah Plateau, battle-cries resounded from all the bastions, and announced the presence of the enemy.[478] The women had climbed upon the roofs, and raised their typical cry by which they express every passionate emotion of joy or grief, 'equally heard at the wedding-feast and at the funeral. This time it expressed their hatred of us, and was meant to arouse the enthusiasm of their champions.'[479] Above the gates Bab-al-Wad and Bab-al-Djeddid flew two red flags of immense size. The same hostile banners had been raised on the very same spots one year before, at the time of Clauzel's expedition.[480] The officers who had been present at that first campaign found on the whole that the aspect of the city was the same; even the Roman bridge, which was said to have been destroyed by Ahmed-Bey, was unaffected.[481]

As the French began to prepare their assault, all the villages far around were in flames, whilst, at the same time, the distinctly audible voice of the imam in Constantine called for prayers 'from the spire of the mosques to the clouds reddened by the flames.'[482]

> Whoever has lived in Mohammedan cities [says Wagner] knows the strange emotion caused by the monotonous, hollow, but far-sounding accents of the Muezzin, calling to prayer from the minaret aloft, in the evening twilight. When in Algiers, from the terrace of my house, I watched the parting sun, and was called from my reverie by the earnest call of the Muezzin, I often fancied I heard the dirge of the sinking orb.[483]

During the evening, the third and fourth brigade passed the River Rummel and took possession of the elevation Coudiat-Aty, at the moment when heavy rain began to fall, which lasted for five whole days.[484] The passage was very difficult: the bed of the Rummel was filled with large stones, and the mountain was steep and slippery. The French advanced under intense fire which killed several men, among them one of the aide- de-camps of Lieutenant-General Fleury, who was torn in two by a cannon-ball.[485] Generals Rulhieres and Fleury, in order to encourage their soldiers, rode to the head of the very difficult path, whilst the wind blinded them with rain.[486] Two battalions posted themselves between the tombs which cover Coudiat-Aty.

---

[477] Ibid.
[478] Ibid. 321.
[479] Ibid, p. 322.
[480] Ibid.
[481] Ibid.
[482] Ibid.
[483] Ibid.
[484] Ibid, p. 324.
[485] Ibid.
[486] Ibid.

On the 7th of October, the Constantine cavaliers made a bolder sally.[487] They attacked in two directions, straight into the thick of the French army. This time the fighting was extremely bloody. The Algerians had surprised the French in no longer defensive position, and inflicted heavy loss on them. In the direction of al-Mansurah, much superior French fire power forced an Algerian retreat, but on the Coudiat Aty, the encounter between the men of Constantine, including in this Turks and Kuluglis, with the Foreign Legion and the Third African Battalion, was fierce and bloody.[488] The French re-organised and counter attacked with fire and bayonets, thus forcing back the Algerians, whose retreat was covered by musket-fire from the city.[489] Just as one group retreated, about three thousand horsemen, mainly Arabs, descended from the mountains east and north of the Coudiat- Aty, to attack the two brigades in the rear and in the flank.[490] Again the fighting was brutal, and only ended when the Chasseurs d'Afrique made a furious charge which forced the Muslims back towards the mountain.[491] In their flight, they made sudden turns and attacked their French pursuers causing them great loss of men.[492]

Constantine was defended by from six to seven thousand armed men, among whom were about 'three thousand Kabyles, savage people, ragged and fanatical, who, roused by the speeches of their Marabuts, several of whom were in the pay of the Bey, had come down from their mountains to take part against the infidels.'[493] They had brought their long muskets and yatagans of various shapes, and were employed as sharp-shooters on the ramparts and on the foremost houses, where they proved useful, as they have 'a practised eye and a steady hand.'[494] But for service in the batteries, the gunners were for the most part Turks or Kuluglis, who had been expelled or had withdrawn from Algiers. The French had been informed that the Ottoman officer Bel Bedjaoui had under his command 2,000 militia men, and that the canons of the Bey were served by 500 Turks who all had great expertise in artillery fire.[495] There were also a few French deserters and prisoners, several of the Foreign Legion.[496] A German, Wendlin Schlosser, from Erfurt, was artillery-officer of the Bey, whilst another renegade: Send, from Dresden, served as gun-smith.[497] The French had learnt that Hajj Ahmed had sixty canons, and that he had cleared an area close to the citadel to

---

[487] Ibid.
[488] Ibid.
[489] Ibid.
[490] Ibid.
[491] Ibid.
[492] Ibid, p. 325.
[493] Ibid.
[494] Ibid.
[495] G. Fleury: *Comment l'Algerie Devint Francaise*; op cit, p. 202.
[496] M. Wagner: *The Tricolor on the Atlas*, op cit, p. 325.
[497] Ibid.

make the defence of the city easier.[498] Everywhere barricades had been set to block the French advance; every street was organised for defence, every opening was armed with a gun, and every house had become 'a stronghold to be taken only at the price of heavy fight.'[499] The chief commander of the town was Ben-Aissa, who descended from the Kabyles, 'but in character and habits,' Wagner says, 'he had turned Turk, for he had lived in Constantine many years.'[500] Under him served the Kaid-el-Dar (the Palace Chief), another Kabyle of signal bravery, restlessly appealing to the enthusiasm of the garrison, and who (it was said) in fact directed the defence.[501] Outside the city, Hajj Ahmed had about three thousand Arab horsemen, and from twelve to fifteen hundred infantry, who encamped east of the city, close to a large country-seat, on which his pennon was raised.[502] Several thousand horsemen were stationed on the heights round the Coudiat-Aty. Another Arab camp was in the neighbourhood of al-Mansurah.[503] It is difficult to ascertain the exact number of Hadj Ahmed's allies round the city, although these could reach eight thousand men, the majority of whom being Bedouin horsemen of the Sahara, led by Bu-Aziz-ben-Ganah, Ahmed's uncle by his mother, whilst the infantry were almost all Kabyles.[504]

On the 9th of October, in the morning at seven o'clock, the French batteries opened an intense barrage from the plateau of Al-Mansurah. Their aim was both to silence the Constantine's batteries, to dismount the cannon, and to terrify the city into submission.[505] General Damremont thought that the inhabitants would capitulate on the very same day; he certainly did not contemplate making a serious attack from al-Mansurah, as the first expedition had already given proof that from this side the storming could not possibly succeed.[506] The French fire was formidable in intensity, and by about eleven o'clock the artillery of the Kasbah and of the al-Kantara Gate had ceased their firing. Most of the cannon had been disabled, and only from Bab-el-Djeddid did a few pieces continue, until the evening.[507] The French mortars seemed to have caused considerable damage to the city, and certainly many casualties. Particular targets were the palace of the Bey and the house of Ben-Aissa. Towards evening, the French tried experiments with Congreve rockets: 'In oblique lines, bursting and hissing, and throwing a flaming light around, those projectiles flew into the very midst of the city.'[508] They were equally loud, destructive, and psychologically very powerful as any new, loud and devastating weapon always is. Despite the heavy fire, the city was no

---

[498] G. Fleury: *Comment l'Algerie Devint Francaise*; op cit, p. 202.
[499] Ibid.
[500] M. Wagner: *The Tricolor on the Atlas*, op cit, p. 325.
[501] Ibid, p. 326.
[502] Ibid.
[503] Ibid.
[504] Ibid.
[505] Ibid; p. 327.
[506] Ibid.
[507] Ibid.
[508] Ibid.

nearer to surrendering. General Damremont had miscalculated the courage of the inhabitants of Constantine: no messenger of truce appeared.

> Though fanaticism does not impart the energy of action to the nations of this country, it gives them the power of endurance. Half the city might have been destroyed; the inhabitants would have borne their disasters with fatalistic indifference, without even entertaining a thought of capitulation [remarks Wagner.][509]

Whilst his city was under fire, Hadj Ahmed, at the head of his cavalry kept attacking the French, focussing most particularly on their artillery supply wagons, seeking to cut them off, and thus break the intense bombardment.[510] As he threw himself and his men into one attack after another, the French responded with fiercer fire.[511] This time the French had the discipline, and above all much bigger and devastating fire power.

The garrison of Constantine made a determined sally on the morning of 10th of October. Turks and Kabyles stealthily approached by a hollow way, and along the deep furrows of the ground, till they neared the batteries. Soon fighting raged. General Damremont, who was on the spot, ordered the Foreign Legion and the "Battalion d'Afrique" to attack with fixed bayonets, and threw himself into the struggle.[512] Many bullets were aimed at him; he was noticeable from the feather in his hat, but none hit him. In a murderous close hand to hand fight, although bravery was missing on neither side, in the end superior fire power and numbers had reason of the Algerians who retreated leaving considerable numbers of their men on the ground.[513]

On the 11th, the batteries began to batter the walls between the gates Bab-el-Wad and Bab-el-Djeddid. Here is the single narrow point where it is possible to create a breach, as here ends the deep ravine which encircles Constantine in every other direction.[514]

Damremont was fully confident that the garrison would now surrender, but he had underestimated their tenacity. *'C'était se tromper sur la nature des Arabes qui sont capables, non de tout faire, mais de tout souffir,'* (It was misunderstanding the nature of the Arabs who cannot do everything but have the resilience for extreme suffering) wrote a young French captain.[515]

Rather than surrendering, the city's defenders made another determined sortie during the day, and at night attacked a French breaching battery which had been

---

[509] Ibid.

[510] G. Fleury: *Comment l'Algerie Devint Francaise*; op cit, p. 205.

[511] Ibid.

[512] M. Wagner: *The Tricolor on the Atlas*, op cit, p. 330.

[513] Ibid.

[514] Ibid, p. 329.

[515] W. Blunt: *Desert Hawk*; op cit, pp. 107-8.

set up only a hundred and thirty yards from the town walls.[516] The city's defenders knew it: an even bigger assault was now about to be launched.

In the morning of 12 October, accurate French fire temporarily silenced the guns opposite the Coudiat-Aty.[517] The breach was already so wide that ten men could storm abreast. Damremont and his suite were early there to watch the progress of the breach. About eight o'clock, he ordered the fire to be discontinued, as a messenger was expected back from the city, who had been sent thither with the summons to capitulate.[518] The letter was carried by a young Muslim volunteer serving with the French, who was hoisted up by ropes on to the battlements.[519] The reply left no doubt that the city was prepared to fight:

> If the Christians are short of powder we will send them some; if they are short of biscuits they may share ours. But so long as one of us remains alive they shall not enter Constantine.[520]
> We shall defend our city and our houses to the last; they shall not become your prey as long as a single defender lives.[521]

When this answer was delivered to the General, he said:
"They are brave men! Well, the struggle will be the more glorious for us."[522]

Towards ten o'clock, the roar of cannon was again heard. The twenty-four pounders and the mortars fired in quick succession, and soon cleared the piles of woolsacks out of the breach. The bombardment was so fierce that the echo, rolling from mountain to mountain, carried the sound as far as to the Desert, over a hundred miles away.[523] Damremont rode off with his staff to the Coudiat Aty in the direction of the city, in order to view with the telescope the effect produced by the fire.[524] He dismounted at an exposed point in full view of the breach. General Rulhières, who stood beside him, pointed out the risk he was running.[525] It does not matter, answered Damremont calmly. At that instant a canon ball rebounded from a rock and hit him in the chest and he fell dead.[526] A moment later General Perregaux, bending over the lifeless body of his friend, was mortally wounded by a musket bullet, and Rulhières received a wound in the cheek.[527] The fire of the Constantine defenders became even more intense as they hit both officers and men around them.[528] Damremont's death was a terrible blow to

---

[516] Ibid, p. 108.
[517] Ibid.
[518] M. Wagner: *The Tricolor on the Atlas*, op cit, p. 330.
[519] W. Blunt: *Desert Hawk*; op cit, p. 108.
[520] Ibid.
[521] M. Wagner: *The Tricolor on the Atlas*, op cit, p. 331.
[522] Ibid.
[523] Ibid.
[524] W. Blunt: *Desert Hawk*; op cit; p. 108; M. Wagner: *The Tricolor on the Atlas*, op cit, p. 331.
[525] G. Fleury: *Comment*; op cit; 207
[526] Ibid.
[527] W. Blunt: *Desert Hawk*; op cit, p. 108.
[528] G. Fleury: *Comment l'Algerie Devint Francaise*; op cit, p. 207.

France, and its repercussions would go on for quite long, and so touched was French public opinion that Berlioz composed his requiem in his memory.

The assault which was to take place on the day was postponed due to Damremont's death until the following, the 13th.[529]
By evening the breach was more than ten yards wide, and it was considered feasible to attempt the assault at daybreak the following morning.

Friday, October 13. In the city the *muezzins* were calling from the minarets, while below in the squares the women, children and old men responded in chorus.[530] A last salvo of artillery was fired, throwing up a cloud of dust round the breach.[531] In a short moment the French main assault began, led by Lamoriciere's Zouavs. The Foreign Legion sounded the storming march; the other regimental bands joined in.[532] From the Arabs and Kabyles encamped among the hills came a fearful, piercing cry which for a moment drowned the drums and the trumpets. A minute or two later the first column was in the breach.[533] In the 25 seconds necessary for crossing the distance of 100 metres which separate the breach from the French army, the attackers became, Fleury says, a choice target of the intense fire of the men of Ben Aissa and Bel Lebdjaoui.[534] Tens of Frenchmen fell dead and wounded.[535] The impetus of their assault and their large numbers soon brought them in close fight with the first line of defenders. A bloody hand to hand fight ensued, the defenders not retreating one pace.[536] The ground was littered with bodies amongst the rubble and dust from the bombardment. Intense fire whizzed from all sides, coming from Algerians scattered amidst the ruins.[537] The invisible marksmen aimed especially at the officers; in consequence, one fourth of the killed were officers.[538] To get over the ruins into the streets, the first troops were compelled to open a path with the bayonet, and to march over corpses. 'The enemy,' says Wagner, retreated from door to door, 'disputing every inch of ground.'[539] Hadj Ahmed had mined parts of the city and their explosions caused havoc amongst the French; in one instance, over forty soldiers and officers were crushed and burnt.[540] Others lived a few moments after the explosion, but their agony was terrible; they had lost their sight, and stumbled about as if in search of the limbs and clothes of which the fire had bereft them; wailing in sounds unlike

---

[529] Ibid.
[530] W. Blunt: *Desert Hawk*; op cit; p. 109
[531] Ibid.
[532] Ibid.
[533] Ibid.
[534] G. Fleury: *Comment l'Algerie Devint Francaise*; op cit, p. 208.
[535] Ibid.
[536] Ibid.
[537] M. Wagner: *The Tricolor on the Atlas*, op cit, p. 334.
[538] Ibid.
[539] Ibid, p. 335.
[540] Ibid.

any human utterance.[541] Ragged Kabyles, likewise blackened by powder, yatagan in hand, could be seen scrambling across the glowing and smoking ruins, to finish off all those 'who still breathed and suffered amidst the scene of destruction and deadly struggle.'[542]

The Fight for Constantine: French victory but at a costly price

The Algerian fighters had retired behind a barricade, which had formed itself of ruins and corpses. From there they launched a murderous musket-fire against the French troops. Combes ordered a company of his regiment to take this barrier by storm, awarding the decoration of the "Legion d'Honneur" to the first who would overstep it.[543]

> The street [says future General St Arnaud] had to be taken house by house, and under a fire all the more terrible since it was impossible to see from which point it came. It was in this street, where we waded up to our knees in corpses and blood, that our losses were heaviest. On reaching it, my first concern was to keep my men close to the walls. But in spite of that, many of them fell, mortally wounded by fire at such close range. Twenty yards up the street we were stopped dead by a continuous cross fire which killed all those who tried to advance. The soldiers were no longer obeying orders promptly.... What a scene it was! What slaughter! Blood stood in pools on the stairs. Not a cry escaped from the lips of the dying. Death blows were given and taken with that frenzy of desperation which makes one clench

---

[541] Ibid.
[542] Ibid; pp. 335-6.
[543] Ibid; p. 336.

one's teeth, which stifles one's cries. The Turks made little attempt to get away; and those who did, made use of every inch of cover to fire on us...'[544] Further down the Street, fully exposed to the enemy's rifles, Combes was urging his men forward. As Saint-Arnaud joined him, the Colonel received a hit. A spasm of pain shook him, but he uttered no cry. As he turned, another ball struck him.[545] Unaided he walked back towards the breach, where he gave a clear account of the situation to General Valée, the new Commander in Chief in place of Damremont. 'The Duc de Nemours, who was standing near, turned to him:

'But you are wounded, Colonel?'

'No, Monseigneur, I am dead.'[546]

Fighting every square metre

Fighting, meanwhile, raged in every corner, every metre disputed with despair and courage. Bel Lebjaoui with his men fought and all died on the spot not surrendering one inch.[547] According to accounts, when overpowered, rather than surrendering, Bel Lebjaoui hurled himself down the nearby ravine, his last words: 'Allah is Great!'[548]

Without one of its finest leader, the city still fought desperately. Each metre was disputed with bayonets, sabres, knives and pistol fire, each house a graveyard were there piled men of both sides.[549] The struggle continued in the galleries and in the yard of the houses; several Kabyles died, arms in hand.[550] A Black woman likewise lay among the corpses: she had been killed by a musket-ball, and held a yatagan and a pistol yet in her hand.[551] Ben-Aissa himself had entrenched himself

---

[544] Saint Arnaud: *Lettres* (1855); in W. Blunt: *Desert Hawk*; op cit, pp. 111-2.

[545] W. Blunt: *Desert Hawk*; op cit, p. 112.

[546] Ibid.

[547] G. Fleury: *Comment l'Algerie Devint Francaise*; op cit; p. 210

[548] Ibid.

[549] Ibid.

[550] M. Wagner: *The Tricolor on the Atlas*, op cit, p. 337.

[551] Ibid.

in the citadel, but he too fought until he was pushed out under heavy fire.[552] Now, at last the city's centre had fallen. The price was horrific: the ground was in a shambles; everywhere piles of corpses, of groaning men living their last moments; dust and smoke; the smell of powder and blood filling the air.

The few surviving defenders now feared the French reprisals against the population; and whilst they retired to continue the fight for another day, they sued for the kind treatment of the population in exchange for cease-fire. The fighting stopped.

> From Coudiat-Aty [Wagner says] we could see the storming columns climbing up the breach before disappearing in the city When, at nine o'clock, we saw the tricolor reared on the Kasbah, we shouted with exultation, and embraced one another; for the first time in my life I felt the power of the consciousness of victory.[553]

At nine o'clock the city surrendered unconditionally.

On 13 October 1837, Constantine was taken with considerable loss of life on both sides. The city had resisted street by street, and defeat was followed up by mass killing and looting on the grandest scale.[554]

4. In the Wake of the French Capture

Wagner, the German scientist (no fervent admirer of the defenders of Constantine whom he calls barbaric and fanatics fighting valiant Frenchmen), who was with the French army, describes the scene:

> The breach was about thirty feet broad. In order to arrive there, one had first to climb an elevation of earth and sand. Many wool-sacks and stones lay strewed about the broken wall; behind the breach we saw ruins of houses destroyed by the explosion. The scorched and mutilated corpses of African and French soldiers lay here so close together, that it was impossible to enter the city without stepping on dead bodies. I never beheld a more frightful sight than this breach: most of the corpses were torn in pieces, some without heads; with others, the features were completely blackened by powder, so that it was impossible to distinguish the white European from the brown Kabyle, and even from the Negro. In the streets, the corpses were less disfigured. Some of the groups of dead were very striking. The struggle had been fought here man to man, and the fallen French soldier rested sometimes on the body of his Kabyle enemy. I can never forget the countenance of an old Kulughli, with a long white

---

[552] Ibid.
[553] Ibid.
[554] M. Morsy: *North Africa*; op cit; p. 137.

beard, whom I saw leaning on the corner of a house in a sitting posture, with eyes and mouth wide open, his left fist raised to the skies, whilst his right hand tightly clasped a pistol. I thought the old man was alive, and was calling for help; but when I approached, I saw that he was a cold grim corpse. The fury of fanaticism, and sometimes the triumph of glutted revenge, that so many enemies had fallen around them, remained impressed on the features of the fallen Mussulmans.

Arriving in the town, over this smoking heap of ruins and corpses, I met a band of plunderers, laden with manifold booty, carpets, burnouses, arms, victuals, and even Arab manuscripts; seeking people to buy them. In the entrance to the first street, a coffee-house was open, where pots of coffee stood yet on the hearth. The Moorish customers had fled, and the French grenadiers emptied now the whole supply, jesting and happy. A long row of Moorish and Jewish shops was already entirely plundered; the soldiers of the Foreign Legion busied themselves here much more than they had done at the storm; but the inhabitants were not injured personally, from the very moment that the struggle had ceased. They stood trembling, without complaint or protestation, gazing at the plunderers of their property. The Jews humbly kissed the hands of the soldiers, who seemed to be greatly amused by such submission.[555]

On the northern side of the city, at the point furthest from the French attack, the rock face drops almost vertically.[556]

Here [says St Arnaud] a hideous spectacle now presented itself to our eyes. Some two hundred women and children lay broken upon the rocks. The Arabs, seeing us take a foothold in the town, and beginning to realize that they had lost, had come there to try to save their women and children. They had attempted an impossible flight down these un-scalable cliffs. Terror increased their haste, and made the undertaking still more perilous. Many women and children had lost their lives in this horrible way. A few were still breathing when we got there. One or two, as if by a miracle, had even reached flat ledges of rock in safety— ledges which led nowhere. By means of chains of soldiers, and by the use of ropes, we rescued them; but their fear of us was the greatest obstacle to our helping them.[557]

On this particular incident, Wagner writes:

The Kasbah, or citadel, is of Roman origin. As the strongest batteries of Ahmed-Bey had been posted here, it was the peculiar aim of the French shells for several days. The missiles had made a dreadful havoc, yet the Roman walls stood out; though pierced by the balls, they did not tumble down. The citadel is built on the extreme edge of a precipice. The rocks

---

[555] M. Wagner: *The Tricolor on the Atlas*, op cit, pp. 339-44.
[556] W. Blunt: *Desert Hawk;* op cit; p. 113
[557] St Arnaud: *Lettres*; in W. Blunt: *Desert Hawk*; op cit, p. 113.

beneath are nearly vertical, and only one path is practicable for men skilled in climbing. Yet many of the ill-fated inhabitants tried to escape this way; some succeeded in descending on ropes; but others were hurled down by the crowd pressing behind on that dangerous spot, and were crushed or maimed by the fall. Whoever had taken that direction could no longer return, as the enemy was raging in the rear, and the stream of the fugitives rolled on. The confusion was yet heightened by the musket-fire of the 17th infantry regiment, which stood on the opposite rock, and shot down the flying multitude. Above five hundred men lost their lives. But in spite of the relentless fire of the French, the people of Constantine carried away their dead; only on some inaccessible projections of the rock there remained a few corpses. On one of these projections, nearly in mid-air, we saw a female lying, who had broken her leg; and a babe, which had remained unhurt. My friend Muralt summoned the French soldiers to make an effort to save the unfortunate woman, and promised a reward to those who should reach her. A Zuave, who spoke Arabic, succeeded after several attempts; but the Mooress refused any help from Christians, and declared she wished to die on that spot with her infant. She only requested a jug of water, which was handed down to her by a rope. She first gave her child to drink, drank herself, and then threw the jug into the abyss. I do not know what became of her. Next day she had disappeared, together with her child.[558]

The French say the Algerians fell by themselves, reality could be otherwise.

---

[558] M. Wagner: *The Tricolor on the Atlas*, op cit, p. 342.

The news of the taking of Constantine was received with great joy in France; the Parisian population soon burst out with the hymn:

> Damremont is dead! But he died with glory; for his country in the field of honour! To him victory is owed; he showed his true worth. Orphaned of its chief, the army, with rage breathes. Forward soldiers! Let's march to the fight! All of us; let us run! Let us fly! And let's challenge death! We enter Constantine![559]

The army remained a week in the city, which the Jews were now busily cleaning up. The Duc de Nemours and Valée established their head-quarters in the Bey's palace, a modern, and externally an unpretentious building, but full of beautiful courts planted with orange, citron and pomegranate trees.[560] Marble fountains, gaily painted tiles, terraces, rich stuffs and glittering candelabra, a lion-pit with twelve lions.[561] Brightly coloured mural paintings decorated the walls-panoramas of Constantine and the great cities of Islam, of naval actions and the like.[562]
But behind the laughter and joy of victory and relief,

> The almost forgotten pleasures of food, warmth and shelter, lay the remembrance of the dead and the wounded-of Damrémont, Perrégaux, Combes and a quarter of the total number of officers who would march no more with the army.[563]

---

[559] G. Fleury: *Comment l'Algerie Devint Francaise*; op cit, p. 212.
[560] W. Blunt: *Desert Hawk*; op cit, p. 113.
[561] Ibid.
[562] Ibid.
[563] Ibid; p. 114.

Four

EMIR ABD AL KADER
(1832-1840)

According to Lane Poole:

> The hero of this sanguinary conflict was 'Abd-el-Kadir, a man who united in his person and character all the virtues of the old Arabs with many of the best results of civilization. Descended from a saintly family, himself learned and devout, a Haj or Meccan pilgrim; frank, generous, hospitable; and withal a splendid horseman, redoubtable in battle, and fired with the patriotic enthusiasm which belongs to a born leader of men, 'Abd-el-Kadir became the recognized chief of the Arab insurgents.[564]

About Abd al-Kader, Churchill says:

> A triumphant warrior, where the most sanguine had a right to despair; a successful ruler in all the difficulties of a course wholly untried; but a warrior whose sword only left its sheath when the first law of our nature commanded it to be drawn; and a ruler who, having tasted of supreme power, gently and unostentatiously desired that the cup might pass from him, nor would suffer more to wet his lips, than the most solemn and sacred duty to his country and his God required.[565]
>
> Warrior, orator, diplomatist, statesman, and legislator, the secret of his force lay in his intellectual grandeur. His letters, his speeches, his conversations, all bear the stamp of their own peculiar freshness and originality. His natural eloquence, enriched by study, matured by meditation, and enhanced by the singular charms and graces of his manner, operated like a spell.[566]

Abd al-Kader (Abd al-Kadir; Abd al-Qadir), unlike Hadj Ahmed, found indeed great admiration amongst the Western audience, and yet, just like Hadj Ahmed, although so much different in character and methods, he also fought the French bitterly. His fight began no sooner the French made inroads into his home region in the western parts of the country in 1832, and would continue for another sixteen years, till late in 1847, a campaign marked by extreme ferocity and destruction.

---

[564] S. Lane Poole: *Barbary Corsairs*; Fisher & Unwin, 1890; p. 305.
[565] C.H. Churchill: *The Life of Abd Al Kader*, Chapman and Hall, London, 1867, p. 152.
[566] Ibid; p. 140.

1. Abd al-Kader Comes Forth

Not long after the French had made their advance in the western parts of Algeria, tribal meetings were held, with the *zawya* of Mascara taking the lead.[567] On 22 November 1832 one such large assembly gathered on the plain of Eghris, not far from Mascara.[568] The assembly included many notables, and Abd al-Kader, a young man of twenty four-five, was seated under an enormous elm tree overlooking the gorge in which the assembly was being held.[569] His old father, Muhi al-Din (1757—1833), rose and walked to the elm tree. In a loud voice he pledged allegiance *(ta'ah)* and submission to his son and gave him the title *Nasir al-Din* (Supporter of the Religion).[570] Next to pledge allegiance to Abd al-Kader was his paternal uncle, 'Ali Abu Talib, followed by Abd al-Kader's brothers and other relatives. Then came the men of religion and the notables, in the order of their rank. When this had been done Abd al-Kader was proclaimed *Amir al-Mu'minin* (Commander of the Believers).[571] Abd al-Kader was now the elected Emir of three powerful tribes of the western province of Oran the Hashim, Gharabah, and Beni Amar.[572] Thus began a career to last sixteen years, during which Abd al-Kader would be, with Hadj Ahmed, the principal leader of the resistance to the French occupation of Algeria.[573]

> Who was Abd al-Qadir, this unknown youth who suddenly was catapulted into prominence? Why was he chosen for the dignity of emir over better-known men? To what extent did his personal background prepare him for his new position? [Asks Danziger.][574]

Abd al-Kader was born in 1808 and, until 1822, lived in the precincts of the family *zawya.* His education was typical, combining excellent religious scholarship with good knowledge of the local tribes.[575] At the age of five he could read and write; at twelve he was proficient in the Qur'an, the Hadeeth (traditional sayings of the Prophet Mohammed). Two years later he attained the highly-prized distinction of

---

[567] M. Morsy: *North Africa; 800-1900;* Longman; London; 1984; p. 138.

[568] The account of this assembly is based on Muhammad b. Abd al-Qadir, *Tuhfat al-Za'ir fi Tarikh al-Jaza'ir wa-al-Amir Abd al-Qadir,* Beirut, 2nd ed, 1964, pp. 155-6 (in subsequent references: *Tuhfah).*

[569] R. Danziger: *Abd Al-Qadir and the Algerians*; Holmes and Meier Publishers; New York; London; 1977, p. 51.

[570] Ibid.

[571] Ibid.

[572] Ibid.

[573] General Boyer, the French commander of Oran, learned of Abd al-Qadir's assumption of leadership less than a week later. General Boyer to Minister of War, Oran, 1 December 1832, AHG: H-18.

[574] The date 26 September 1807 is given in *Tuhfa,* p. 932, and in a biography of Abd al-Qadir written in Syria in the 1890's and authorized by Hashim, a son of Abd al-Qadir: Marie d'Aire, *Abd el-Kader quelques documents nouveaux, lus et approuvés par l'officier en mission aupres de l'émir,* p. 242. Most French historians, apparently relying on Leon Roches, *Trente-deux ans a travers l'Islam (1832-1864),* vol. 1, p. 140, wrote that Abd al-Qadir had been born in 1808; it seems that the date given by Abd al-Qadir's own sons is more reliable, especially since the rendering from the Islamic to the Christian date in Roches is erroneous. For a severe criticism of Roches' book as a historical source, see Marcel Emerit, "La Légende de Leon Roches," *Revue Africaine,* vol. 91(1947), pp. 81-105.

[575] M. Morsy: *North Africa*; op cit; p. 138.

being a *Hafiz*, or one who knows the entire Qur'an by heart.[576] By the time he was seventeenth he was noted for his remarkable strength and agility.

> The perfect symmetry and compactness of his figure his height being about five feet six inches; his bony make, his broad, deep chest, all bestowed him with a frame formed for untiring activity, and capable of enduring the utmost fatigue.[577]

No-one could match him in horsemanship, a graceful rider, his superiority in all feats of horsemanship requiring 'the keenest eye, the steadiest hand, and the greatest efforts of muscular power.'[578]

> Touching his horse's shoulder with his breast, he would place one hand on its back, and vault over to the other side; or, putting the animal to its full speed, he would disengage his feet from the stirrups, stand up in the saddle, and fire at a mark with the utmost precision. Under his light and skilful touch, his well-trained Arab would kneel down, or walk for yards on his hind legs, its fore ones pawing the air, or spring and jump like a gazelle.[579]

In 1827, Abd al-Kader performed the Pilgrimage to Makkah with his father and stayed two years in the East. In the course of his education, he acquired a great love of books and learning, and this was to remain a dominant feature of his personality.[580]

The French had advanced into western Algeria, taking Mers El-Kebir in 1830, and entered the Kasbah of Oran in 1831.[581] As in other parts of Algeria, French rule was cruel and sanguinary. General Boyer, known as Pedro the Cruel after the infamous Spanish king of old Castile, ruled the neighbourhood by terror.[582] His campaigns of mass arrests and killings, besides other depredations only alienated the Algerian population. Resistance soon began to grow, and was initially led by Abd al-Kader's own father. Thus, on 17 April 1832, 400 horsemen and fifty foot soldiers from both Gharabah factions, led by Muhi al-Din, made a surprise attack on a detachment of 100 French soldiers on patrol near Oran.[583] The Algerians killed some but suffered heavier casualties.[584] Although it became obvious right then that the French had the numbers, and above all the superior military power to inflict considerable loss on the Algerians should the latter challenge them, this incident was the first salvo of resistance to the French in the interior of Oran province.[585] It established a strong link between the fight against France and

---

[576] C.H. Churchill: *The Life of Abd Al Kader*, op cit, p. 2.
[577] Ibid.
[578] Ibid, pp. 2-3.
[579] Ibid.
[580] M. Morsy: *North Africa*; op cit; p. 138.
[581] See R. Ageron: *Histoire de l'Algerie*; op cit. p. 13. C. A. Julien: *Histoire de l'Algerie*; p. 104.
[582] C.R. Ageron: *Modern Algeria*, op cit, p. 12.
[583] R. Danziger: *Abd Al-Qadir and the Algerians*; op cit, p. 61.
[584] General Boyer to Minister of War, Oran, 21 April 1832, no. 2958, AHG: H-12.
[585] R. Danziger: *Abd Al-Qadir and the Algerians*; op cit, p. 61.

unity amongst local tribes, the latter brought together through the concept of Jihad, that same concept that had at all times and in all places united the otherwise divided, weak, and most often warring Muslim communities or tribes.[586] A few days later, at a large assembly held on 23 and 24 April 1832, with the participation of many tribes, convened at a location between Mascara and Oran, Muhi al-Din called on the participants to attack the French to fulfil the duty of jihad. The call was enthusiastically endorsed.[587]

On 1 May 1832 Muhi al-Din had 10,000 men under his command, ready for an attack on Oran.[588] According to the rules of Islamic warfare, he had to invite the enemy to join Islam before attacking them.[589] He therefore sent a message to General Boyer, commander of the French forces in Oran, in which he offered him the choice of becoming a Muslim together with his men, and surrendering the city peacefully, or leading his forces out of the town to fight the Muslims.[590] Boyer's reply came from the mouths of the French garrison's guns. From the 3rd to the 8th of May 1832 the Algerians attacked Oran daily.[591] Due to Muhi al-Din's advanced age and physical weakness, it was Abd al-Kader who led the attacks. It was then that he demonstrated impressive courage in the face of enemy artillery fire and considerable skill in fighting.[592] These fighting qualities on top of his wisdom and learning considerably enhanced his reputation, legitimising him as the successor of Muhi al-Din.[593] That time would soon arrive, but until then, the father continued to lead the attacks on Oran. After a while, though, despite his large troops and the heavy loss of fighters' lives, the Algerians failed in front of Oran.[594] Still more attacks were mounted on the city on 31 August, 19 September, 23 October, and 10 November 1832.[595] These were no more successful than the previous ones, but they let everyone appreciate Abd al-Kader's courage and military abilities.[596] And so, on 22 November 1832, as already described, at the age of twenty-four, he was acclaimed by some of the tribes in the region of Mascara as 'sultan of the Arabs'.[597] Devout and courageous, the young leader declared his first task to be the *jihad* or holy war upon the infidel.[598]

General Boyer received the news of Abd al-Kader's accession to power around the 26th of November 1832. His first reaction was one of disdain, stating that even the

---

[586] Ibid.
[587] General Boyer to Minister of War, Oran, 25 April 1832, no. 2984, AHG: H-13.
[588] General Boyer to Minister of War, Oran, 2 May 1832, no. 4425, AHG: H-13.
[589] E. Tyan, "Djihad," *EI* (2), vol. 2 (1965), p. 539.
[590] Copy of the message enclosed with: General Boyer to Minister of War, Oran, 2 May 1832, no. 4425, AHG: H-13.
[591] For the details of these skirmishes, see General Boyer's reports to the Minister of War, 3-18 May 1832, AHG: H-13.
[592] *Tuhfah*, p. 151.
[593] R. Danziger: *Abd Al-Qadir and the Algerians*; op cit, p. 62.
[594] General Boyer to Minister of War, Oran, 16 May 1832, no. 3359, and 18 May 1832, no. 3363, AHG: 11-13.
[595] Details in General Boyer's reports to the Minister of War, dated 3 September, 22 September, and 25 October 1832, AHG: H-17, and 10 November 1832, AHG:H-18.
[596] *Tuhfah*, pp. 147, 151-3; Bellemare, p. 32.
[597] C.R. Ageron: *Modern Algeria*, op cit, p. 12.
[598] Ibid.

sultan of Morocco had had great difficulty in imposing his authority over his subjects and that therefore the "usurper," Abd al-Kader, had no chance at all of asserting his rule in the province.[599] Boyer knew that Abd al-Kader intended to unite the tribes of the province against the French and to impose law and order, but he failed to understand the religious aspects of his accession, assuming that his title was that of *bey,* in continuation of Ottoman tradition.[600]

Upon his assumption of power, Abd al-Kader decided to discontinue his father's war tactics of mounting frontal attacks on French-controlled Oran. These were very costly and were completely ineffective as the French had much superior fire-power, artillery in particular, to repulse any assault by Algerians however strong their numbers. His other priority was to extend his rule over those Muslims who had not yet submitted to his authority.[601] He achieved this within a few days after his election. On 25 November 1832 he entered Mascara triumphantly and established his seat of government in the beylical palace.[602] The taking of Mascara changed Abd al-Kader's position. Before that, he was merely a chief of three semi-nomadic tribes, with no seat of power of any sort. Now, three days after his election, he was in possession of a centrally located town, whose history went back to the 10th century, which for almost a century had been the capital of Oran province, and which commanded the plain of Eghris, one of the most fertile regions of Algeria.[603]

In this position, Abd al Kader could put into effect his tactical military genius. One night with a hundred picked horsemen, he laid an ambush a short distance from Oran, at a spot through which the French were accustomed to send their relief of cavalry to the outposts.[604] When a squadron of Chasseurs made their appearance, Abd al Kader led on the charge, routed them, slaying several, and taking thirty prisoners.[605] On the occasion of this fight, Abd al Kader once more proved his horsemanship and fighting capacities as he was able to face and disarm a Chasseur thrusting at him with his lance, which Abd al Kader held tight under his left arm, before dealing him a deadly blow with his sword.[606]

On the 3rd of December, 1833, Abd-al-Kader and General Desmichels, who both led their troops in person, fought a hard-contested fight in the plain of Tlelat, to which the Emir had formally invited the French.[607] But this battle remained without result. The field-artillery of the French caused heavy loss amongst

---

[599] R. Danziger: *Abd Al-Qadir and the Algerians;* op cit, p. 73.
[600] General Boyer to Minister of War, Oran, 1 December 1832, monthly report, AHG: H-18.
[601] R. Danziger: *Abd Al-Qadir and the Algerians;* op cit, p. 73.
[602] Ibid.
[603] For a succinct description of Mascara, see G. Yver, "Mascara," *EI,* vol. 3 (1936), pp. 314-5 (incl bibliography).
[604] C.H. Churchill: *The Life of Abd Al Kader,* op cit, p. 34.
[605] Ibid.
[606] Ibid.
[607] M. Wagner: *The Tricolor on the Atlas,* op cit, p. 264.

Algerian horsemen; but the French columns had after all to retreat for lack of provisions, and were followed and harassed by the restless Algerian cavalry to the walls of Oran.[608]

Realising the importance of Abd al Kader, General Desmichels, the commander of the French forces in Oran, endeavoured to turn him into his protégé as the champion of the liberation of the country from 'the hated Turks.'[609] On 26 February 1834, General Desmichels concluded with him an agreement which recognised his authority over the territory in the district of Oran outside the towns controlled by the French, namely Oran, Arzew, and Mostaganem.[610] Once again there were two treaties — one public, in French and Arabic, and the other secret, in Arabic only, which Desmichels did not communicate to Paris.[611] By means of this subterfuge, the general was able to announce to the central government the submission of the province of Oran and the freedom of trade, even though he had in fact signed an agreement by which he recognised the sovereignty of Abd al-Kader as *Amir al-Mu'minin* (Commander of the Faithful), the traditional title of the Caliph, and granted him monopoly on trade at the port of Arzew, not to speak of a commitment to provide the Emir with aid.[612] Indeed, Desmichels went so far as to provide him with arms, thanks to which Abd al-Kader defeated the surviving forces of the Bey of Oran on 12 July 1834.[613]

2. Battle of Macta (June 1835) and Aftermaths

Demischels' tactics did not work in the end, and the Emir's power in just a year increased so much as to threaten French interests. General Trezel, who succeeded Demischels, adopted a policy aiming at weakening the Emir by trying to detach the more important chiefs from him.[614] General Trezel in earnest began to hold negotiations with the most influential Sheikhs of the Duairs and Zmelas, who lived near Oran, combining offers with threats until he succeeded in persuading them to abandon the Emir.[615] Abd-al-Kader, informed of those proceedings, sent one of his Aghas with some troops towards Oran, in order to force the Duairs and Zmelas, both semi-nomadic tribes, to strike their tents, and to carry them away into the interior, where they could not come into contact with the French whether for good or evil.[616] The tribal leaders decided instead to throw their lot with the French and hastily informed Trezel, also asking for his protection against

---

[608] Ibid, p. 265.
[609] C.R. Ageron: *Modern Algeria;* op cit, p. 12.
[610] J.M. Abun-Nasr: *A History of the Maghrib*, Cambridge University Press, 1971, p. 242.
[611] C.R. Ageron: *Modern Algeria*, op cit, p. 12.
[612] Ibid.
[613] Ibid.
[614] M. Wagner: *The Tricolor on the Atlas*, op cit, p. 271.
[615] Ibid, p. 272.
[616] Ibid.

'the persecution of Abd-al-Kader.' Trezel, a man of energy, immediately gathered all his troops, and at their head marched on the 16th of June, 1835, from Oran; proceeding about twenty miles to the south in order to cover the territory of the tribes.[617] As the French approached, the Agha of the Emir retreated, and General Trezel moved forward to the plain of Tlelat, where he concluded a formal treaty with the Duairs and Zmelas, according to which these tribes entered the service of France.[618] Trezel now wrote a letter to Abd al Kader warning him not to interfere with the tribes that had recognised French sovereignty. Abd al-Kader answered that his religion 'forbade him to leave Muslims under the sway of infidels, and that he was determined to pursue the rebel tribes up to the walls of Oran.'[619] At the same time he recalled his representative from Oran, in return for the French Consul in Mascara, which amounted to a declaration of war.[620] Taking the initiative, Trezel at the head of a powerful army decided to finish with the Emir, and advanced to the banks of the Sig. Abd al Kader, who was encamped there with his troops, knew of the French progress and called for Jihad, all the faithful to join the war against the French.[621]

The first engagement took place in the wood of Muley-Ismael, half way between Oran and Mascara, the biggest military encounter in the west. The battle was hotly contested, the two sides fighting even from bush to bush.[622] Once more French artillery took the upper hand, forcing the Algerians out of the wooded area; but the French suffered severe loss, including the death of Colonel Oudinot, who commanded the cavalry.[623] The chief of Abd-al-Kader's cavalry, his Khalifa, was likewise slain.[624]

The French army halted for a short time on the banks of the River Sig; but General Trezel who had thought the campaign would be over swiftly, now found himself short of provisions, and having to transport the wounded.[625] He took the direction of Arzew towards the coast. But when his weary troops reached the banks of the streamlet Macta, they were suddenly attacked by the whole force of Abd-al-Kader.[626] The French columns were thrown into confusion by assaults coming from all directions at once, and several companies which were meant to occupy the hills flanking the way were pushed back. Just then panic seized the Foreign Legion, and men of one of its battalions began shouting 'Sauve qui peut!' (Run for your Life!), thus causing greater confusion in French ranks.[627] This was

---

[617] Ibid.
[618] Ibid.
[619] Ibid.
[620] Ibid.
[621] Ibid.
[622] Ibid.
[623] Ibid.
[624] Ibid; pp. 272-3.
[625] Ibid, p. 273.
[626] Ibid.
[627] Ibid.

the moment seized by Abd al Kader's men to cause further chaos and loss in French ranks. One battalion fought bravely, but it was composed of Poles, Germans, Dutch, and Spaniards, and commanded by French officers whose orders they did not always understand.[628] In the midst of great confusion, the wagons in which the wounded were transported became stuck in the swamps of the Macta. The men in charge of them, seized by panic, fled, thus abandoning their wretched comrades to the daggers of Algerian horsemen.[629] Order and discipline collapsed amongst the French; no order was obeyed; men strayed in every direction; the yelling of the Algerians adding to the panic.[630] Whole companies and battalions fled towards Arzew. Commander Saint Fargeau, who had been present at the greatest battles of the Empire, at Liitzen, Dresden, and Leipzig:

> In spite of powder, smoke, and roaring of cannon, those great battles were by far less dreadful than the scenes on the Makta.[631]

In their extremity, some of the men began to sing the Marseillaise; others prayed; a few yelled shouts of courage; Algerian warriors cut through the rabble.[632] The mounted rifles (Chasseurs d'Afrique) made a decisive stand and cut down the Algerian assault.[633] It still ended in a French disaster. Five hundred men and officers had been slain according to the most conservative estimates (the real figure being many times higher). The demoralising impact was beyond calculation.[634] The Algerians now realised the French were not invincible even in pitched battles. Even more, the Emir's prestige had sharply risen; and all the tribes, including those that had earlier doubts as to his authority and capacity of leadership, now turned to him.[635] General Trezel, despite his personal bravery and great capacity for command, was still removed from command. But public indignation in France turned against the Governor of Algiers, 'whose weakness and indulgence' had given such power to Abd-al-Kader, and had caused the defeat on the Macta.[636]

Following this defeat, and precisely one year before he turned his attention to the east and Constantine, Marshal Clauzel on 6 December 1835 attacked Mascara, the Emir's capital. Abd al-Kader had evacuated it the day before, and so Clauzel withdrew from the city two days later after setting it on fire lest the Emir decided to re-occupy it.[637] Systematic burning of towns and cities by the French would become the norm.

---

[628] Ibid.
[629] Ibid.
[630] Ibid.
[631] Ibid. p. 274.
[632] Ibid.
[633] Ibid.
[634] Ibid.
[635] Ibid.
[636] Ibid.
[637] J.M. Abun-Nasr: *A History of the Maghrib*, op cit, p. 242.

On 13 January 1836, Clauzel led a similar expedition to Tlemcen, on the pretext that the *kulughlis* in it sought French help against the Arabs.[638] (In truth, following the French arrival) the Kuluglis sent Abd al-Kader word privately that they only awaited the departure of the French to give him up the citadel.[639] It was the intention of Clauzel to occupy the town, as he was anxious to establish a direct communication between Tlemcen and the seacoast.[640] The mouth of the River Tafna was the nearest available point for this purpose, but the ground in the middle was mountainous. As soon as he set out to do this, he found himself in presence of Abd al Kader with his entire force.[641] This time the two great armies hurled one against the other with great force. For ten successive days battle raged. The Algerians were obstinately tenacious, and the French equally the same. In Algerian tactics, hills, ravines, rocks, and rivers were seized and defended, according to the necessities of the moment.[642] Despite superior fire power, courage and discipline soon deserted the French. Clauzel was defeated and driven back to Tlemcen with considerable loss. After placing a garrison in the citadel under the command of Captain Cavaignac, he returned with his column to Oran, harassed to its very gates by Abd al Kader.[643]

That same year, on another front where the Emir was not involved, General d'Arlanges, seeking to suppress rebellious tribes, went by sea to the mouth of the Tafna, where he established a camp. On a reconnaissance mission in the direction of Tlemcen, his column was suddenly attacked and met with severe loss.[644] The column, nearly exterminated, desperately sought and awaited relief from Oran.[645] Now, it would seem, the Algerians no longer feared French canon.

> The Kabyles of the Tafna [says Wagner] fought as desperately as the tribes near Bujia; they often advanced up to the mouth of the cannon, and the yatagan constantly crossed the sabre.[646]

Soon the French had their revenge. At the battle of the Sikkak, fought on 6 July 1836, they crushed the regular army of Abd al Kader.[647] The French commanding officer was Bugeaud, in not too long to rise to great prominence. Months after this success, there took place one of the greatest reversals in French colonial history: the Constantine debacle. The situation had also deteriorated in the Mitidja, the long, narrow fertile plain in the vicinity of Algiers. The security of the city, which stands on a promontory of low hills between the western half of this plain and the

---

[638] Ibid.
[639] Ibid.
[640] C.H. Churchill: *The Life of Abd Al Kader*, op cit, p. 96.
[641] Ibid.
[642] Ibid.
[643] Ibid.
[644] M. Wagner: *The Tricolor on the Atlas*, op cit, p. 280.
[645] Ibid.
[646] Ibid.
[647] C.R. Ageron: *Modern Algeria*, op cit, p. 13.

sea was under threat. French settlements, which depended on possession of the Mitidja, were now subject to raids by the Hadjuts, whom Clauzel had boasted he would wipe out within two months of his arrival.[648] This situation brought both Emir and the French to a settlement, both sides hoping to win time for the next round.

3. The Treaty of the Tafna and its Impact

Bugeaud volunteered to approach Abd al Kader and to attempt to negotiate a treaty.[649] On the 15th of May 1837, led by himself, the army, carrying supplies for forty days, marched to Tlemcen, delivered the powder needed by the blockaded garrison, and proceeded north towards the River Tafna.[650] Previously diplomatic transactions had been initiated by Marshal Clauzel, but had not led to any result; Bugeaud resumed negotiations by using the services of the Jew, Ben-Durand, the close man of the Emir, who knew how to ingratiate himself with the French generals.[651] But as all the messages to and fro did not progress, Bugeaud selected another negotiator in the person of Sidi-Hamadi-ben-Seal.[652] The disagreements were over the supremacy of the province of Titteri (northern central Algeria with its capital Medea), claimed by Abd-al-Kader, whilst the French Government had marked the River Cheliff as his boundary eastwards. General Bugeaud, used to act independently, conceded this to the Emir.[653] The Minister of War had insisted that Abd al Kader should pay a yearly tribute to the French; but the Emir refused, and again, Bugeaud yielded to the Emir.[654] The French General was eager to settle matters as fast as possible.[655] At last, on the 30th of May, a treaty was signed by the two parties, and a final interview arranged for the next day between the General and the Emir. The main points in the treaty were the following:

Emir Abd al Kader acknowledges the sovereignty of France in Africa. France retains the possession of Oran, Arzew, Masagran, Mostagenem, and Algiers; of the Sahel, and the plain of Mitija from the right bank of the Chiffa to the Wad-el-Kadderah, and the territory beyond that river; besides the cities of Blida and Koleah.[656]

---

[648] Ibid.
[649] W. Blunt: *Desert Hawk*; op cit, p. 95.
[650] M. Wagner: *The Tricolor on the Atlas*, op cit, p. 290.
[651] Ibid.
[652] Ibid.
[653] Ibid.
[654] Ibid.
[655] Ibid.
[656] Ibid. p. 291.

The Emir has the administration of the provinces of Oran and Titteri, and of the parts of Algeria not included in the above-mentioned boundaries; but he is not allowed to enter any other part of the Regency.[657]

The Emir provides the French army thirty thousand bags of wheat, as many bags of barley, and one thousand cattle heads; but the city and citadel of Tlemcen, together with its cannon, will be delivered to him; and he is allowed to buy arms, powder, and brimstone, in France.[658]

A secret article stipulated thirty thousand pieces of local Algerian currency to General Bugeaud. This treaty was sent to France for ratification, of course without the last mentioned secret article.[659]

There was also a discrepancy between the Arabic and French text of the treaty; the Arabic granting the Emir more than the French; but once the French text was ratified, the French government insisted that no publicity should be given to the Arabic text, which was declared lost until 1951, although in fact several copies existed.[660]

Such was the Treaty of the Tafna, 30 May 1837, which recognised Abd al-Kader as the sovereign of two-thirds of Algeria, and claimed to establish peaceful coexistence between 'this immense Arab state and the two little corners which Bugeaud had kept for France.'[661] In the secret text, Bugeaud had also undertaken to deliver 3,000 rifles to Abd al-Kader, to exile the chiefs of the Turkish *makhzan* tribes, and to confine the Douair tribe to a restricted territory.[662] In return, 180,000 gold francs were to be paid to Bugeaud, of which he intended 100,000 to meet the cost of road-building in his parliamentary constituency in the Dordogne.[663]

The peace of Tafna enabled the Emir to consolidate his rule in the greater part of the districts of Oran and Titteri and to establish his government in them.[664] The Emir's system of government took on side the tribal structure of society. He himself held supreme authority over a federal structure of tribes. His *khalifas* (deputies) governed the major districts under his control, but the immediate control of the tribes was left to their leaders who were granted the title of *agha*.[665] The emir's revenue derived primarily from the taxes and his monopoly on trade in the territories he controlled.[666] After Clauzel's attack and capture of Mascara the emir lost a permanent political base, but he kept an economic capital at Tagdempt, an emporium of trade between the hinterland and the south, where

---

[657] Ibid.
[658] Ibid.
[659] Ibid.
[660] C.R. Ageron: *Modern Algeria*; op cit; p. 15.
[661] Ibid.
[662] Ibid.
[663] Ibid.
[664] J.M. Abun-Nasr: *A History of the Maghrib*, op cit, p. 244.
[665] Ibid.
[666] Ibid.

he struck his coins and kept his stores of provisions and ammunition.[667] His central government, just as his army, were both mobile. His camp became his capital which he moved about according to political and military necessities. His standing army was small, never exceeding 10,000 men, but it was reinforced by tribal auxiliaries usually drawn from regions where he was engaged in battle.[668] Both auxiliaries and regulars were shock troops whose characters and tactics were better suited for surprise attacks than for sustained fighting, where superior French firepower always gained a greater advantage.[669]

Now, Abd al Kader was regrouping his partisans, building his state on strong lines, preparing for the next round, which he was convinced would eventually come.[670] Step by step, through personal prestige and skilful diplomacy, including the help provided by the French in the way of weapons, which gave him a greater advantage over potential rivals, Abd al-Kader was able to bring the people under his banner as far out as the borders of Constantine.[671] The organisation he set up had resistance to the French as its objective and was organised on a traditional tribal and religious model.[672] He set up citadels in tribal territory to provide protection to civilians and to serve as stores both for food and for military equipment.[673] The places of concentration were judiciously chosen; even where he built his granary-citadels (Tafraut, Sa'ida, Taza, Bughar, Tagdemt) have historical tradition behind them.[674]

At Tagdemt (just south of Tiaret, the famous Berber fortress of the Middle Ages), Abd al-Kader set up his other, stationary, capital. It was a rocky stronghold overlooking a river, the Wadi Mina.[675] When in the late 7th century the Muslims entered Algeria, and in the centuries after, the town rose to become a seat of government; it had a college, and attracted doctors and poets.[676] The wars between various local rulers towards the close of the 10th century doomed it to final destruction and oblivion.[677] The town which Abd al Kader raised from its ruins, nine centuries later, was sixty miles to the south-east of Oran. Judging from the remains of its walls, it must have been ten miles in circumference.[678] Its old Roman vaults were soon turned into stores for ammunition, sulphur, saltpetre, brass, lead, and iron; and for all the machines, implements, and utensils. A musket manufactory turned out eight muskets a day, the work of French mechanics

---

[667] Ibid.
[668] Ibid.
[669] Ibid.
[670] M. Morsy: *North Africa*; op cit; p. 139.
[671] Ibid; p. 140.
[672] Ibid.
[673] Ibid.
[674] Ibid.
[675] Ibid.
[676] C.H. Churchill: *The Life of Abd Al Kader*, op cit, p. 124.
[677] Ibid.
[678] Ibid.

procured from Paris at good salaries.[679] A mint struck off silver and copper coins, ranging in value from five shillings to two-pence, and bearing on one side the inscription, "It is the will of God; I have appointed him my agent;" on the other, "Struck at Tagdemt, by the Sultan Abd al Kader."[680] These coins carried greater political than economic symbol, i.e asserting the independence of the Muslim Algerian state. Had Abd al Kader been allowed time to complete his programme, it was his aim to have made Tagdemt not merely a place of strength, but a seat of learning; to have established a library and founded a college. Writing later after his defeat by the French, he said with great sorrow:

> But, [to use his own expression,] God did not so will it. The books which I had brought from all parts of the east for this institution, were taken when the French king's son seized my Smala (mobile tent camp); and to my other misfortunes was added that of being able to mark the traces of the French column, on their return to Medea, by the torn and scattered leaves of the books which it had cost me so much time and pains to collect.[681]

Of course the French were aware of the Emir's efforts, and they themselves were preparing for the next round with him.

4. Fighting Resumes (1839-1840)

The Peace Treaty of the Tafna was simply not viable. The French ceased to recognise the treaty from the day when, having at last captured Constantine, they decided not to keep peace with the Emir. Nevertheless, the truce held for another two years.[682] Uncertain political conditions in France, and the necessity to assemble a strong force to deal with the Emir were possible reasons for such a delay. Now, in 1839, they were at last ready to face him, by claiming rights in the interior by the force of arms.[683]

Marshall Valee despatched in the month of February, 1839, Commandant de Salles to Abd al Kader's head-quarters, who was then at Miliana, to give his approval on some disputed territory in exchange for the continuation of the peace treaty.[684] Although a continuation of the peace was of vital importance to the Emir, in order to enable him to complete his work of organisation, yet to yield the disputed territory was to him a moral and political impossibility.[685] Politically

---

[679] Ibid, p. 125.
[680] C.H. Churchill: *The Life of Abd Al Kader*, op cit, p. 125.
[681] Ibid, p.127.
[682] C.R. Ageron: *Modern Algeria*, op cit, p. 15.
[683] C.H. Churchill: *The Life of Abd Al Kader*, op cit, p. 163.
[684] Ibid; p. 168.
[685] Ibid.

and strategically it was impossible for him, because the territory in question, once ceded to the French, would give them free means of communication between the provinces of Algiers and Constantine, and would thereby make their possessions more compact, and increase their aggressive power.[686] Morally it was so also, because, not only was it repugnant to his own sense of honour to yield, it would also harm his status and influence amongst Algerians.[687] He had already repeatedly calmed many anxious voices by the assurance that France would never dare to go beyond the limits granted to her in the plain of Algiers, and it was on the strength of this assurance that the military and religious chiefs had consented to the peace. Without their consent, he could not modify the treaty.[688]

In the meantime, the French had acquired more reinforcements. Valee had asked for and obtained more troops, and by the end of the Summer of 1839, he had 50,000 men besides local troops.[689] Valee now thought of imposing French dictate by a show of military force, the army marching through disputed territory. He decided that the march was to start from Mila, north-west of Constantine, penetrate the pass of the "Iron Gates," which cut through the mounts of the Bibans, two hundred kilometres west of Constantine, 130 east of Algiers, and eighty from the sea.[690] And so, late in October 1839, the French army set off under the command of the Duke of Orleans and marched through that said territory.[691] Valee himself joined the troops at some point, and in the process meeting very little resistance from the Algerians, who had little knowledge of both march and breach of the treaty. Early November 1839, the column of thousands of men entered Algiers to the acclamations of the European population as great victors, and on the 4th of November the event was joyfully celebrated.[692] With this action, the French had broken the treaty they had ratified.

The tribal chiefs were summoned by Abd al-Kader on what measure to take. The decision to declare war was taken and officially announced on 20 November 1839.[693]

The first few months of the war witnessed severe French setbacks. It began on 20 November 1839 with a strong assault by large contingents on the French settlements and establishments in the Mitidja Plain near Algiers.[694] Within a few days most of the farms and installations set up by the *colons* in Algiers province were destroyed, and all the Europeans in the area were forced to flee to Algiers

---

[686] Ibid.

[687] Ibid; p. 169.

[688] Ibid.

[689] G. Fleury: *Comment l'Algerie*; op cit; p. 224.

[690] Ibid; p. 225.

[691] Ibid.

[692] Ibid; p. 226.

[693] M. Morsy: *North Africa*; op cit; p. 141.

[694] R. Danziger: *Abd Al-Qadir and the Algerians*; op cit, p. 224.

with great loss of life among settlers and soldiers alike.[695] At the same time, local forces devastated European establishments in the provinces of Oran and Titteri and disrupted communications between the isolated French army camps in the countryside, most of which had to be abandoned.[696] Even the coastal towns occupied by the French came under attack, and for the first time, an action on the sea, allowed on 26 January 1840 a small Algerian gunboat stationed in Cherchel (west of Algiers) to capture a French merchant ship and seize its contents.[697]

Abd al-Kader's carefully prepared and well-executed offensive completely took the French by surprise and brought the Emir for a few months closer than ever to the fulfilment of his principal objective: squeezing the French out.[698] With the important exception of those outposts in Constantine province, the French were confined to a few coastal towns.[699] Abd al-Kader's success was in large measure due to his maintaining the lifeline of arms supplies from Gibraltar through Morocco, with the secret good will of Morocco's sultan, who still wanted the French out of Algeria.[700] By March 1840 Abd al-Kader, supported by virtually all the tribes of the interior of western and central Algeria, had reached the apogee of his power.[701]

Nonetheless, Abd al-Kader's basic military and economic weakness vis-à-vis the French soon became obvious. France by 1840 was with Britain the world leading power with vast economic resources, a good industrial foundation, and a powerful navy, all in all capable of sustaining any conflict. Her power to shift men and equipment from one area to another, and to provide her army with great, even seemingly limitless, supplies was another of her great advantages. While the number of Algerian troops fighting under the Emir had by early 1840 reached the upper limit of approximately 80,000 (most of whom were irregulars), the French had a comparatively unlimited reservoir of highly trained and well-equipped soldiers at their disposal.[702] By March 1840 reinforcements from France had increased the forces in Algeria from less than 40,000 to over 58,000, a figure which subsequently was to increase to upwards of 100,000-despite heavy casualties.[703] Of course France had a much larger population to draw from, Abd al Kader did not; moreover, apart from his neighbouring western parts, and some central areas, logistically he could not call on the people of the eastern side, just as Hadj Ahmed could not on those of the west, for French possessions and territorial and military control stood as an obstructing block in the middle.

---

[695] Ibid.
[696] Ibid.
[697] Ibid.
[698] Ibid.
[699] Ibid.
[700] Ibid.
[701] Ibid.
[702] Ibid.
[703] Ibid.

Another weakness of Abd al-Kader's army was its inability to fight a pitched battle against the French, whose artillery was capable of annihilating their opponent's forces. After considerable losses of regular soldiers in frontal clashes around Blida, especially in the battle on 31 December 1840, Abd al-Kader ordered his khalifas to avoid such clashes.[704] Instead, when facing large French concentrations, they were instructed to retreat, harass the flanks, cut communication lines, and inflict as many casualties as possible.[705]

The war also undermined the economic life of the Emir's state. The French army had the main-land, i.e France, for a constant supply of all the wares and provisions, as well as the funds it required; the Emir had only his state which was now part of the front-line, always exposed to devastation and destruction of its resources, a method the French soon put to full and lethal effects. The profitable trade with the French-occupied towns and with pro-French indigenous tribes also ceased, while the internal trade in Abd al-Kader's realm was reduced from large-scale, long-distance commerce to local tribal markets.[706] This greatly reduced economic activity and caused a sharp drop in his revenues just when he needed them most.[707]

Governor General, Valée, began the counterattack with the occupation of the port of Cherchel on 15 March 1840. The town had been evacuated by Abd al-Kader on the eve of the attack, and Valee left a garrison in it.[708] Valée then marched east, on the town of Medea, and despite heavy loss of troops, still inflicted a defeat on Abd al-Kader's regulars, and occupied the town on 17 May.[709] On 9 June, Valée's forces occupied Miliana and left there a garrison. Abd al-Kader had forced the town's residents to abandon it.[710]

Despite these setbacks, the Emir was able to record some successes which brought in the end a stalemate. Military operations by Valée were now confined largely to the re-supply of his garrisons stationed in the occupied towns and to minor engagements with the Emir's forces.[711] The situation was far from pleasing the French government, and so, the victor of Constantine, Valee, was recalled on 29 December 1840, and was replaced by an old hand in Algeria: General Bugeaud, victor of the Battle of the Sikkak and the man who had signed the Tafna Treaty.[712]

*****

---

[704] Ibid, p. 225.
[705] Ibid.
[706] Ibid.
[707] Ibid.
[708] Ibid.
[709] Ibid.
[710] Ibid.
[711] Ibid.
[712] Ibid.

Whilst the Emir fought primarily in the west, although somehow leaderless, Eastern and Central Algeria remained quite active. Colonel Saint Arnaud in his letters from Jijel constantly cites the state of warfare involving the local tribes and his forces. In one letter from the forward French positions, dated 18 May, 1839, he wrote:

> Ah dear brother, what a job as ours. From the time I arrived here, what a situation, what a burst of emotions and sorrows. Every day, brother, without exception, for five and six hours we are involved in 'a fight of titans.' We are attacked from all directions, and always are obliged to charge with bayonets. We have won positions covered by Kabyles who fight hand to hand, and who even when dying bite you, and still hit at you with their ebbing limbs.
>
> These people are the bravest on earth. They rush towards us to be blasted by our artillery fire only ten paces away. Once, a father fell; his two sons rushed to give him cover; and whilst we were thrusting our bayonets in them, they were still shielding him.[713]

Another letter sent on 12 June 1839:

> We don't spend a single night without a fight. On the 9th, they started the party at 2 in the morning and only finished at seven. There were more than 2,000 of them. Always beaten, always losing so many people, and yet they always find recruits. We, on the other hand, we fall in numbers, we get tired, and diseases are on us.[714]

Further west, in Greater Kabylia, fighting was all the while raging with greater intensity. There we have the accounts of the German officer, Clemens Lamping, who was fighting alongside the French.

> Our friends, the Kabyles, [he writes in September 1840] come down from the neighbouring mountains to pay their respects to us. They greet us from afar with a torrent of friendly epithets, such as 'haluf' (swine), &c., which is quickly followed by a shower of balls. We are no less civil in our turn, allowing them to approach within a short distance, when we treat them to a volley of musketry and a few discharges from the field-pieces.[715]

Then, he describes at good length the French punitive operations against the tribes, in which he was also involved:

> The Commandant marched up into the mountains one night with the whole garrison to chastise the Kabyles for their insolence. We started at midnight without stopping and in deep silence, up hill and down dale until just before daybreak, when the crowing of cocks and the baying of dogs gave us

[713] St Arnaud: Lettres de St Arnaud; 2 vols; Michel Levy; Paris; 1855; vol 1; pp. 215-218.
[714] Ibid; p. 221.
[715] Clemens Lamping: *The French in Algiers. Soldiers of the Foreign Legion; Prisoners of Abd el Kader;* tr. from German and French by Lady Duff Gordon, London; 1855; p. 24.

notice that we were close upon a tribe. We were ordered to halt, and two companies with a few field-pieces were left behind on an eminence.

After a short rest we started again, and the first glimmer of light showed the huts of the tribe straight before us. An old Kabyle was at that moment going out with a pair of oxen to plough; as soon as he saw us he uttered a fearful howl and fled, but a few well-directed shots brought him down. In one moment the grenadiers and voltigeurs, who were in advance, broke through the hedge of prickly pear which generally surrounds a Kabyle village, and the massacre began. Strict orders had been given to kill all the men and only to take the women and children prisoners: for we followed the precept of "an eye for an eye, a tooth for a tooth."[716]

A few men only reeled half awake out of their huts, but most of them still lay fast asleep; not one escaped death. The women and children rushed, howling and screaming, out of their burning huts in time to see their husbands and brothers butchered. One young woman with an infant at her breast started back at the sight of strange men exclaiming "Mohamed! Mohamed!" and ran into her burning hut. Some soldiers sprang forward to save her, but the roof had already fallen in and she and her child perished in the flames.[717]

We then returned with our booty, and it was high time, for other tribes of Kabyles came flocking together from every side, attracted by the noise. We were forced to retreat in such haste that we left the greater part of the cattle behind. The fire of the companies we had stationed in our rear with the field-pieces at last gained us time to breathe. We however had but few killed and wounded.

A few days after, a deputation was sent by the survivors with proposals for the exchange of the women and children against cattle, which was accepted. It is a point of honour with the Kabyles not to leave their women and children in the enemies' hands. They most conscientiously ransomed even the old women whom we would willingly have given them gratis.[718]

He moves onto another scene:

The incessant heat had already dried up all the fountains and springs within the line of the blockhouses, so that we were forced to drive the cattle beyond it to a stream which flows from the mountains and never fails. We advanced as usual en tiralleurs to cover the watering-place, but we had scarcely reached the further side of the stream when we were greeted on all sides by yells and bullets. The Kabyles had hidden themselves in the brushwood close by, and occupied an eminence opposite to us. In order to make use of our strongest weapon, the bayonet, which is much dreaded by the Kabyles, we advanced up the hill with levelled

---

[716] Ibid; p. 26.
[717] Ibid.
[718] Ibid.

bayonets and took it at the first attack. But scarce had we reached the top when we received a heavy fire from all sides, the Kabyles having surrounded us in a semicircle. In a moment we had several killed and wounded and were forced to retreat faster than we had advanced, the Kabyles pressing furiously on our rear. The commanding officer exclaimed: "Sauvez les blesses! Sauvez les blesses!"[719]

A non-commissioned officer close beside me had been shot through the jaw; he had completely lost his senses, and was reeling round and round like a drunken man. I seized him under the arm and dragged him towards the nearest blockhouse into which the company retreated. We were the very last, and the Kabyles yelled wildly close behind us while their bullets whistled in our ears; I was not hit however, and succeeded in bringing my charge safely home, conscious of having done my duty as a soldier and as a man.[720]

In the meantime, further South, Hadj Ahmed was still fighting together with the few faithful who had survived the loss of Constantine. In fact, soon after the fall of the city, the French realising how in him they could have a formidable ally to subdue eastern and southern Algeria, still tried to persuade him to accept French sovereignty in return for the restitution of his former position as the local ruler of the Beylik.[721] He refused, once more. He remained active in the surrounding mountains together with Ben Aissa, who, too, had managed to leave Constantine.[722] Under repeated French assaults, Ben Aissa was left with hardly any troops, without any base, hounded from one place to another; enemies surrounding him from every direction, and had to surrender in 1838.[723] Against French promise to offer him safe conduct, he was soon deported far away from his country to the Island of St Marguerite.[724]

Hadj Ahmed with a small group of faithful followers retired to the southern marches of Algeria where he fought on for another eleven years.[725] He refused any compromise or offer from the French that could have, Temimi remarks, 'sullied the religion and values of his country.'[726] He fought the French and their local allies who, much keener than him to keep their realms and positions, had thrown their lot with the French.[727] He kept the same warrior spirit with courage and resignation, and even with pride.[728] Losing supporters one after the other, he

---

[719] Ibid; p. 27.
[720] Ibid; p. 28.
[721] J.M. Abun-Nasr: *A History of the Maghrib*, op cit, p. 243.
[722] W. Blunt: *Desert Hawk*; op cit, p. 114.
[723] A. Temimi: Le Beylik de Constantine; op cit; p. 288.
[724] X. Yacono: Les Premiers Prisonniers Algeriens de l'Ile de St Marguerite 91841-1843); in *Revue d'Histoire Maghrebine*; No 1; Tunis; 1974; pp. 53-6.
[725] M. Morsy: *North Africa*; op cit; p. 137.
[726] A. Temimi: Le Beylik de Constantine; op cit; p. 205.
[727] Ibid.
[728] Ibid.

constantly appealed to the Ottoman Sultan for support 'to continue the Jihad from the Sahara,' running from one part to another, his enemies on his heels. In one of his letters to the Ottoman Minister of the Navy, he wrote:

> We accepted with resignation this decision of the Almighty (the fall of Constantine), and in order to sustain the Muslim community and lessen its sorrows, we retired with a great number of Muslims who have joined us, leaving behind our friends, dearest and all we had in this life. We had vowed to defend the faith ... Everywhere we are surrounded by foes... Help us fight for the faith... If you want Islam to prevail in this country save it from French hands; give me support; help us now, or those who still support us will abandon us; if you do not give me any support, I have no means with which to fight... It should be clear now that your servant (Hadj Ahmed) would never attach himself to the French... If you grant us your help, you must know that we need 4000 men and 4 canons. If these reach Sfax (Tunisia), they would soon get to us and will help us defend ourselves... Should your support reach me, those who are still fighting by my side would still do.... I have sent you all the letters that the French have sent me asking me to rally myself to them, and make peace with them. But I have refused to accept their offers, and when you will read them you will understand how long I have waited for your help, trusting in Allah and His Prophet.[729]

It was a lost cause to then rely on Ottoman assistance. The condition of the Ottoman Empire was growing even more sorrowful by the year, and had it not been for the Crimean War 1853-1856 and the perversions of international politics, which gave it a lease of life, it would have collapsed right then. Long gone were the days when Ottoman Turkey replied to even much less fervent calls than those of Hadj Ahmed for assistance in the defence of Islam.

---

[729] *Basvekalet Arsivi* (Archives of the Presidency of the Council in Istanbul); in A. Temimi: Le Beylik de Constantine; op cit; pp. 258-62.

Five

TOTAL WAR
(1841-1847)

M. Louis Veuillot said about Bugeaud: 'His house and home was the abode of simple sweet Christian virtues, all powerful over his soul.'[730]

Writing in February 1841 from Kabylia, Clemens Lamping, said:
> We had only taken three prisoners, for in the heat of the skirmish the soldiers cut down every one. Some, indeed, had even cut off the heads of the wounded with their own yataghans. The Commandant Superieur rewarded these heroes with five Franc pieces, and stuck the heads over the city gates, where they remained until the stench became intolerable. Truly I almost begin to think that we have learned more of the barbarous manners of the Kabyles, than they of our humanity and civilisation.[731]

1. War of Annihilation

General (later Marshal) Bugeaud was to put in place a policy of total occupation. He had already in the earlier period leading up to the Tafna Treaty fought against Abd al-Kader, and defeated him at the Sikak.[732] The war, in his view, could only be won by creating a climate of terror by the destruction of villages, the burning of fields, and wholesale slaughter.[733]

This is the claim found in all modern narrative of French colonial history in Algeria, that makes it seem that Bugeaud, alone, was responsible for the policy of war of annihilation of Algerian society. This claim that puts blame solely on him is wrong on the following accounts:
-Firstly his was the practice of all French officers as will be seen below.
-Secondly the same policy of mass extermination of natives was adopted before him and after him. Previous and subsequent chapters will show this.
-Thirdly he, like all officers who carried this policy: Pelissier, Lamoriciere, St Arnaud, Randon, and Mac Mahon (besides Bosquet, Camou, Yusuf, of course, Renaud and virtually everyone else) were all raised to the highest positions of

---

[730] Count H. Ideville: *Memoirs of Marshal Bugeaud from his Private Correspondence and Original Documents*; 2 vols; edited from French by C.M. Yonge; Hurst and Blackett; London, 1884; vol 2; p. 44.
[731] Clemens Lamping: *The French in Algiers. Soldiers of the Foreign Legion; Prisoners of Abd el Kader;* tr. from German and French by Lady Duff Gordon, London; 1855; p. 32.
[732] M. Morsy: *North Africa*; op cit; p. 141.
[733] Ibid.

power subsequently, including ministerial positions. The only one who was never promoted was Montagnac but only because he was killed in combat in September 1845. These promotions, instead of demotions, utterly contradict the generalised claim of such French-Western narrative that these officers' deeds created revulsion in French opinion (with the exception, of course, of the usual one or two who get repelled by such things.)

-Fourthly the war of extermination fitted precisely with overall French policy. The aim was no to end insurgency but to destroy the very foundations of Algerian life, including basic means of survival in order to ease mass eradication of natives and free their lands for European settlement. Saint-Arnaud informs us in his letters 'I shall burn everything.., kill everyone!'[734] And that was precisely what he and his fellow officers and men did, and were rewarded for it.

Thanks to the long government of Soult as Prime Minister and Guizot as Minister of Foreign Affairs, Bugeaud remained Governor-General of Algeria for nearly seven years, February 1841 to September 1847.[735] He received all the assistance he asked for, and maintained the army in the country at a strength always above what was provided for in the budget, 83,000 in 1842 rising to 108,000 in 1846, besides the various corps of native auxiliaries, about 10,000 strong.[736] His period in Algeria was, Abun Nasr remarks, a decisive one in Algerian history and not only because of the destruction of Abd al-Kader's authority.[737] Under his governorship, more native land was taken for the benefit of European settlers, and gradually Algeria was absorbed into the political and administrative structure of France.[738]

The method of war which La Moricière, the commander in Oran since 1840, had pursued, was now generalised throughout the country.[739] The aim was to methodically ravage all territory not yet under French control.

> We shouldn't run after the Arabs but prevent them from sowing, harvesting and grazing.[740]

It was the same picture of systemic destruction of every means of survival that emerges in all accounts of the time. Montagnac, writing to his brother on 27 July 1842, said:

> We left Mascara and settled near the Mina River, four days away from Mascara. We harvested from 22 June until 5 July the lands of a hostile tribe. It gained us 800 quintals of barley and 400 quintals of wheat.[741]

---

[734] Ibid.
[735] C.R. Ageron: *Modern Algeria*, op cit; p. 18.
[736] Ibid.
[737] J.M. Abun-Nasr: *A History of the Maghrib*, op cit, p. 245.
[738] Ibid.
[739] Ibid.
[740] C.R. Ageron: *Modern Algeria*, op cit, p. 19.
[741] De Montagnac: *Lettres d'un soldat*; Librairie Plon Paris; 1885; p. 260.

Page after page Montagnac speaks of the same, and doing the same from one end of the country to the other; now on 15 March, 1843, in Eastern Algeria, precisely in Skikda (Philipeville as it was then called), seizing thousands of livestock, burning hamlets and ruining the local tribes.[742]

Saint-Arnaud, likewise, does and says the same:

> We are among the mountains between Miliana and Cherchell. We have fired few shots, but we are burning all the *douars,* all the villages, all the huts. The enemy flees before us, taking his flocks with him' (April 5 1842). 'The Beni Manacer's country is superb... We have burnt everything, destroyed everything. Oh! This war, this war! How many women and children, seeking refuge in the Atlas snows, have died there of cold and misery.... Our casualties were five killed and forty wounded' (April 7, 1842). 'We lay waste, we burn, we plunder, we destroy the crops and the trees. As for engagements, few or none; just a hundred or two wretched Arabs who fire on the rearguard and wound a few men' (June 5, 1842). 'When I last wrote I was among the Brazes. I laid waste and burnt everything. Now I am among the Sindgads. The same thing on a grand scale; it's a real public granary.... A few tribesmen brought in their horses as tokens of submission. I refused because I wanted a general submission, and began burning once more' (October 1, 1842). 'Here I am with my little army, burning the *douars* and huts of the insurgents, raiding their silos and sending to Miliana all the corn and barley that I draw from them... A few shots have been fired. Today I am making a halt to continue emptying silos and burning villages and huts. I shall leave them no peace till they submit' (October 5 1842). 'I shall not leave a single tree standing in their orchards, not a head on the shoulders of these wretched Arabs.... Those are the orders that I have received from General Changarnier, and they will be punctually executed. I shall burn everything, kill everyone...' (January 18, 1843). 'On the 4th I reached Haimda. I burned everything in my path and destroyed the pretty village, but it was impossible to proceed further . . . When day dawned we saw that two foot of snow had fallen. No sign of a track, nothing; just snow, and more snow. I started off, and we had hardly made a quarter of a mile when we came upon a horrible sight . . .. heaps of bodies huddled together, frozen to death during the night. They were the Beni—Naâseur whose villages and huts I had burnt, whom I had driven before me...' (February 8, 1843).[743]

Here he is in the region of Bejaia in 1844, from his letter to his brother dated 2 October 1844:

> 15 Leagues of Bejaia, the region is stunning. There are beautiful orange orchards, which my vandalism is going to cut down. I wish I could send you this beautiful forest to Noisy; your wife will be so happy. Today, I am

---

[742] Ibid; pp. 291-98.
[743] W. Blunt: *Desert Hawk*; op cit, pp. 167-8.

burning the properties and the villages of the Ben Salem, and Bel-Cassem or Kassi.

You can tell Rousset (A Royal Court Lawyer, childhood friend of Saint Arnaud) that I have burnt and destroyed so much. He is right to call me Goth or Vandal.'[744]

A year later from western Algeria in his pursuit of Bou Ma'za:

Au bivouac d'Aïn-Méran, 15 August 1845.

On 9th beginning of blockade of Arabs in their caves (between Tenes and Mostaganem, in the west.) On 12, I seal everything. And then I create a vast graveyard. Earth will cover the bodies of these fanatics for ever. Nobody has gone down to check, only a confidential report to the Marshal. Dear Brother, nobody has as kind and humane disposition as me. Between 8 and 12 I have been sick. But my conscience reproaches me nothing. I have only done my duty as a commander. Tomorrow, I will do it, again.[745]

In Greater Kabylia, in 1845, he is still at it:

Following one of the many large encounters: The enemy had left a thousand or so corpses, which supposes many more were killed and wounded. Now we set 40 villages on fire. The fires were gigantic, fed by olive oil which the Kabyles produce in large quantities, stored in large containers, and which now because of the intense fire explode; all the corpses are now consumed by fire; it causes a huge stench in the air... unbearable vapours of burnt blood.[746]

Also in Kabylia, but another unit, the Foreign Legion, and here we have Clemens Lamping:

After a hot forced march, we saw on a mountain top, which formed a plateau, a great heap of stones which we knew to be a town. In two hours we were close upon it. Our battalion and several others climbed the steep hill, in order to enter the town from above, while the rest of the column attacked it from below. "We were driving the Bedouins before us all the time. At length we reached the walls, but to our astonishment no one appeared to defend them, and the gates stood wide open. Suspecting a stratagem, some of us climbed to the top of the walls to look into the town. The nest was empty, and the birds flown; as usual we had come just too late. The whole column poured into the town, which was I think called Callah, and the soldiers eagerly ransacked the houses. The owners could not have been gone long, for the kuskussu on the hearth was still hot. A few fowls, cats, and lambs, which the Kabyles had left behind in their hurry, and two rusty cannons, were all the spoil. After taking as much wood as was wanted to cook our supper, we set fire to the town. We then

---

[744] H. Alleg et al: *La Guerre d'Algerie*, op cit; p. 66.

[745] St Arnaud: Lettres de St Arnaud; 2 vols; Michel Levy; Paris; 1855; vol 2; p. 37.

[746] P. Gaffarel: *Lectures Geographiques et Historiques sur l'Algerie et les Colonies Francaises*; Garniers Freres; Paris; 1886; p. 224.

bivouacked on an eminence at a distance, where we slept as soundly as if we had performed some glorious action.[747]

The same unit, but this time further west:

A few days afterwards we started again to throw provisions into Milliana, and to lay waste the plains of the Chellif with fire and sword. It was exactly harvest time. In order to cut off from the Bedouins all means of existence, it was of course necessary to drive away their cattle and to burn their corn. Before long, the whole plain looked like a sea of fire.[748]

The same Clemens Lamping:

The prisoners, chiefly old men, women and children, were driven with the cattle, under a special guard, in the middle of the column; it was heart-rending to see women and children, unaccustomed to walking and barefooted, compelled to follow the rapid march of the column, over rocks and briars. Their feet were soon torn and bleeding, and they dragged themselves along with the greatest difficulty. They seldom made any complaint: only when one of their number dropped from fatigue, and was left behind, they all uttered a loud wail.[749]

Elsewhere in Kabylia, Generals Camou and Bosquet between them burnt 300 towns and hamlets, cut down orchards, and massacred entire tribes, both foes and friends.[750] Back in the Oran region, it was Cavaignac and Pelissier who slew, burnt, and did much else besides.[751] On one day alone, 12 May, 1843, Colonel Pelissier brought in two thousand prisoners of both sexes, four or five hundred mares, seven or eight hundred asses, twelve thousand head of cattle.[752] To the east of the Ouarsenis, meanwhile, Changarnier was 'punishing' the Beni Fera, taking 2000 prisoners, eight thousand sheep, and eight hundred cattle.[753] At Medea, it was Colonels Korte and Yusuf who were slaying, burning, and on one day alone, on 29th of June, 1843, plundered away 15,000 head of cattle.[754]

Throughout the country, the tribes were on the run with their old and young, their sick and malnourished, their flocks and their possessions, and the French chasing, in all seasons, and at all times. There was no abode or sanctuary. Pelissier earned himself great notoriety and plaudits for his walling and smoking in caves whole tribes that had sought refuge in them.[755] It was in the Dahra region, that this future Marshal of France and Governor-General of Algeria, now Colonel Pélissier, rose to fame[756] In the month of June 1845, in hot pursuit of the Ouled Riah, he forced

[747] Clemens Lamping: *The French in Algiers*; op cit; p. 54.
[748] Ibid; p. 72.
[749] Ibid.
[750] H. Alleg et al. *La Guerre*; op cit; 77.
[751] Ibid; pp. 66 and 69.
[752] Count H. Ideville: *Memoirs of Marshal Bugeaud*; op cit; p. 72.
[753] Ibid.
[754] Ibid.
[755] H. Alleg et al: *La Guerre*; op cit; pp. 66 and 69.
[756] C.R. Ageron: *Modern Algeria*, op cit, p. 20.

them to seek refuge, as they had always done in moments of crisis, in an elaborate chain of grottoes in the Dahra mountains. At first they refused to submit; but seeing that their situation had become hopeless, they agreed to give themselves up and to pay a considerable indemnity, on condition that their lives were spared.[757] Pélissier had resolved to 'smoke out the rebellious tribesmen,' and so refused their terms, ordering the sealing off of all openings, and setting fire to brushwood at the main entrance to the caves. All night long, 'by the light of a brilliant moon, the murderous flames were fed. The soldiers pushed the heaps of wood towards the mouth of the cave as if in an oven.' A terrible spectacle offered itself to the French when at last the smoke began to clear and it became possible to enter the grotto.

> Bodies lay heaped together in the furthest recesses of the caves—women with their infants in their arms, young men and old, girls, children—their blackened faces convulsed with the agony of their suffering before they died. All of them were naked. Blood came out of their mouth. Babies lay amongst dead sheep and sacs of beans. Many piled onto each other resembling a boiled mass. In places children lay under the clothes of their mothers who had sought to protect them.'[758]

According to an eye witness:

> What brush should paint this picture. In the middle of the night, lit by the moon, a corps of French troops kept an infernal fire, whilst the sounds of moans and groans of men, women and children inside the cave, as well as of animals; the cracking sound of the rocks which calcinated began to crumble; there were lying bulls, asses, sheep... beside the animals piling up, we could find men, women, children. I saw a man dead, his knee on the ground, his hand grabbing the horn of a bull. In front of him was a woman holding a child in her arms. This man had been asphyxiated at the moment when he sought to preserve his family from the rage of the animal. We counted 750 bodies.[759]

Writing to Marshal Soult, Minister of War, Bugeaud justified the act:

> Before administering and civilising and colonising, it is necessary that the native population accepts our rule. A thousand examples have shown they would only do so if we use force. The use of force itself is powerless if it does not hurt people as hard as their interests. Philanthropic deeds will perpetuate war and the spirit of rebellion, and then we would never accomplish our benevolent goal.[760]

The Minister himself, Soult, defended the acts of Pelissier:

> I deplore what has happened. In Europe such an act would be detestable and abhorrent. In Africa, on the other hand, it is war itself.[761]

---

[757] W. Blunt: *Desert Hawk*; op cit, p. 195; P. Gafarel: *Lectures Geographiques et Historiques*; op cit, pp. 217-20.
[758] Ibid.
[759] H. Alleg et al: *La Guerre d'Algerie*, op cit, p. 66.
[760] P. Gafarel: *Lectures Geographiques et Historiques*; op cit, p. 220.
[761] H. Alleg et al: *La Guerre d'Algerie*. op cit, p. 69.

> This was the well devised strategy. It consists, [Alleg et al. explain] in the destruction of any form of opposition by starving the country though devastation, confiscation of harvest and livestock, burning hamlets and villages, massacring the largest number of people possible, whether fighting men or not, spreading such terror that they either submit or disappear.[762]

The war of devastation, which Ageron notes, seemed justified by immediate success, in the end only served to prolong the conflict, and resulted in the permanent alienation of the Algerians from the French.[763] And, indeed, the response from tribal sheiks was this:

> What is this spirit that impels France, calling itself such a powerful nation, to come and make war upon us? Has she not territory enough? What loss will the land she takes be to us in comparison with what is left us? She will march forward, and we shall retire; but she will be compelled to retire, and we shall return. And you, Governor of Algiers, what harm can you do us? In fighting you lose as many men as we do. Sickness decimates your army every year. What compensation can you offer your king, and your country, for your immense losses in men and money? A little land and the stones of Mascara. You burn, you waste our harvests, you cut our barley and wheat, and rob our silos..... We shall fight when we think fit: you know we are not cowards. For us to meet all the forces you drag along with you would be madness; but we shall weary them and harass them, and destroy them in detail; our climate will do the rest. Send man against man, ten against ten, a hundred against a hundred, a thousand against a thousand, and you will see if we recoil. Do you see the wave rise when a bird brushes it with its wing? This is the image of your passing over Africa.[764]

And it was precisely this spirit that made the eradication of Algerians an impossibility, for they refused to be fair game to the same ideology that had done the same and succeeded elsewhere.[765]

2. The Progress of the Military Campaign: 1841-1844

In July, 1841, Saint-Arnaud was commanding the rear-guard in a march from Mostaganem to Mascara; it was the hottest time of the year, and the men were completely exhausted. Algerians were hovering about the rear-guard and, though

---

[762] Ibid, p. 70.
[763] C.R. Ageron: *Modern Algeria*; op cit; 19.
[764] Count H. Ideville: *Memoirs of Marshal Bugeaud*; op cit; vol 2; p. 25.
[765] D. E. Stannard: *American Holocaust; The Conquest of the New World;* Oxford University Press; 1992.
W. Howitt: *Colonisation and Christianity*: Longman; London; 1838.
Ward Churchill: *A Little Matter of Genocide*; City Lights Books; San Francisco; 1997.

rifle-fire drove them back, they continued to follow at a distance, confident that the French could not escape them.

> Not for a general's epaulettes would I live those next ten hours again, [he wrote.] Hardly had the firing ceased when stragglers began to drop out of the ranks, by scores, by hundreds, from every corps and every regiment. The wretched Light Infantry Battalion which was having its first taste of African warfare was in complete chaos. It formed the van, and was therefore nearly two leagues ahead of me; but I picked up its men in the rear-guard. I saw the most hideous scenes of weakness and demoralization. I saw soldiers throw away their arms and equipment and lie down to await death—certain and dishonourable death. Forced to their feet, they stumbled on for a hundred yards, only to fall again, overcome by the heat, worn out, weakened by fever and dysentery. In order to try and avoid me they threw themselves down away from the track, in the thickets, among the ravines. I followed them and took their rifles and their packs; I made my *zouaves* drag them along. . . Many begged me to kill them so that they should not die at the hands of the Arabs. I saw some of them clasp the barrels of their rifles in a voluptuous frenzy as they tried to place them in their mouths; never have I found suicide easier to understand... That day, a day I shall never forget, I understood the Macta, Tafna, all the disasters of Africa.[766]

The French principal objectives were to occupy what they saw as Abd al-Kader's centers of power, first and foremost, his new capital, Tagdempt, and the old capital of Mascara.[767] The Emir understood the futility of direct confrontation. So, wisely, he evacuated Tagdempt, which was occupied on 25 May 1841 and rased to the ground.[768] Moving from there, French columns inflicted devastation on the tribes of the Hachem and the Flitta and territories deemed loyal to Abd al-Kader, occupying all the towns in the western Tell.[769] On 30 May 1841 Bugeaud entered Mascara, which had also been abandoned, and left in it a garrison before returning to Mostaganem.[770] At the same time, General Baraguey d'Hilliers occupied two additional third-line towns, Boghar and Taza before razing them with their fortifications and factories.[771] A network of permanent posts kept conquered districts under control; another controlled the supply of grain from the north to the nomads of the south, thus keeping the borders of the desert under surveillance.[772] While three commanders based in Mascara, Tlemcen, and Mostaganem gave the chase to the Emir between Tlemcen and the littoral,

---

[766] St Arnaud: *Lettres*; in W. Blunt: *Desert Hawk*; op cit, pp. 168-9.
[767] R. Danziger: *Abd Al-Qadir and the Algerians*; op cit, p. 225.
[768] Ibid.
[769] C.R. Ageron: *Modern Algeria*, op cit, p. 19.
[770] R. Danziger: *Abd Al-Qadir and the Algerians*; op cit, p. 225.
[771] Ibid.
[772] C.R. Ageron: *Modern Algeria*, op cit,19.

Bugeaud established in 1842 a base at al-Asnam (renamed Orleansville) to curtail the Emir's movements in the Dahra mountainous regions.[773]

Sorely weakened, the Emir kept moving ahead, at times launching raids, trying to remain on the offensive.[774] Often bewildered by his daring and refusal to come to terms, the French, still maintained their methodical progress.[775] Their work of destruction was constant and systemic. The Emir still kept fighting, but around him the whole social structure had been shattered by the violence of the conflict. In the words of the *sheikh* of the Beni Urag:

> I will tell 'Abd al-Qadir: I have lost six sons in battle; the tribe has sacrificed everything, we can do no more...[776]

By the spring of 1843, the Emir had lost his last fortified post, Teniet. The most crushing blow came, however, in May 1843 when a small French detachment fell on the *Smala* (Abd al Kader's tented, mobile capital), which included the wandering population of faithful servants, officials, craftsmen, and tribes, besides Abd al-Kader's family-some 30,000 persons.[777] The French attack was a complete surprise and in the panic that ensued, they overran the camp with little difficulty or loss of life. Abd al-Kader's mother and wife escaped in the confusion, but most of the camp surrendered.[778]

After three years of struggle Abd al-Kader, at the end of his resources, was obliged to take refuge in Morocco to save what remained of his *Smala*.[779] 'The serious warfare is over,' declared Bugeaud optimistically in July 1843, and went off in the spring of 1844 to subdue the western slopes of Kabylia, the high mountain massif to the east of Algiers which still recognised the authority of a *khalifa* appointed by the emir.[780] Writing from his bivouac: de Manselt-el-Maëlha, 17 Octobre 1844, Saint Arnaud, again:

> We fought around Dellys; the Kabyles have lost heavily: we are walking on their corpses. These people fight very well. They fought us from close range.[781]

Abd al-Kader was well aware that isolation ultimately spelt defeat. Just as Hadj Ahmed had looked to the east for support, so he looked to the west. Moroccan support became ever more crucial.[782] He was not truly in search of political backing or even military help but merely seeking an open frontier so that his

---

[773] J.M. Abun-Nasr: *A History of the Maghrib*, op cit, p. 246.

[774] M. Morsy: *North Africa*; op cit; p. 141.

[775] Ibid.

[776] Ibid.

[777] Ibid.

[778] Ibid. 113.

[779] C.R. Ageron: *Modern Algeria*, op cit; p. 19.

[780] Ibid.

[781] St Arnaud: Lettres de St Arnaud; 2 vols; Michel Levy; Paris; 1855; vol 1; p. 551.

[782] M. Morsy: *North Africa*; op cit; p. 142.

troops could find refuge there or use Moroccan territory as a military base, whilst relieving the pressure on the severely affected Algerian side of his support.[783] In November 1843, with the remnants of his army, he thus crossed over into Morocco. The French reaction was not slow. General Bugeaud marched westwards and occupied Lalla Maghniya, on the right bank of Wadi Kis, a few miles beyond the frontier.[784] This had the immediate effect of stirring up the Moroccan tribes, and national indignation was such that Sultan Abd al-Rahman had to send the army out under the command of Sidi Muhammad, his nephew.[785] The royal camp was set up on the bank of Wad Isly, near the town of Wujda (Oujda). In response, in August 1844, the French sent a squadron under the Prince of Joinville to the shores of Morocco bearing an ultimatum.[786] The Prince nonetheless decided for a more persuasive method and thus on 6 August 1844 shelled the harbour of Tangier, following this up by a similar attack on al-Sawira on 16 August.[787] Bugeaud, not to be outdone and in spite of orders to the contrary, crossed Wad Isly on 13 August and attacked the Moroccan camp. Once more, French military superiority was obvious. By noon the battle was over. The Moroccans were crushed; the French captured the camp and took many prisoners.[788] This won for Bugeaud the title of Duke of Isly, whilst at the same time it brought to light Moroccan military weakness.[789] The Treaty of Tangier which followed outlawed Abd al-Kader, and opened the way to the definition of the frontier between Algeria and Morocco by the convention of Lalla Maghnia on 18 March 1845.[790] The Moroccan Sharif complied with French requests concerning Abd al-Kader who was formally declared an outlaw on Moroccan soil.[791] The Emir who had taken refuge among friendly tribes in the mountainous region of Wadi Muluya had to cross back into Algeria.[792] Nevertheless, in the course of that year fighting broke out once again right across the 'pacified' regions at the call of the brotherhoods.[793] This was the precursor of a much larger uprising inside Algeria.

3. 1845, Year of the General Uprising

Leaving Morocco, Abd al-Kader reappeared in the Oran region, achieving some success around Sidi Brahim.[794] French methods however had so enflamed

---

[783] Ibid.
[784] Ibid.
[785] Ibid.
[786] Ibid.
[787] Ibid.
[788] Ibid.
[789] Ibid.
[790] C.R. Ageron: *Modern Algeria*, op cit, p. 19.
[791] M. Morsy: *North Africa*; op cit; p. 142.
[792] Ibid.
[793] C.R. Ageron: *Modern Algeria*, op cit, p. 19.
[794] Ibid, p. 20.

popular hostility that even as the Emir's forces waned, the banner of resistance was taken up by others.[795] In 1845, armed opposition flared up throughout Algeria, the tribes of the high plains to the south of the Tell and those of the Saharan Atlas on the edge of the desert rose again at the end of the year.[796] In the hinterland of the coast, the mountains of the Dahra, the valley of the Chelif and the range of the Ouarsenis rose against the French under the leadership of a young *sharif*, Mohammed Ibn Abd Allah, known as Bou Ma'za.[797] He pledged that he would rid Algeria of the French within the year.[798] His movement spread through the Chelif and the Ouarsenis, threatening the new French centre of Orleansville.[799] There were other such risings, the most important of which were in the regions of Hodna and Titteri.[800]

This 'great insurrection' seemed to call everything back into question. One French army after another attacked the areas where Bou Ma'za's support was found or suspected with the same zeal as before.

Algiers, 24th April, 1845, From Bugeaud to 'My Dear Saint-Arnaud'

> The Beni-Hidja tribes deserve the most severe and most exemplary punishment. You must perseveringly hang on to them like a plague. Deprive them of all their harvests, cut down their fruit-trees of all kinds; they must be ruined for a long time, unless they consent to give up their guns, and horses, and a large war contribution.[801]

To his wife, he also wrote:

> To the Maréchale Duchesse d'Isly:
>
> Ouarsènis, 9th May, 1845, on the Oued-Lira.
>
> My Love, — Today we entered upon the territory of the insurgents. They have not yet fired a shot at us. The chief event hitherto is a great storm we encountered yesterday as we came to our bivouac, that lasted five hours. We destroy our enemy's harvests as much as we can. Saint- Arnaud writes to me that everything is nearly finished to the east of Tenès.[802]

Bou Ma'za seemed to be everywhere. His namesakes swarmed. Colonel Saint-Arnaud 's correspondence shows many of them; he says,

> All these sherifs appear and vanish. I hunt the sherifs to death, and they come up like mushrooms. It is a perfect maze, one cannot find one's way. Besides the oldest Bou-Maza we have Mohammed-bel-Cassem, Bou-Ali, Ali-Chergui, Si-Larbi, Bel-Bej, and I get lost in them. I have killed Ali-Chergui

---

[795] M. Morsy: *North Africa*; op cit; p. 142.
[796] C.R. Ageron: *Modern Algeria*, op cit, p. 20.
[797] Ibid.
[798] C.H. Churchill: *The Life of Abd Al Kader*, op cit, p. 236.
[799] M. Morsy: *North Africa*; op cit; p. 142.
[800] Ibid.
[801] Count H. Ideville: *Memoirs of Marshal Bugeaud*; op cit; vol 2; p. 158.
[802] Ibid; p. 163.

among the Medjaja, and Bou-Ali among the Beni-Derjin, and I should be glad to catch Ben Hinni.[803]

On the 20th of September a Mohammed ben Abdallah arose in the Djebel Dira, in the southern part of the Tittery, and soon, was involved in bitter fight with the French. Hunted down by General Marey, he was driven back into the Kabyle Djurjura, where, in November, he fought General d'Arbouville's troops from Setif, as well as Marey's.[804] He joined with the Kabyle Ben Salem in keeping French eastern flanks under constant duress.[805] General d'Arbouville, like Saint-Arnaud, upon the Chelif, reported several other chiefs also called Bou-Ma'za. We find another Mohammed ben Abdallah in the west before General Cavaignac.[806]

On the 3rd of November 1845 a Sherif of only twenty, specially called Bou-Ma'za of the Beni-Zoug-Zoug, stirred up the tribes of the Chelif between Orleansville and Milianah, and showed himself at the Ouled-Segris. He was caught. The French owned paper, the *Moniteur Algérien* writes:

> This man, not more than twenty or twenty-two years of age, is incredibly fanatic and arrogant. He claimed to be a brother of the original Bou Ma'za. He replied fearlessly to his cross-examiners the day before his execution:
>
> Q. What have you to blame the French for? Theft, exaction, injustice, crimes? Tell the truth without fear.
>
> A. None of that; the Arabs hate you because you are not of their faith, because you are strangers. You now come to take their country, and to-morrow you will want their wives and children. The Arabs asked my brother, 'Lead us, let us begin the war again; everyday that passes makes the Christians stronger; let us finish them this moment.'
>
> Q. A great many Arabs know what to think of us, and are devoted to us.
>
> A. There is but one God. My life is in His hand and yours; I will speak openly to you. Every day you find Mahommedans tell you that they love you, and are your servants. Do not believe it. They lie to you from fear or interest. Every time that there comes a Sherif who they think is able to conquer you they will follow him, and even would attack you in Algiers.
>
> Q. How can the Arabs hope to conquer us, led by chiefs who have no army, no cannon, no treasures?
>
> A. Victory comes from God; when He chooses He makes the weak to triumph, and brings down the strong.[807]
>
> The man was condemned to death by court-martial on the 15th of November. He has been supposed to be the brother of Bou-Ma'za, because

---

[803] Ibid; p. 199.
[804] Ibid; p. 200.
[805] Ibid.
[806] Ibid.
[807] Ibid; pp. 199-200.

he stated it upon his trial. But 'Arab fanatics' often call themselves each other's brothers without there being anything but a spiritual connection.[808]

The main Bou Ma'za was keeping the French on toes. A murderous engagement took place on the 10th of January 1846 between General Herbillon and the Ouled-Djellal, whom Bou-Ma'za had just visited.[809] On another side, General Marey-Monge, commanding at Médéa, fell upon the Ouled-Naïl, who, following Abd al-Kader, had received Bou Ma'za, and given him assistance in men and food.[810] Some days afterwards, Bou-Ma'za himself was chased between Tiaret and the forest of pines and gigantic cedars of Teniet-el-Had, where his escort was routed, and his treasure captured.[811] The French army was busy 'raking, combing and subjugating,' the country while flying columns set off in pursuit of the elusive Emir and Bou Ma'za.[812] It had now become customary to wall and smoke to death tribes that sought shelter in caves.[813] Close fight was also frequent. Writing to his brother from Oued Mogrelas (Dahra region) on 18 March 1846, St Arnaud said:

> I had learnt that Bou Ma'za was two leagues away from me. Early in the day I set off with four battalions, artillery, cavalry, after him. I came across him on the hills to my right. Hard fighting ensued. The ground was horrific. We could only climb with great difficulty. Bou Ma'za was with 400 cavaliers and 600 Kabyles, and launched a bloody attack on my cavalry. They held firm giving me time to reach the scene of the worst clashes. 'The chasseurs' are following me on foot. In a short moment it was intense fighting. I had enemies behind me and in front of me. We charged. Bou Ma'za was forced to withdraw. We followed. In the fighting, he (Bou Ma'za) was shot and the bullet shattered his arm. I have killed so many of them.... There were still many enemies surrounding us but refusing to come down to us. I have begun to cut down the beautiful orchards and burning the superb villages under the eyes of the enemy.[814]

Three columns, under Colonels Ladmirault, Saint-Arnaud, and Pelissier, first marched through the Dahra, and afterwards in the Ouarsenis.[815] Other generals and their units were marching in and around neighbouring regions. Bou-Ma'za, finding himself pressed by General Pélissier, Colonels Saint-Arnaud, and Canrobert, rode into the mountains on the left bank of the Chélif, escorted by 34 horsemen. He was carried stretched out upon a mule, as his wound was in a very bad state.[816] Saint-Arnaud planned to return to Orléansville with some of his

---

[808] Ibid; p. 200.
[809] Ibid; p. 235.
[810] Ibid.
[811] Ibid.
[812] C.R. Ageron: *Modern Algeria*, op cit, p. 20.
[813] M. Morsy: *North Africa*; op cit; p. 142.
[814] St Arnaud: Lettres de St Arnaud; 2 vols; Michel Levy; Paris; 1855; vol 2; pp. 82-3.
[815] Count H. Ideville: *Memoirs of Marshal Bugeaud*; vol 2; op cit; p. 165.
[816] Ibid; p. 224.

force, then would enter the Ouarsenis by the Oued-el-Ardjens. The plan was to hunt for Bou-Ma'za among the Ouled-Bou-Sliman, and then march in the direction other generals were coming from to fall on the people driven towards him.[817] It was a systematic sweep.

After few flights, his wounded arm turning into a great obstruction, Bou Ma'za surrendered in April 1847. In the years that followed, on the outbreak of the Crimean War (1853-1856), Bou Ma'za asked leave of Napoleon III to fight for the Ottomans against the Russians. The Emperor not only gave his permission but also presented him with a beautiful sword. Thus, by a curious turn of fortune, the old enemy of France found himself fighting side by side with Saint-Arnaud and the very men who for two years had been his greatest enemies. Nothing more was heard of Bou Ma'za after the war, and it is presumed that he lost his life during the Anatolian campaign at the head of a Turkish corps of volunteers.[818]

4. Abd al Kader's Final Years of Resistance (1845-1847)

> Abd al Kader is being pursued: Camou is after him; Yusuf is running after him; Renault, too; everyone is hunting him down.[819]

In a letter to his brother, Saint Arnaud wrote:
> I have received a letter from the Marshall (Bugeaud) who is very happy with my measures... Abd al Kader is trying very hard to rally the tribes, but what headaches and pains it is causing them: they are all broken, shattered by war, but they still are listening to him because they love him and do not like us.[820]

In the wake of the local uprisings, French forces were redeployed and this brought Abd al-Kader a brief respite. A few signal victories, notably at Sidi Brahim in September 1845, revived flagging hopes.[821] It was on that occasion that Colonel Montagnac was slain with his troops.[822] Abd al-Kader renewed his efforts to bring the tribes to unified action, but he was largely unsuccessful although he found cooperation among the Kabyle tribes of the Djurjura and the Ulad Sidi Shaykh of the south-west.[823] He was being hunted from all sides and by all, though. Yusuf was chasing him from Tiaret to Teniet-el-Hâd; Lamoricière from the Tell to Tiaret; Marey was at Boghar; d'Arbouville from Setif to Medea.[824] From

---

[817] Ibid.

[818] W. Blunt: *Desert Hawk*; op cit, p. 201.

[819] St Arnaud: Lettres de St Arnaud; 2 vols; Michel Levy; Paris; 1855; vol 2; p. 83.

[820] Ibid; p. 106.

[821] M. Morsy: *North Africa*; op cit; p. 143.

[822] For details of his death, see introductory chapter by his nephew in Montagnac: *Memoirs*; op cit.

[823] M. Morsy: *North Africa;* op cit; 143.

[824] Count H. Ideville: *Memoirs of Marshal Bugeaud*; vol 2; op cit; p. 203.

Orléansville Bugeaud himself had gone to the Nahr-Ouassel, as the Chelif is called in the upper part of its course. Not finding the Emir, he went to Boghar, making Pelissier take his place, who had just taken a great convoy to Tiaret, and replaced Lamoriciere, gone to Mascara.[825]

The Emir, finding the line impenetrable in the west and centre, endeavoured to break through on the East, performing a miracle of boldness and speed. He suddenly made his appearance with his father-in-law, Ben-Salem, upon the Sebaou and the Isser, where he had not been seen since the treaty of the Tafna.[826] He had left the Sahara in February, 1846, followed by part of the Beni Hassan, passed, unobserved, through the Wady Isser to the east of Medea, very far inside north central Algeria, and, making a punitive descent on the Beni Hadoura, who served the French, reached the Djurjura, where the Kabyles stood ready to fight by his side.[827] With a force of 5,000 warriors, accumulated 'as if by magic,' says Churchill, he now swept down into the plains, ravaged and destroyed the French colonies, and advanced to within four hours of Algiers itself. The French generals were all the while looking for him in the high ground of the Tell hundreds of kilometres further inland.[828] Soon they realised their error. On the 7th February, he encamped at the foot of the Djurjura, and while he was engaged in late night prayer, he heard the French order to charge. In the quickest of times, the French were upon him.[829] He sprang on his horse and called on his men to rally. The Chasseurs closed around him, and began to pounce on him. He fought them single-handed, two horses shot under him in succession.[830] He fought on foot, soon surrounded by his men. He became lost in the confusion of the fighting, and helped by the darkness of the night managed to escape.[831]

It did not take the French long to respond to the Kabyles by the means they knew best. Dawson Borrer, an Englishman fighting amongst the French narrates:

> By half-past 4 a.m. eight battalions, "sans sacs," with some mountain guns, a small body of cavalry, and some hundreds of the "Goum Arabe," were toiling up the first heights, the Marshal having decided to attack and destroy the numerous towns of the Beni-Abbas, said to lie behind them. These villages were numerous, and generally situated upon commanding summits, the slopes, where possible, being cultivated with corn and olives. Lofty isolated towers, square at the base, then carried up in an octagonal form, overlooked these villages from the hills around. These peculiar

---

[825] Ibid.
[826] Ibid; p. 204.
[827] C.H. Churchill: *The Life of Abd Al Kader*, op cit, p. 247.
[828] Ibid.
[829] Ibid, p. 248.
[830] Ibid.
[831] Ibid.

structures were probably holy places of resort during peace, and during war served for watch-towers and defence.

The villages were all surrounded with walls of about twelve feet in height, and composed of stones cemented together with mud mingled with chopped straw, a strong fence of thorny bushes crowning them, and impenetrable hedges of the prickly pear growing along their base.

The narrow streets were soon crowded with French troops, ravishing, massacring, and plundering on all sides. Neither sex nor age was regarded; the sword fell upon all alike. From one house blood-stained soldiers, laden with spoil, passed forth as I entered it. Upon the floor of one of the chambers lay a little girl of twelve or fourteen years of age: there she lay, weltering in gore and in the agonies of death: an accursed ruffian thrust his bayonet into her. God will requite him. In another house a wrinkled old woman sat crouched upon the matting, rapidly muttering, in the agony of fear, prayers to Allah, with a trembling tongue. A pretty child, of six or seven years old, laden with silver and coral ornaments, clung to her side, her eyes streaming with tears as she clasped her aged mother's arm. The soldiery, mad with blood and rage, were nigh at hand. I seized the fair child: a moment was left to force her into a dark recess at the far end of the building; some ragged matting thrown before it served to conceal her; and whilst I was making signs to her mother to hold silence, soldiers rushed in: some ransacked the habitation; others pricked the old female with their bayonets. "Soldiers, will you slay an aged woman?" "No, monsieur," said one fellow, "we will not kill her; but her valuables are concealed, and we must have them."

In nearly every house were vast jars of oil (for the Kabailes make, consume, and sell vast quantities,) often six or seven feet in height, and ranged in rows around the chambers. Holes being rapped in all these jars, the houses were soon flooded with oil, and streams of it were pouring down the very streets. When the soldiers had ransacked the dwellings, and smashed to atoms all that they could not carry off, or did not think worth seizing as spoil, they heaped the remnants and the mattings together, and fired them. As I was hastily traversing the narrow streets to regain the outside of the village, disgusted with the horrors I witnessed, flames burst forth on all sides, and torrents of fire came swiftly gliding down the thoroughfares; for the flames had gained the oil. An instant I turned, the fearful doom of the poor concealed child and the decrepid mother flashing on my mind. It was too late; who could distinguish the house amongst hundreds exactly similar? The fire was crackling, blazing, with increased fury, and there was no time to lose. The way of the gateway was barred with roaring flames. Scrambling to the terrace of a low building I threw myself over the wall.

>The unfortunate Kabyle child was doubtless consumed with her aged parent. How many others may have shared her fate![832]

From the same region, another officer wrote:

>Order was given to deliver a war of devastation... So our soldiers acted with ferocity... women, children were slaughtered, homes burnt down, trees razed to the ground, nothing was spared... Kabyle women wore silver bracelets to the arms and around their ankles. Soldiers cut all their limbs, and they did not always do it to the dead only.[833]

French high authorities at best had knowledge of such acts. They certainly condoned them and even ordered them. Marshal Bugeaud, writing to his wife:

River of Bougie, eleven leagues from the town. 18th May, evening.

>My Love, — I write you four lines, for I am very busy, and it is oppressively hot. Our business goes well, and so does my health. The events have restored my energy. I have asked General de Bar to show you my reports to the Minister; so I will not tell you what we have done. I say no more than that our troops were splendid, and that I am far from having lost their confidence. I shall bring you various jewels of the Kabyle ladies, and a carpet that have been given to me. Our soldiers have taken a great deal of booty, and our goums still more, because they were not fighting, and pillaged the villages that our soldiers had carried.[834]

Late in 1846 we find Abd al Kader far in the hinterlands of Algeria. He had hoped to recruit his forces amongst the tribes of the Sahara, but the French had forestalled him. Wherever he went, their various armies seemed to be waiting for him. All previous loyal and friendly tribes to him: the Beni Nail, the Beni Shaib, the Beni Hassan, who used to provide him with whatever he sought for his men, and with whom he had often found shelter in the hour of need, all now fell under French control.[835] And so harsh was the French retribution on the supportive tribes that the impact was immediate and disastrous as far the Emir and Algerian resistance went. The French ransacked, devastated and slew en masse, and also selectively amongst the leadership in particular.[836] Abd al Kader visited a large and powerful tribe at the southern extremity of the Sahara, and there their chiefs and imams thronged about him, and assured him of their warmest sympathies.[837] They also offered him temporary hospitality, but at the same time asked him not to entail upon them the horrors of war. Abd al Kader received their bequests with composure. Accompanied by his faithful escort, he now rode further north to his stronghold (Deira), on the Moulouia, in Morocco.[838]

---

[832] Dawson Borrer: *Narrative of a campaign against the Kabailes of Algeria;* Spottiswoode and Shaw, London, 1848; pp. 92-104.

[833] P. Gaffarel: *L'Algerie*; op cit; p. 77.

[834] Count H. Ideville: *Memoirs of Marshal Bugeaud*; op cit; vol 2; p. 245.

[835] C.H. Churchill: *The Life of Abd Al Kader*, op cit p. 249.

[836] Ibid.

[837] Ibid.

[838] Ibid; p. 250.

These were the last moments of his resistance. The defeat of Abd al-Kader was the result both of the waning resistance in Algeria and the now determined hostility of the Moroccan Sultan who felt personally threatened by the sort of popular enthusiasm the Emir could stir up.[839] More importantly, following the treaty agreed in the wake of the Battle of Isly, the Moroccan sultan was now forced to abide by the conditions of the conquering power.[840] The 4th article of the treaty stipulated that:

"Hadj Abd al Kader is placed beyond the pale of the law throughout the entire extent of the empire of Morocco, as well as in Algeria. He will, consequently, be pursued by the main force, by the French on the territory of Algeria, and by the Moroccans on their own territory, till he is expelled therefrom, or falls into the power of one or other nation. In the event of Abd al Kader falling into the hands of the French troops, the Government of his Majesty the King of the French engages itself to treat him with respect and generosity. In the event of his falling into the hands of the Moorish troops, his Majesty the Emperor of Morocco engages himself to restrict his abode, for the future, to one of the towns on the western coast of his empire, until the two Governments shall have concerted such measures as will prevent the possibility of his resuming arms, and troubling the tranquillity of Algeria and Morocco."[841]

The days of fraternity, of holy sympathy, were now truly gone. Mouley Abderahman saw himself daily surrounded with fresh difficulties as the French Government hourly demanded the literal execution of its treaty.[842] Rumours circulating in Morocco that Abd al-Kader intended to carve out a state for himself in the Rif and to usurp the sultanate were used to justify the Moroccan authorities' cooperation with the French in hunting him down.[843]

When, in July 1846, Abd al-Kader and his men once again withdrew into Moroccan territory, they were attacked by the Moroccan army.[844] The Algerians won the day, but a number of Algerian refugees in and around Fes were massacred. Abd al-Kader's faithful *khalifa*, Bu Hamidi, who was at court negotiating, died mysteriously, and it is assumed that he had been poisoned.[845] The emir was forced to move to the left bank of the Mulouya only to find himself pursued by the Moroccan troops, and the forces of General La Morcière awaiting him on the right bank of the river.[846]

Abd al Kader at length received the following imperial mandate:

---

[839] M. Morsy: *North Africa*; op cit; p. 143.
[840] C.H. Churchill: *The Life of Abd Al Kader*, op cit, p. 256.
[841] Ibid.
[842] Ibid, p. 257.
[843] J.M. Abun-Nasr: *A History of the Maghrib*, op cit, p. 247.
[844] M. Morsy: *North Africa*; op cit; p. 143.
[845] Ibid.
[846] J.M. Abun-Nasr: *A History of the Maghrib*, op cit, p. 247.

"Abd al Kader must either surrender himself in person to Sultan Abderahman, or return to the Algerian desert. In case of refusal or delay, the imperial armies will march against him."

The last link was thus broken between him and his only hope. He stood at bay, alone.[847]

Calmly he realised he had nowhere else to go, and now he could no longer rely on his brothers, whilst the faithful, long-tried, and devoted Ben Salem was a voluntary prisoner in the French camp.[848] His whole available force barely amounted to 2,000 men, but among these there were 1,200 horsemen, the flower of the Algerian cavalry. Most of these men, also, had been his inseparable companions, who shared in all his hardships and dangers throughout the whole of his career.[849] Then there took place the final blow: Bou Ma'za's surrender in April 1847, together with the strengthening of the French position on the frontier, made the emir's return to Algeria very difficult.[850] At the same time, the other great leader, Hadj Ahmed, to the east, had been reduced to a fugitive, fighting more or less alone, riding from one hostile region to the other, the French closing down on him.

Now Abd al-Kader had no other place to turn to, hounded from all sides. Moved by the plight of his followers, who included the wounded, women and children, a harsh winter making their plight even worse, he decided to negotiate honourable conditions for surrender.[851] On 23 December 1847, terms were agreed between Abd al-Kader and the French general, Lamoricière. The Governor of Algeria, the Duke of Aumale, son of the King of France, pledged his word that Abd al-Kader would not be made prisoner but would be allowed to go into exile to a Muslim land.[852]

The poignancy of these final moments of Abd al-Kader's resistance is caught in the following extracts by Churchill:

> Towards the end of the third week of December 1847, on a very rainy day, leaving his Deira in momentary security, Abd Al-Kader now turned towards the hills of the Beni Snassen a tribe which yet adhered to him in part. His indomitable cavalry followed in anxious silence, suffering, wearied, and exhausted. The rain fell in torrents. Heavy and conflicting thoughts preyed on the mind of the wandering chief. Though the French were seen in the distance, occupying the principal pass of the Kerbous, there were yet narrow defiles through which he could emerge into the Sahara. He might yet try his fortunes. But to what end? he thought despairingly. How was he to persevere in the struggle? What force had he

---

[847] C.H. Churchill: *The Life of Abd Al Kader*, op cit, p. 257.
[848] Ibid, p. 258.
[849] Ibid.
[850] J.M. Abun-Nasr: *A History of the Maghrib*, op cit, p. 246.
[851] M. Morsy: *North Africa*; op cit; p. 143.
[852] Ibid.

at his command? On what assistance could he calculate? Then his thoughts reverted to his aged mother, his wife and children, his helpless followers, who were within three hours of the French camp, and might probably enter it before long, as prisoners of war. In no extremity had Abd al Kader ever found himself so hopelessly pressed. He felt the crisis of his fate had come. What he meant to determine, he knew he must determine quickly.

He sounded a halt. He ordered his men to close up. When they had surrounded him, he thus commenced a conference which he had that moment resolved to open:

"Do you remember the oath you took at Medea eight years ago, at the renewal of the war," he said "the oath that you would never forsake or abandon me, whatever might be your dangers or sufferings?"

"We all remember it, and are ready still to adhere to it."

"That oath," pursued Abd al Kader, "I have ever considered to be binding on me towards you, as well as on you towards me. It is this feeling alone which has made me persevere in our struggle up to this hour, even against hope. I was resolved that no Muslim, of whatever rank or degree, should ever be able to accuse me of binding you to any engagement which I on my part was not equally prepared to fulfil; or to say that I had not done all in my power to insure the triumph of the cause of God. If you think I can yet do anything, tell me. If not, I ask you to release me from the oath I made you mentally, when I solemnly demanded yours."

"We all bear witness before God, that you have done all that it was in your power to do for His cause. At the day of judgment God will do you justice."

'If that is your opinion, we have now only three courses open before us either to return for the Deira, and with it be prepared to encounter every obstacle; or to seek out a path for ourselves into the Sahara, in which case, the women, children, and wounded would not be able to follow us, and must fall into the hands of the enemy; or, lastly, to submit."

"Perish women and children, both ours and yours, so long as you are safe and able to renew the battles of God. You are our head, our Sultan; fight or surrender, as you will, we will follow you wherever you choose to lead."

Abd al Kader paused for a few moments, and then with deep emotion:

"Believe me, the struggle is over. Let us be resigned. God is witness that we have fought as long as we have been able.

'Sultan,' was the universal reply, 'let your will be done.'

The rain was still falling so incessantly that it was impossible for Abd al Kader to write down his demands. Taking a piece of paper, he affixed his seal to it, and immediately dispatched it with two horsemen, who were commissioned to show the seal to the French General, as a sign of authorisation on his part for demands which they were to make in his name verbally.

During the night of the 21st December, General Lamoriciere had been informed both of the arrival of the Deira within the French frontier, and of the direction which Abd al Kader and his little force had taken. To the Deira he at once sent assurances of safety. The prize was important. But the concentration of any amount of men against the camp of Abd al Kader would have been of little permanent avail, if the redoubtable chief himself were yet at large. Without a moment's delay, therefore, Lamoriciere started in his pursuit, at the head of a small column of infantry and cavalry.

He had scarcely marched three hours when he was unexpectedly joined by Ben Khouia, a lieutenant of his Arab Spahis, accompanied by the two emissaries of Abd al Kader. The latter showed him their master's seal and stated his demands. Lamoriciere was overjoyed. He granted everything. But, as in the case of Abd al Kader, the rain prevented him from stating his consent in writing, and his seal was not in his possession. In this emergency he gave his sword, and the seal of Commandant Bazaine, to the emissaries, to be presented to Abd al Kader in token of the acceptance of his conditions.'[853]

After receiving the pledge of the Duc d'Aumale, the king's son and Bugeaud's successor as governor-general, that he would be given a safe passage either to Alexandria or Acre in Palestine, on the 25th December, 1847, Abd al Kader, his family and followers, embarked in the Asmodeus frigate for Toulon.[854] All his personal effects, his baggage, his tents, his horses, mules, and camels, had previously been sold by the French authorities for 6,000 francs.[855] But even this little sum was afterwards only given to him in instalments, and even then the manner in which each instalment was disbursed was object of strict investigation.[856] General Lamoriciere accompanied him on board, and generously made him a present of 4,000 francs. Abd al Kader, in return, gave him his sword.[857] But due to public pressure the French government kept him in confinement in France until 1852, when Napoleon III had him released. He first resided in Bursa, in Turkey, and then, following the earthquake which largely destroyed the city, he settled in Damascus where some of his descendants still lived.[858]

Thus with the surrender of Abd al-Kader in 1847, the capture of Bu Ma'za the same year and the surrender of Hajj Ahmed Bey the following year, ended the initial phase of Algerian resistance.[859] French victory had only been obtained at

---

[853] C.H. Churchill: *The Life of Abd Al Kader*, op cit, pp. 262-6.
[854] J.M. Abun-Nasr: *A History of the Maghrib*, op cit, p. 247.
[855] C.H. Churchill: *The Life of Abd Al Kader*, op cit, p. 270.
[856] Ibid.
[857] Ibid.
[858] J.M. Abun-Nasr: *A History of the Maghrib*, op cit, p. 247.
[859] M. Morsy: *North Africa*; op cit; p. 143.

the expense of a long war and continuous military efforts, in 1846 the army in Algeria totalling 108 000 men, a third of the total armed forces.[860] The manner in which the operations were carried out destroyed opposition, but also created a new and permanent rancour.[861] Even before the early resisters had surrendered, new opposition groups had appeared. In this period, the French had acquired the reputation of tyranny, injustice, and bad faith, a reputation that would persist.[862] Bad faith was all the more deeply resented because it involved religious betrayal as when mosques were converted into churches.[863]

---

[860] Ibid.
[861] Ibid.
[862] Ibid.
[863] Ibid.

Six

ALGERIAN RESILIENCE
(1848-1871)

He was buried next morning with no kind of ceremony, and I followed him to the grave alone. It is well for him that he is at peace! His spirit was too gentle to bear the sight of all this cruelty and wretchedness. One must case one's heart in triple brass to bear existence here at all. (Clemens Lamping writing on the suicide of his friend.)[864]

1. Resistance in the North

The Arab carries nothing but his rifle, his cartridges, and a knife to cut off your head... They flee, they attack with equal speed and fury; we are always at a disadvantage. We wage a war that brings us no glory, and which in the long run is as costly as the battle of Austerlitz.' (A French officer)[865]
The courage of the Kabyle enemy and the great skills they lay ambushes. They are serpents, who whilst crawling through the undergrowth, from one rock to the other, without being seen until they reach our men, and then fire without missing. We see the smoke but the shooter is invisible. (Colonel Montagnac)[866]

Hadj Ahmed paid dearly for his defence of his country, his faith and culture, and refusing compromise and half solutions.[867] The French, instead of offering him exile to a Muslim country as they had promised him, held him in guarded residence.[868] Before then, in the last few months of his struggle, in 1848, a year after Abd al-Kader's surrender, Hadj Ahmed was an old and sick man, no longer even able to ride on horseback. Most of his men and all his private papers had fallen into French hands.[869] He negotiated honourable conditions of surrender with the French commander of Batna. He was first taken to Constantine where he saw his empty and ruined palace, then to Algiers.[870] In 1850 he died poisoned.[871]

---

[864] Clemens Lamping: *The French in Algiers. Soldiers of the Foreign Legion; Prisoners of Abd el Kader;* tr. from German and French by Lady Duff Gordon, London; 1855; p. 29.
[865] In W. Blunt: *Desert Hawk;* op cit, p. 198.
[866] De Montagnac: *Lettres d'un soldat;* Librairie Plon Paris; 1885; p. 100.
[867] A. Temimi: Le Beylik de Constantine; op cit; p. 205.
[868] Ibid.
[869] M. Morsy: *North Africa;* op cit; p. 137.
[870] Ibid; p. 138.
[871] A. Temimi: Le Beylik de Constantine; op cit; p. 205.

Modern writers, Morsy notes, have on the whole failed to acknowledge Hajj Ahmed's great role in the Algerian resistance.[872] In fact, it was not just him, but the whole story of Algerian resistance to colonisation and its true scale that have been passed in great silence. With the exception of Emir Abd al Kader (whom Western opinion has eulogised, not because of his role in the Algerian resistance, but because of his subsequent protection of Christians in Damascus after his exile there,) this page of Algerian history remains vastly ignored. The French and other Westerners are not to blame for this. Responsibility rests squarely with the Algerians, who have miserably failed to bring to knowledge the great pages of their history. Much worse, whenever dealing with their history, they follow the colonial method: they pick on the negative aspects of their own and their history (which are unavoidable in any nation's history,) and then focus all attention on them. They, especially some leading individuals and media sold out to France, also conceal the crimes of their colonial masters, and exaggerate the contribution of the one or two Frenchmen who had been less inhuman to their people. In words, the Algerians dealing with their colonial history, as a rule (as there are exceptions) is one of the most pathetic, if not the most pathetic, in the world, that makes one sick.

By the time of Hadj Ahmed's and Abd al Kader's defeats (in 1847-8), France had slain a large portion of the Algerian population, and had thoroughly devastated the country from one end to the other, and yet:

> In all these years of miserable guerrilla warfare, in which such well-known commanders as Bugeaud, Pelissier, Canrobert, St. Arnaud, MacMahon, and many more, learned their first demoralizing lessons in warfare [says Lane Poole,] the only people who excite our interest and admiration are the Arab tribes. That they were unwise in resisting the inevitable is indisputable; but it is no less certain that they resisted with splendid valour and indomitable perseverance. Again and again they defeated the superior forces of France in the open field, wrested strong cities from the enemy, and even threatened to extinguish the authority of the alien in Algiers for ever.[873]

Indeed, in contrast to Algerian valour, the proud recollections of the French generals of their deeds makes whoever sifts through their memoirs ask themselves one thing only: how on earth did Algerians survive? Let's make the briefest intrusion into a couple of such French glorious pages:

---

[872] M. Morsy: *North Africa*; op cit; p. 138.
[873] S. Lane Poole: *Barbary Corsairs*; op cit; p. 304.

Some Deeds of Saint Arnaud:

General Saint Arnaud led one of the largest French contingents from one part of the country to the other in this inexhaustible fight. We begin with him in Blida in September 1848.

'I am leading another operation this evening to chastise thieves and bad heads of some tribes: I know the Arabs: hit them hard first and explain later.'[874]

Months later he is in Kabylia. He writes to his brother from his bivouac on 16 May 1849:

'I have made a rude visit to the Beni Seliman: I have slain thirty of their men, and burnt their village.[875]

'I burn myself in Kabylie,' he notes in frustration. 'I burn myself not from the sun but from the degenerate Kabyle fire, because their country is a fortress that fifteen men could defend against an army.'[876] Then, in a letter dated 29 Oct 1849 'we have killed the pseudo Bou Ma'za in Kabylia but three more Bou Ma'za have risen, all of them preaching the holy war.'[877] So, he keeps chastising the Kabyles.

In May 1850, he is further south, in the Nemenchas, writing to that same brother from Ain M'Toussa: 'I have descended on the Nemenchas as they were fleeing; I have killed twenty good horsemen and a sheikh, and taken from them 15,000 sheep, 400 camels, and 75,000 francs. They will pay all costs of my operations and for a fort in Khenchela. I hope they (the government) will be happy in Algiers and Paris.[878]

(He had left Kabylia a while before, but fighting had been raging there.) He is extremely saddened at the news he received on the 3rd of June, 1850: the death of a high officer and good friend of his: 'I have bitterly mourned that dear friend's death however glorious. To reach so high, to lead well, and to die from the bullet of an obscure Kabyle. It would have been much less painful had he been killed in Russia or in England, I would have had fewer regrets.'[879]

Then in the same letter: when I wrote to you yesterday at five pm, 'I did not know that a few hours later the oasis of Oueldja would have ceased to exist.' They had killed a French soldier and wounded another. 'I invested the place at midnight then at 3.30 in the morning I struck; we entered the town, and at 5 am, Oueldja was under my total control; we set all dwellings on fire... corpses on the ground; I expel the women and children to the next oasis to teach the Arabs a lesson. Oueldja no longer exists.'[880]

---

[874] St Arnaud: Lettres de St Arnaud; 2 vols; Michel Levy; Paris; 1855; vol 2; p. 186.
[875] Ibid; p. 203.
[876] Ibid; p. 206.
[877] Ibid; p. 224.
[878] Ibid; p. 278.
[879] Ibid; p. 286.
[880] Ibid.

He is in Lesser Kabylia in the late spring of 1851, and this time writing to his wife:
9 and 10 May 1851:

'I am going to descend on the Djidjelli-Bougie sector and I am going to hit them hard. The Kabyles are going to try hard to defend their homes which I am going to set on fire. The troops cannot wait.' P.s. My men have just left, and now I can see the villages burning.'[881]

Days later on 15 May (1851) he writes to his brother from Djidjelli (Jijel):

'From Mila to Djidjelli, everywhere I found the Kabyles in rebellion. They attack us from all sides. Everywhere I pass I burn every village I come across. From 12 till 15 June, I fought every day from 5 in the morning until evening, hill by hill. I only took a break at al Aroussa to rest my men and to spread terror around me.'[882] On the 13th (of May) things were 'extremely difficult and costly for us the Kabyles having penetrated our lines. I was told it would be a promenade, the whole country is in a boiling mood; between Bougie and Setif, the Beni Seliman, whom I chastised two years earlier are in rebellion again; Bejaia has been attacked, and Bou Baghla (the leader of the latest rising) is leading 6,000 Kabyles.'[883] 'I have to unblock Djidjelli, then move onto Collo (further east towards Bone).

On 25 May, he tells his brother 'of the greatest campaign ever undertaken in Africa' around Djidjelli was 'the hardest and most beautiful.'[884] It have been fighting every day from day break till dark, 'fighting every square metre' of space with the tribesmen. 'I have left behind me a vast trail of fire. All the villages have been burnt down, about 200 of them. All the gardens have been destroyed; all orchards; all olive trees cut down.' I rested my men on the 17 and 18 May, then on the 19th, I began dealing with the tribes south of Djidjelli.'[885]

Then on the 20th, he noted the weakness in Algerian tactics, and liaised with General Bosquet who was also fighting nearby. Whilst the latter made a move that confused the local Algerian fighters, Saint Arnaud sent his elite forces to difficult terrain, and there deployed the weapon that had constantly decimated the Algerians: artillery barrage followed by bayonet charges. There he cut off the locals' retreat and took the upper hand, decimating their ranks.[886]

That was only for a while, for Djidjelli and its environs whether west towards Bejaia, or east towards Skikda, or south towards Mila and Constantine would soon come forth again with more fighters and fighting. General Randon, his successor, would have to fight time after time in that region in subsequent years.[887]

---

[881] Ibid; p. 325.
[882] Ibid; p. 326.
[883] Ibid; p. 328.
[884] Ibid; p. 331.
[885] Ibid.
[886] Ibid; p. 332.
[887] A. Rastoul: *Le Marechal Randon; D'apres ses Memoirs et Documents Inedits*; Firmin Didot; Paris; 1890.

Saint Arnaud is on his way to Collo, but he has, first, to fight the Beni Habibi, east of Djidjelli. Writing on 11 June 1851 to his wife, he speaks of the operation which involved not just he and his men, but also other generals and their armies. The French sought to catch the Algerian fighters in enveloping operations, and in large measure succeeded, for wherever the locals sought a way out or sanctuary, one army was waiting for them with its ever much superior fire power. In the meantime, everywhere their villages and crops were ablaze. 'I burnt down their superb villages, and now we are cutting down the olive trees,' Saint Arnaud gloats.[888] But only a few kilometres towards the sea, at al Kennar, east of Djidjelli, the locals inflicted serious loss to his forces.[889] His reaction was, understandably, to lay waste everything he came across, informing his wife on 28 June 1851: 'I have just received the mail from France. Everyone is happy with my work. The Prince, the Minister everyone is loading me with congratulations. I have been promoted to the rank of General of Division.'[890]

He turns his attention to Collo on the road to Philipeville (Skikda). He writes on 5 July (1851):
'I have continued my works, and success belongs to me. I have undertaken in Africa one of the hardest and longest expeditions ever undertaken. I will be General of Division. How great it is to become one.'[891]
Then on 10 July he announces proudly to his brother: 'I am sending you a copy of the letter signed by the president. This letter says I am general of Division; there it is dear brother: the third star. Now, what are they going to give me.'[892]
Then, again on 23 July 1851, writing to his brother: 'You know now I am general of division. I have received my diploma. Here it is now my objective fulfilled, my career accomplished. I have reached the highest rank in the army... I rest therefore, dear brother, this rank the result of hard and blessed labour.'[893]

Randon, Camou, and other Generals Devastate Greater Kabylia (mid 1850s onwards):

Bou Baghla led the rising in 1851. In spite of the French onslaught that left neither dwellings standing, nor humans or beast alive, nor trees on the ground, he was still able to keep alive the spirit of resistance amongst the tribes even after his death in 1854.[894] A decade earlier, Bugeaud, had tried to subdue the region by an atrocious war of devastation and wanton cruelty, and yet, rising after rising

---

[888] St Arnaud: Lettres de St Arnaud; 2 vols; Michel Levy; Paris; 1855; vol 2; p. 341.
[889] Ibid; p. 342.
[890] Ibid; p. 345.
[891] Ibid; p. 346.
[892] Ibid; p. 347.
[893] Ibid; p. 349.
[894] J.M. Abun-Nasr: *A History of the Maghrib*, op cit, p. 251.

and total insecurity (for the French) have remained the outcome.[895] The war, now nearly 25 years, descended into interminable acts of brutality.[896]

> The conquest had been carried out by men who in acting against the Algerian enemy committed the worst excesses, which, as a rule, were ignored by their commanders. This is the case, of course, when such commanders themselves did not give the orders for such excesses to be committed [admits Ageron]. Whilst the conquest proved more costly in human lives than any other colonial conquest, from the point of view of the conquered the consequences were even worse. Algeria was devastated, and its economy ruined by raids which were both systematic and continuous, with the raiders pillaging stores of grain, carrying off livestock and felling trees. Recurrent epidemics decimated an undernourished population, whilst the cultural damage was equally bad, and its consequences were even longer-lasting.[897]

It is impossible to depict all the French devastation of Kabylia. Randon's memoirs of the 1850s are crammed with accounts of his and other French generals campaigning in this region. Only brief mentions are made here.

On 17 June 1854, different French army corps led by Generals Camou and Mac Mahon fought Kabyle tribes. Camou fought the Beni Menguellet, Beni Yenni, Beni Aissi and the Beni Raten.[898] Mac Mahon came to blows with the Beni Thourag, the Illilten, the Beni Hidjer. In the wake of bitter fighting Camou captured Taourirt and two other villages, whilst Mac Mahon captured the villages of the Beni Thourag. All were burnt down.[899] On 18 and 19th June, taking advantage of early morning thick fog, the Kabyles reinforced their positions. At sunrise, fighting resumed even more fierce than before. French artillery had reason of Kabyle courage; Algerian fighters refusing to give ground, dying on the spot.[900] Victorious, the French, as per usual, set alight all villages, and cut down the orchards. As they withdrew, surviving Kabyle troops fell on them; the French prevailed but at high cost.[901]

In 1856 it was Generals Gastu and Yusuf, who descended on the region, and again, there took place the same bitter fighting, accompanied by widespread destruction of much that had survived previous encounters.[902] Then General Chapuis descended on the Beni Raten: 'never had their land been so despoiled by any invader,' remarks Randon in his memoirs.[903]

---

[895] P. Gaffarel: *Lectures Geographiques et Historiques sur l'Algerie et les Colonies Francaises*; Garniers Freres; Paris; 1886; p. 43.

[896] C.R. Ageron: *Modern Algeria*, op cit, p. 21.

[897] Ibid.

[898] A. Rastoul: *Le Marechal Randon; D'apres ses Memoirs et Documents Inedits*; Firmin Didot; Paris; 1890; 132.

[899] Ibid.

[900] Ibid.

[901] Ibid.

[902] Ibid; p. 146.

[903] Ibid; p. 147.

In 1857, the French decided to finish with the Kabyle uprisings. Three armies led by Mac Mahon, Yusuf, and Renault crushed everything in their path. The military campaign is described at great length by Randon.[904] He emphasises French gallantry, and also Algerian determination, fighting to the last, whilst all around them their land was set ablaze, and all that they had planted, generations of labour, was now cut down.[905] The Ait Iraten were particularly hit, ruined by fighting and war indemnities.

These are the lines from a Kabyle poem retained in French:

Le Français , quand il se met en marche,

roule comme les flots d'une rivière;

il a fait avancer de nombreux bataillons,

des zouaves plus encore que des autres;

il s'est abattu sur nous,

comme la glace sur la neige lorsqu'elle couvre et durcit la terre.

...

Comprenez, ô vous qui savez comprendre.

L'Alger des Zaouas est tombé.

Ce qui arrive aux Aït-Iraten ne s'est pas vu depuis le commencement du monde.[906]

Which translates:

The Frenchman, when he marches,

Rolls like the flows of a river;

He moves forward many batallions;

Of Zouaves more than others;

He fell on us,

Like ice on snow, when it covers and hardens the land.

...

Understand oh you who can,

Algiers of the Zaouas has fallen.

What happened to the Ait Iraten has not been seen since the world began.

The Bani Iraten defeated, crushed, other tribes geared themselves for the fight. They, Randon says, 'gathered their men,' and 'the most fanatical men of Algeria rushed to support,' and all agreed to stand at the village of Isheriden.[907] The battle of Isheriden took place on 24 June 1857.

> Marshal Mac Mahon raised his camp at five in the morning. The Brigade of Bourbaki leading the march, the army advanced on a plateau nine hundred metres from the enemy. The position occupied by the Kabyles was

---

[904] Ibid; 160 ff.
[905] Ibid; 162.
[906] Ibid; 172-173.
[907] Ibid;170.

formidable. At the foot of mount Isheriden and to the right was a profound ravine seeming un-crossable. To the left the ground was broken and dominated by two hills with steep slopes, one ending on a rock, the other by a path leading to the village. Here the Kabyles had built extremely strong defences, which were very difficult to breach, and which, moreover, could help the defenders should they wish to retreat. Then, above the first line of defence the Kabyles had set up further systems that could fire at will at the attackers. All these defences were reinforced with heavy rocks, large tree trunks, doors, and 4,000 of the bravest men of Kabylia.

The attack began with intense French artillery fire together with Congreve missiles and every shell from every engine available, mercilessly pounding the defenders. When it was felt only a few of them had survived, the first brigade was thrown forth with immense resolution. However just about a hundred metres from the defences it was broken by intense fire. The Kabyles had only withdrawn to more secure spots during artillery fire, but now, back in force, they were sweeping the French with fire, shouting cries of war. The French fought very hard to keep to their ground.

Just then, coming to the rescue was a regiment of the Foreign Legion which attacked the defenders from the side, seeking to outflank them on the right. Now the Kabyles were threatened with envelopment. The fire from both sides was intense but the foreign elements managed to reach the top at times being exposed, at others protected by the ground. After a while they reached the defenders, and there took place a terrific hand to hand combat. The fighting took its toll on both sides. The foreign regiments (highly trained and men whose trade was to fight) managed to have the upper hand. Now the Kabyles realising what was happening to their right slowed their fire, which was used by Zouav units to launch themselves forward, and there followed yet another hand to hand fierce fight with yatagans and bayonets. Taking the upper hand, both Zouavs and Foreign Legion hurled themselves towards Icheriden, which they managed in the end to capture. The enemy, now surrounded from all sides, still managed to retire to the mountain on its only line of retreat towards the valley of Beni Yenni and the path which went from Icheriden to Ageumoun Izen. Even in their retreat, the Kabyles still managed to inflict losses on the exposed French troops until these could at last reach safe entrenchments.[908]

---

[908] Ibid; 170-172.

*****
Algerian Valour

When one reads through the French officers' accounts, one realises that all parts of the country, from north to south, and east to west, competed between each other in valour alone. One can pick many accounts by the French and their allies to highlight this. The Englishman Dawson Borrer who was fighting with the French in Greater Kabylia tells us this:

> There still remained one more village at hand to be stormed; it was that one mentioned as occupying so commanding a position. It being out of the question for the cavalry to mount the height, and the attempt being moreover perfectly unnecessary, they remained where they were, and three small columns of infantry, composed of the Zouaves, the Chasseurs d'Orleans, and the "Tirailleurs Indigenes," were led to the attack. The defence made here was more obstinate than in the former villages; for this was the forlorn hope of the enemy; this was the point whither the fugitives had fled, and the only place of refuge left for their wives and families. Congreves hissed through the air, and burst over the doomed stronghold, doing considerable execution; yet did the defenders pour down from the terraces of their houses an incessant fire upon the ascending troops, who advanced, however, with the utmost intrepidity, throwing forward clouds of skirmishers, firing in return as best they could, and toiling onward perseveringly towards the summit, though frequently obliged to use both hands and knees in their progress. One Zouave, whom I happened to be remarking, zealously labouring upwards to the attack, received a ball, apparently in his head; for, leaping from the ground, he fell over backwards, and made a series of somersaults down the ascent into a ravine below.

> Finding their enemies rapidly gaining the height, and that one detachment was upon the point of taking them in the flank, the Kabailes might now be seen retreating in despair from the village, turning and firing at intervals as they retired to the heights beyond. Two or three of the soldiers, mounting to this attack, fell dead struck by no ball. Desperate exertion and intense heat had killed them. The summit once attained, however, the lust of plunder gave strength to the troops; and dashing over the walls and through the gateways, the scenes which had taken place in the villages below were again acted over, but with increased attendant horrors; for was it not the refuge of the women and the aged? Ravished, murdered, burnt, hardly a child escaped to tell the tale. A few of the women fled to the ravines around the village; but troops swept the brushwood; and the stripped and mangled bodies of females might there be seen.

> An instance of feminine daring worthy of record was reported to have taken place in this village. A soldier entering a house for plunder found there a Kabyle; rushing on to cut him down, a woman came forth, and shot the soldier dead with a pistol. A curious instance of sang-froid on the part of an aged woman, during these scenes of blood, is also remarkable. Massacring, burning, and plundering going on around her, she still sat coolly in her dwelling hard at work, making cous-coussou, and paying no sort of attention to anything but her seething-pot. Most fortunately for this old hag, an officer was the first who came upon her; and, struck with her extraordinary conduct, made prisoner of her as a curiosity; yet was she very savage at being disturbed during her culinary operations; and it required considerable effort to tear her from her pots and pans to save her life. Some Israelite artisans, workers in silver and in iron, trusting to their black turbans and their unwarlike character for mercy, fled not upon the taking of

this village. It was false confidence; for the soldiers, neither distinguishing nor wishing to distinguish them from Moslems, fell upon and slew them.[909]

*****
Why did the French officers do what they did?

True, the French were serving 'civilisation,' their country, and their faith, Christianity, when they slew en masse the 'barbaric Algerians.'

However, there were also less 'noble' objectives:

In 1854, Colonel Desvaux, who was dreaming of his second star, attacked Tuggurt but was delayed, and was beaten to the objective by Commandant Marmier who himself was dreaming of his fifth promotion. Tuggurt was entirely sacked. Marmier got his fifth promotion, and Desvaux, too, got his two stars.[910]

In the meantime, Marshal Randon who had problems to find sleep in front of St Arnaud's rise to fame, went in his own way to get the same gratifications and launched himself on Kabylia in 1857, burning all that was left to burn.[911] It was during that expedition that someone came to inform General Yusuf that another tribe had arrived to make its submission. 'Not yet,' answered Yusuf. 'Wait a little. There is to our left that brave colonel who had got nothing yet. Let's leave him that tribe to punish, and once his fame and promotion are secure, then we will grant the *aman* (security following submission.)[912]

*****

2. Resistance in the South

The inhabitants of the Za'atcha oasis to the south-west of Biskra, led by a religious scholar, called Bu Ziane, rose against the French in 1848.[913] On 7 October 1849, General Herbillon, commander of the province of Constantine, and four thousand French and indigenous soldiers arrived before Za'atcha with enough munitions and supplies for a very long operation.[914] Soon other contingents poured in until eight thousand men were gathered in front of the Oasis, blockading it from all sides. In earnest in order to starve the place and undermine the resolve of the population, Herbillon ordered the date palm trees to be cut down.[915] In the desert landscape, one imagines the scale or the effects of destruction, not just in terms of cutting down food supplies, but in ecological and aesthetical terms.

---

[909] Dawson Borrer: *Narrative of a campaign against the Kabailes of Algeria;* Spottiswoode and Shaw, London, 1848; pp. 109-111.
[910] Le Comte d'Herisson: *La Chasse a l'Homme, Guerre d'Algerie*; Paul Ollendorff; Paris; 1891; p. 347.
[911] Ibid.
[912] Ibid.
[913] J.M. Abun-Nasr: *A History of the Maghrib*, op cit, p. 251.
[914] A bibliographical notice devoted to General Herbillon is found in R. Peyronnet: *Livre d'or des Affaires Indigenes, 1830-1930,* Algiers, Soubiron, 1930, 2; pp. 142-4.
[915] J.A. Clancy Smith: *Rebel and Saint,* University of California Press; 1994, p. 114.

The siege understandably had its toll on the place, and as it dragged on, an outbreak of cholera, introduced by battalions arriving from other parts, decimated, first, the army, claiming hundreds of lives.[916] There remained great numbers of soldiers, though, and the siege went on, its effects on the Algerians worsening with time, especially through the Winter months, which can be arduous especially for a place deprived of supplies, and under constant heavy bombardment. This did not break the resolve of the defenders, including women, during the fifty two day ordeal.[917] Not only did the latter exhort their men to fight bravely, as was the custom in the Sahara, they also took up arms and fought alongside them.[918] Once more Algerian defenders showed the same qualities of good organisation and indifference to death, especially in the many sorties they effected against the besiegers.[919] Soon, though, cholera caught up with the defenders as well, and due to the siege conditions and bombardment the effects were much worse than on the French.[920] The French had also poisoned much of the water supply network feeding the Algerians, whose ordeal was made worse by sharpshooters and artillery fire. Here, as on other fighting grounds there become obvious the huge discrepancy in war technology. The French were armed with the more sophisticated and accurate 'carabine a tige,' a bolt action rifle; the Algerian defenders only used antiquated muskets of uncertain quality.[921] Once the oasis was entirely encircled and cut off from the rest, its doom became certain.[922] Now the moment of the final assault had arrived.

The Assault on the Za'atcha. In the picture we capture the sight of cut palm trees. Only survived those within the walls.

[916] Ibid, p. 115.
[917] Ibid.
[918] Ibid, p. 116.
[919] Ibid, p. 115.
[920] Ibid, p. 116.
[921] Ibid.
[922] AMG, Algerie 13; Herbillon: Relation, 89; Perret: Recis 2; 21-2; and Bocher: Le Siege: 87-9.

According to a participant:

> On 25 November 1849, the French launched the assault at seven in the morning. It was led by the chasseurs and the Zouaves... After making a breach in the defence, they hurled themselves through it, and after fierce fight found themselves in the city centre. ... Now there remained the task of fighting for each square metre with Arabs who were ready to sell dearly their skin.. In the midst of loud sounds of war, the French tried to reach the roofs of the houses. They were met by intense fire from all sides, from behind walls, through the small apertures, windows, and even through the flooring from beneath them. The first wave of attackers was annihilated; those who followed rushed with open bayonets against the defenders. A terrible carnage followed where no quarter was given and no distinction made between civilian or fighter... The leader of the uprising, Bu Ziane was still leading the fight from his house in the town centre, where he had managed to retreat with his family and a group of close followers to the gate of the Za'atcha. Commander Laverande led the assault which was met by thick fire from the defenders. The place, according to the French, was defended fiercely by a group of 'irreductible fanatics.' The Zouaves attempted to carry the place by ascending the neighbouring houses and launching their assault, but were repulsed. A canon was placed in face of the gate about to blow it up, but the defenders blew it instead together with the men serving it. A sac of explosives was brought forth, but the soldiers who volunteered to fire the fuse were killed. A daring officer managed to fire the fuse which caused a formidable explosion bringing the defence wall crumbling. 150 Algerians, men and women were now out of cover in front the attackers. The Zouaves rushed forward without hesitation, and yet again no quarter was shown to the multitude shot and bayonetted to death. An Algerian, with distinguished features, but with wounds in the leg was seen stepping leaning on one of his companions. It was Bu Ziane. He sat in the Arab manner and began to recite his prayers.
> Commander Laverande sought orders from his superior, General Herbillon, who ordered Bu Ziane should be shot. The commander called four Zouavs and ordered them to aim for the heart. Before giving the order Laverande asked Bu Ziane for his final wish or what he wanted to say:
> 'You defeated us. Allah alone is Great. May His will be done.'
> Laverande helped Bu Ziane to rise against the wall. The four Zouavs fired at once. Bu Ziane fell dead.

(It is also accounted that the French troops captured Bu Ziane's mother, wife, his daughter and two young sons, and had them massacred before his eyes before killing him.)[923]

> In other parts of the town [pursues the eye-witness], the soldiers were fighting fiercely every corner; and anywhere their progress was held back, they lit bags of powder and blew up the walls which fell on those inside. Those who did not die at once perished suffocated in the caves where they had sought refuge. The soldiers, thirsting for revenge, entered every house, searched every corner, and took no prisoner, nor did they allow anyone to escape. The Arabs had been surrounded by a circle of fire. None of them got away.'[924]

Bu Ziane's head was severed from his body and was offered as a prize to General Herbillon who had it displayed on the gatepost for all to see.[925] It was not just his head as modern Western narrative tells us, but as contemporary accounts show, it was also his lieutenant's, Si Musa, and Bu Ziane's young son. The town was thoroughly demolished, all its gardens destroyed, hundreds upon hundreds of bodies were uncovered.[926] The French army chose to raze the Oasis to the ground and none was ever allowed to reside there again.

The French, however, as in many, if not most, places, left a message of their passage:

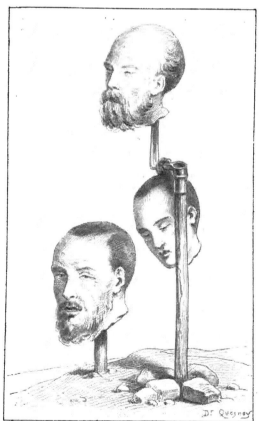

Heads of Bu Zian, his son's, and Si Musa's.
Other than highlighting French barbarism, of course, this sight, it must be reiterated was generalised, systemic, and did not just apply to men but also to women, whose limbs were severed not just to impress or terrorise Algerians but simply out of greed, and utter disregard for Algerian life. We know these things, again, not thanks to modern French or other Western historians, always keen to attribute barbaric acts, including beheadings, to Muslims alone, but thanks to French military officers themselves, whose memoirs are full of such incidents of which they speak proudly.

[923] In J.A. Clancy Smith: *Rebel and Saint*, op cit, p. 116; the text can be found in P. Gaffarell.
[924] Souvenirs de l'Expedition dans les Zibans en 1849; *Revues des Deux Mondes*, 1851.
[925] J.A. Clancy Smith: *Rebel and Saint*, op cit, p. 116.
[926] Ibid.

The fall of Za'atcha had a disastrous impact on surrounding areas, as their livestock, in particular, besides their gardens, were destroyed. Many of the survivors fled Algeria for Tunisia and even to more distant lands, seeking to escape vengeance, disease, and the devastation inflicted on the whole region, where some ten thousand palm trees, the very basis of the economy, were systematically cut down by the French.[927] That same year, 1849, a sheikh called publicly on the people to emigrate to Syria; some three thousand eventually departed for the Ottoman ruled East.[928]

Then the French decided to march on Laghouat.

The French objectives for the capture of Laghouat were thus expressed in the literature of the time. The town did not just have a strategic military value, it was also well situated for other purposes. It was a commercial station of great importance, well positioned on the banks of Wadi Djeddi in the middle of the Algerian desert.[929] Laghouat, also according to the sources then, had an abundance of very high quality waters in an arid surrounding, which, of course, was the difference between life and death. It was the centre of the caravan route which went into every direction, and where Nomad tribes exchanged various products of the land as well as manufactured objects. This to France was essential as Laghouat, in her hands, would be turned into a great market for French manufactured products from whence they could be distributed in the neighbouring countries thanks to the visiting caravans and merchants.[930]

The French excuse for taking the city came in 1852 when the locals rose against the excesses of the *agha* appointed by the French. The leader of the uprising, Muhammad b. 'Abd Allah from the Awlad Sidi al-Sheikh tribe, led his men into battle, again with little means other than the same old weaponry and the enthusiasm of his and his men's.[931] Outnumbered and outgunned, the citizens of Laghouat put up yet another epic fight. The French took the upper hand in December 1852. First, they occupied the town before moving on from there to crush all opposition in the whole region of Suf.[932] Again, accounts of the time speak of very bitter fighting and Algerian resistance from house to house. The French painter and writer, Eugene Fromentin, who visited Laghouat soon after its fall in 1852, wrote:

> Every house bore the remains of the terrible fight. Every stone was as if ripped apart by bullets and canon fire. Men fought in every street, in every

[927] Ibid, p. 117.
[928] C.R. Ageron: L'Emigration des Musulmans Algeriens et l'Exode de Tlemcen (1830-1911), *Annales Economies Societes Cultures* (AESC) 22, 2, 1967, 1047-66.
[929] P. Gaffarel: *Lectures Geographiques et Historiques sur l'Algerie et les Colonies Francaises*; Garniers Freres; Paris; 1886; p. 236-238.
[930] Ibid.
[931] J.M. Abun-Nasr: *A History of the Maghrib*, op cit, p. 251.
[932] Ibid.

garden, in every house. When the time came to bury the Muslim dead, they were so many that in some streets they constituted as if barricades. Muslim corpses were simply dragged on masse, and were thrown anywhere that could be found, in wells principally. One well alone was filled with 256 corpses.[933]

For a long time the city could not be entered because of the stench of death.[934]

When the rising of the Sharaqa (eastern) branch of the Awlad Sidi al-Sheikh tribe occurred in March 1864, this branch of the tribe had accepted French rule, and its chief at the time of the rebellion, Sulaiman b. Hamza, had been appointed by the French shortly before the rebellion.[935] The same Sulaiman b. Hamza himself led his tribesmen into rebellion when his *khuja* (chief assistant) was beaten up in public by officers of the *Bureau Arabe* of Geryville.[936] In April 1864 the Algerians defeated a column of French troops near Jabal 'Amur (Amour), killing the commanding officer and all but three of his men. Subsequently the uprising spread into Flitta territory, the Dahra, and eastern Kabylia.[937] The French reacted as ferociously as they did before, and by the end of the year the uprising had been quelled, but groups of the Sharaqa tribesmen remained un-subdued and continued, when pursued by the French, to take refuge with the Gharaba (western) branch of the tribe.[938]

*****

The Dirty Work

We had caught four Arabs last night, says the French officer. One of the four was guilty of attempt at evasion, and was tried and condemned to death by Yusuf. Towards 4, a picket made of Spahis and an indigenous Brigadier acting as guards and executioners, took the unfortunate man to the site for his execution. He had his hands tied behind his back. He was made to kneel forward. The Brigadier hit with his sword which cut through the man's neck by about an inch and half. The Arab fell, his neck open, blood gushing out, whilst he still repeatedly chanted:

La Ilaha ila Allaah, Mohamed Rasul Allah. (There is no Deity but Allah, and Mohammed is the Prophet of Allah.)

A second blow, then a third, and still his head was not entirely severed. Then the Spahi took the head from the beard and sought to saw it off, but without effect.

'Use a knife!' yelled another indigenous Spahi. Which the brigadier nonchalantly did. Thus was the head finally severed. Justice was accomplished, and Yusuf added yet another exploit

---

[933] P. Gaffarel in H; Alleg et al: *La Guerre d'Algerie*; op cit; 79-80.
[934] Ibid; p. 80.
[935] J.M. Abun-Nasr: *A History of the Maghrib*, op cit, p. 252.
[936] Ibid.
[937] Ibid.
[938] Ibid.

to his account. Then the head rolled down on the ground. A soldier, a Corsican, cut off the ears to receive his rewards, for Yusuf pays for the ears of Muslims that are brought to him.[939]

Yusuf, raised by the Dey of Tunis, pampered even, by him, converted to Catholicism, married a French woman, and served France with a zeal far higher than that of other French officers, that is even if the French had nothing for him other than contempt.

'If the imbecile,' as Montagnac called him, 'of whom, we (the French) want to make a great hero had any notion of our tactics.'[940]

Yusuf fought for the French throughout Algeria. Other than his cruelty, he earned himself a reputation of being a slimy Arab who sought by all means to be accepted by the French, most of whom not only despised him but utterly loathed him as can be found in the accounts of the officers and officials, and not just Montagnac's, Le Comte d'Herisson's most particularly.[941] Yusuf was particularly despised by the German Wagner who marched with the French in their expedition against Constantine.[942] And of course he was extremely hated by the Algerians themselves for not just his cruelty, but most of all for being one of those who caused them some of the worst harm in the destruction of all that they owned. In one razia against the Ouled Nail, he took 25,000 sheep, and 600 camels, which represented the loss of all that sustained the tribe, condemning it to slow death out of want.[943] Yusuf was promoted to the rank of general. Yusuf is never alone. There are many Yusufs to this day.

3. The Uprising of 1870-1

I cannot withhold my sympathy from that magnanimous rebel Sidi Ahmed-el-Mokrani, who led the last fight made by the Berbers for freedom. Too generous to strike at France while she was defending herself against German aggression in 1870, he further gave notice to the Government of his intention to open hostilities before the first shot was fired in 1871. C'etait magnifique mais ce n'aitait pas la guerre (it was magnificent but it was not war), and when El-Mokrani fell after much bloodshed, the ribbon of the Legion of Honour, bestowed on him in the hope of converting a chivalrous enemy into a friend, was found tied to his horse's tail. Some months after my tour in Kabylia I stood beside his grave in the sunlit cemetery of Belcourt. Out of El-Mokrani's heart grows a great tree, a sturdy carob, and, like himself, more easy to break than to bend.[944]

The bloody rebellion that in Algeria followed the withdrawal of the French garrison in 1871, and flickered along the margin of the desert and up and down the length of the Atlas with the uncertain movement of all Arab actions, is already almost forgotten. But El Mokrani lives.[945]

---

[939] Le Comte d'Herisson: *La Chasse a l'Homme, Guerre d'Algerie*; Paul Ollendorff; Paris; 1891; pp. 128-9.

[940] De Montagnac: *Lettres d'un soldat*; Librairie Plon Paris; 1885; p. 84.

[941] Le Comte d'Herisson: *La Chasse a l'Homme*, op cit.

[942] M. Wagner: *The Tricolor*; op cit.

[943] Le Comte d'Herisson: *La Chasse a l'Homme*; op cit; p. 134.

[944] R. Devereux: *Aspects of Algeria*; London; J.M. Dent and Sons; 1912; p. 27.

[945] L. March Phillips: *In the Desert, the Hinterlands of Algiers*; Edward Arnold; London; 1909; p. 11.

Following the call of Sheikh al-Haddad, the Holy War was proclaimed against the French. It is held that 600,000 Algerians (out of a total population of less than four millions) took part in this massive rising.[946] One of its main causes was the mutiny of Spahi regiments refusing to take part in the French war against Germany.[947] It was in January 1871, that the Spahis under French service mutinied in the east of Constantine, and made their junction with the ally tribe of the Hanencha.[948] Together these forces besieged the French stronghold of Souk-Ahras (in the vicinity of modern Tunisia).[949] The uprising was centered in Kabylia, but it quickly spread over an area about 300 km long from the suburbs of Algiers to the heights of Collo in the north east, and southwards as far as the desert.[950] This insurrection was the result of a long preparation by secret cells in a vast network which, according to French official reports, was established from Constantine to as far as Greater Kabylia.[951]

Greater Kabylia was the land of Mohammed al Mokrani, lord of the Medjana, who in March 1871, called for the fight against the French.[952] The Mokrani tribe had already fought against the French when they first landed at Sidid Ferruch and Staoueli.[953] Al Mokrani was a chief who had formerly accepted an office under the French Government, and had been the friend of French officers. Although he was an Algerian patriot, he thought himself bound by those obligations and those ties of friendship to take no advantage of the moment when France was fighting Prussia in Europe.[954] French army units had left Algeria for the European front, but al-Mokrani let that opportunity pass, and only when peace with Germany was declared did he issue a formal defiance, and after an interval of forty-eight hours led his men against the invaders.[955] In a letter to General Augeraud, he reminded him that he continued to serve France whilst she fought Prussia, and did not want to increase her troubles. But now that peace was declared, he was free to act otherwise. To Captain Olivier, he told, 'today, I am getting ready to fight you, let everyone take his gun.'[956] He even offered to conduct the French civilians to places of safety under the protection of his own militia.[957]

The 1870-1871 uprising degenerated into a war of devastation much worse than previous ones. Fighting was fierce alongside the multiple front-lines. This insurrection which stretched from the coast to the southern regions of M'zab,

---

[946] H. Alleg et al: *La Guerre;* op cit; p. 80.
[947] M. Morsy: *North Africa*; op cit; p. 157.
[948] H. Alleg et al: *La Guerre;* op cit; p. 80.
[949] Ibid; p. 81.
[950] J.M. Abun-Nasr: *A History of the Maghrib*, op cit, p. 255.
[951] Statistiques Generales de L'Algerie, 1867-1872; in H. Alleg: *La Guerre;* op cit; p. 81.
[952] Ibid.
[953] A. Rambaud: L'Insurrection Algerienne de 1871; *Extraits de la Nouvelle Revue*; Oct-Nov 1891; p. 11.
[954] L. March Phillips: *In the Desert, the Hinterlands of Algiers*; Edward Arnold; London; 1909; p. 11.
[955] Ibid.
[956] A. Rambaud: L'Insurrection Algerienne de 1871; *Extraits de la Nouvelle Revue*; Oct-Nov 1891; p. 19.
[957] Ibid.

Biskra and Tuggurt had involved 340 military engagements. Each Algerian stronghold had to be captured at great cost in close combat through barricades and bayonet charges; fighting which took place in mountains, oases, steppes, and all sorts of landscape.[958] Despite the bitterness of the fight, the Algerians, unlike their foes, adhered to a strict level of chivalrous conduct (despite a few excesses here and there on the part of some bands). The leaders of the insurrections did all in their power to keep the insurrection within an Islamic framework, a true jihad insists Rambaud, where it obeyed the strict rules of the Qur'an, that is to only kill the fighters and spare the innocent, women, children, and the old, to respect one's word, or ceasefire, and to avoid acts of cruelty.[959] Commander Rinn insists, all leaders of the uprising did their utmost to respect these rules.[960] Everywhere, Rambaud, just as Rinn,[961] make specific observations on how the Algerian fighters warned and guided to safety European settlers when these were under threat. They even equipped them with mules to carry as much as they could and reach points of safety. They always before attacking, in obedience of Islamic rules of warfare, offered their opponents the chance of peaceful and bloodless surrender.[962] Rambaud dwells on the instances of Europeans, including army officers, who fell in insurgents hands and who were kept under protection, some of them kept amongst families, which, however poor, shared all they had with them.[963] In the regions of Dellys, Bordj Menail, in particular, countless European civilians were kept in safety by the same population that was fighting fiercely the French soldiers.[964] It was the same throughout the Algerian territory. And yet these same people who protected Europeans were subsequently condemned to death by French courts.[965]

Unlike their Algerian foes, the French distinguished themselves by their usual war methods. Hundreds of villages that had either escaped, or just been rebuilt after the destruction of the previous phase were set ablaze, and their populations systematically massacred; even greater numbers were displaced en force, and whole regions were emptied of their populations. Expressing European settler's opinion, the local newspaper, *The Seybouse,* insisted:

> Terror must hang over the abodes of these murderers (Algerians). Repression should be so ferocious as it should acquire a sinister status in the memory of these tribes, and that it guarantees security to (European) immigrants.[966]

---

[958] Ibid; p. 54.
[959] Ibid; p. 59.
[960] Ibid.
[961] L. Rinn: *Histoire de l'Insurrection de 1871 en Algerie*; Alger, Librairie Adolphe Jourdan; 1891.
[962] A. Rambaud: L'Insurrection Algerienne de 1871; op cit; p. 59.
[963] Ibid; p. 60.
[964] Ibid.
[965] Ibid.
[966] Seybouse, in H. Alleg: *La Guerre*; op cit; p. 83.

*****

Al Mokrani's Death

Whilst French troops advanced from victory to victory towards Bouira, al Mokrani and his cavalry approached that same spot.[967] On 5 May 1871 the two sides met on the Wadi Suffla. General Gerez saw on the neighbouring hills around 300 cavalry standing by a banner. There was al Mokrani leading an army of about 8,000 men.[968] French fire, including artillery, was met by Algerian resolve. It was during a lull soon after that Al Mokrani was killed. According to an account, when it was time for prayers, he dismounted, did his religious dues, then, soon after, as he was inspecting the ground, a company of Zouavs that had reached a neighbouring height opened fire from a distance of 700 metres. A bullet hit al Mokrani straight between the eyes just giving him time to utter: 'There is no Deity but Allah,' and fall onto the ground.[969] Three of his men rushed to lift him up and were all killed. His body was carried to Ouelaa of the Bani Abbes. He was buried in a grave with no inscriptions.[970] According to another version, realising defeat was unavoidable, al Mokrani dismounted from his horse and led his last charge on foot. He was shot through the forehead.[971]

*****

The surrender at the end of June 1871 of the aged Rahmaniyya chief, Sheikh Haddad and his son and war-chief 'Aziz, opened the way for the subjugation of Kabylia.[972] Bou Mazrag, who led the southern branch of the resistance, was captured in June 1872. The last fighter, Bou-choucha fought on longer than anyone and was captured on 31 March 1874, was condemned to death and executed.[973] In the course of suppressing the uprising the French lost 2,686 men. The loss of Muslim lives was beyond computation. Economically, also, the Algerians were ruined.[974] The settlers insisted that 'the rebels' should be tried as criminals before French courts whose juries were entirely French, and that the economic repression should ensure that the Muslims would no longer have the means to 'rebel again.' There was mass execution of `rebels' and suspects, and considerable numbers, chosen at random, were condemned to deportation abroad.[975] Bou Mazrag was first condemned to death, then to perpetual exile in New Caledonia, where he remained and sought to found a Kabyle colony there.[976] The retribution hit Algerians very hard in other ways. A war indemnity of 36.5 million Francs was imposed on 298 peasant communities; a fine that ruined

---

[967] L. March Phillips: *In the Desert, the Hinterlands of Algiers*; Edward Arnold; London; 1909; p. 11.

[968] Ibid.

[969] J. A. Rambaud l'Insurrection de 1871 in P. Bernard and F Redon: *Histoire, Colonisation, Geographie et Administration de l'Algerie*, Librairie Adolphe Jourdan; Algiers, 1906; p. 74.

[970] Ibid.

[971] L. March Phillips: *In the Desert, the Hinterlands of Algiers*; op cit; p. 11.

[972] J.M. Abun-Nasr: *A History of the Maghrib*, op cit, p. 255.

[973] A. Rambaud: L'Insurrection Algerienne de 1871; op cit; p. 52.

[974] J.M. Abun-Nasr: *A History of the Maghrib*, op cit, p 255.

[975] M. Morsy: *North Africa*; op cit; p. 159.

[976] A. Rambaud: L'Insurrection Algerienne de 1871; *Extraits de la Nouvelle Revue*; Oct-Nov 1891; p. 53.

them.[977] In addition all the lands of the tribes that had taken part in the 'rebellion' were sequestrated by a decree of 31 March 1871 in accordance with the principle of tribal collective responsibility.[978] Alsatian and Lorraine emigrants were settled on 100,000 hectares of sequestrated lands in the Summam Valley and the regions of Setif and Constantine.[979] It is 500,000 ha which passed into French hands in total.[980] In large measure, the money paid by Muslims went to the colons to pay for supposed damages inflicted on their farms, and also to finance further colonisation.[981] Greater Kabylia was particularly hit. Besides the lands of the Zaouias, the best Kabyle lands were taken by the French, most particularly those of the Valley of Sebaou and Wadi Sahel. The lands which the French had no use for were repurchased by their former owners, when they could. The others were distributed to European colons. The Kabyles were thrown onto sloppy, unproductive lands.[982] When Governor-general de Gueydon arrived in Algeria, he sought to find ways to make the Kabyles pay some of the costs of the war. Whilst the council admitted that 'the Arabs had nothing,' the governor was not satisfied.[983] He subsequently demanded another ten millions of francs from them under the threat that whatever they had kept would be ravaged, and they had to pay.[984] Another fine exceeded 25 millions, so much so that in the end more than 60 millions found their way to the colonial treasure chest.[985] The Algerians were ruined.

This did not mean the end of Algerian uprisings. In 1881, Sheikh Bou-Amama led another great rising in the southern parts of Oran, threatening French possessions in the vicinity of Saida and the south of Oran, and once more it took extreme measures to quell this uprising.[986]

Still refusing French dictate, the Algerians rose again. The First World War in particular, saw recurrent uprisings by Algerians incensed by French policy to raise armies amongst them to fight the Germans.

> France [wrote one such Algerian fighter] enlists our children and sends them to death. They are put in the front lines where the worst and most violent assaults and counter-assaults occur... Why are we fighting the Germans? It is because France has relegated us to the rank of animals...[987]

---

[977] M. Morsy: *North Africa*; op cit; 159.

[978] J.M. Abun-Nasr: *A History of the Maghrib*, op cit, p. 255.

[979] Ibid.

[980] A. Rambaud: L'Insurrection Algerienne de 1871; op cit; p. 53.

[981] J.M. Abun-Nasr: *A History of the Maghrib*, op cit, p. 255.

[982] A. Rambaud: L'Insurrection Algerienne de 1871; op cit; p. 52.

[983] Count H. Ideville: *Memoirs of Marshal Bugeaud from his Private Correspondence and Original Documents*; 2 vols; edited from French by C.M. Yonge; Hurst and Blackett; London, 1884; vol 2; p. 92.

[984] Ibid.

[985] Ibid; pp. 92-3.

[986] H. Alleg: *La Guerre*; op cit; p. 84.

[987] Lettre addressee a un haut Dignitaire Italien, dated 25 September 1914. Cited by O. Depont in his report on the insurrection in the Aures Mountains.

These uprisings stretched through the Aures mountains, in 1916, and many other parts of the south of Algeria. Pictures of mass executions of Algerian prisoners remain a poignant reminder of the spirit of resistance and refusal to submit shown throughout.[988]

> The earthly- happiness of the Arab, and his images of Paradise, do not suit us, because the direction of our soul has always been different from that of his. Could the French sceptic, in accepting the life of the Arab, buy likewise all the simplicity of his mind, and all the intensity of his faith, half of the army of Algeria would be ready for the exchange. (Wagner)[989]

4. What was the frame of mind of those who inflicted what they inflicted and still inflict on Muslims

What comes out in regard to colonial history in modern narrative, as in the case of Algeria, is that French policy was confused, that France was not committed to colonisation of the country, that her policies shifted from the humane to the excessive at times as a reaction to Colon pressure and political necessities, that those French officers guilty of excesses were generally an oddity (the usual bad apples) or not conforming to French central policy. We are also informed that such few French excesses were outcomes of acts committed on the spur of the moment, generally following atrocities committed on the French by Algerians, and so on and so forth. When we examine the officers' and other contemporary accounts, however, we realise that this narrative is lying, and that, as a rule, French scholars/historians, and their gullible/sold out followers, including Algerians, are all crooked.

The accounts by French officers involved in the colonial war, and those of their contemporaries give us the fundamental reasons why Westerners have acted towards Muslims the way they did over the centuries, and still do. Unless we understand this matter we cannot understand colonial history. Unless we understand this matter, there is no end to the practice of Western violence against Muslims, and counter action by Muslims, some such counter action also being of the execrable sort. So, here, unlike any other work on French colonisation of Algeria, or related matters, let's go inside the minds of those who did things to Algerians, or condoned them, or justified them. To be one hundred per-cent true to these sources, let those concerned tell us their thoughts themselves, only translate their words and thoughts from French into English (which is mostly the case here) as accurately as possible.

---

[988] In H. Alleg et al: *La Guerre*, op cit; p. 166.
[989] M. Wagner: *The Tricolor on the Atlas*, op cit, p. 157.

We begin with the devoutly Christian, Colonel Montagnac (All leading French officers in Algeria were devout Christians.) In a letter full of tender feelings for his family, just as all other letters to them, and again, praising the Lord, adding his prayers of an old soldier, hoping the Lord would accept them,[990] 'my only fortune,' he says, as he does repeatedly, 'is to love you just as I love God;' calling on his Aunt Therese to pray to God;[991] adding tenderly words towards his religiously devout, good, family. Then he changes subject, and moves onto Algeria and Algerians, and his tone also changes abruptly.[992]

> These acts (i.e his destruction of Algerian life and mass killing of Algerians) which seem abject to you, brave people, you who live in peace in your industrial city, fine; but here, in this country, where snakes crawl over the ground, where wolves are everywhere, death must reap all the time. This is why even the kindest heart can become ferocious when it is forced to take this heavy responsibility of securing the tranquility of the country. A few days ago, at midnight, I made a descent two leagues and half from here (Ghazaouet, near Oran)... I only found women and little children in the camp. I took the lot (i.e he made them march) in the middle of the night in the midst of very heavy rain. My heart bled to see the little girls, the women, the little children stuck in the mud and the thick bush lacerating their flesh, but I had to silence all feelings of humanity. I was suffering, believe me. Each time I have to use the means that shatter my old heart in order to tackle (Arab) crimes, to keep tribes under control, tribes which only understand this bloody justice. What I inflict on them, in fact, are only roses compared to what their former chiefs, under the regime of the Turks and Abd al Kader inflicted on them.[993]

Obviously Montagnac's mind was letting him down on so many of his claims, but one important thing he should have realised was that if the Turks and Abd al Kader had truly inflicted worse on Algerians, Algerians would have never fought France, especially with the fierceness they did and would have instead seen her as their liberator.

We return to Pelissier's smoking of Algerians to death, an incident already narrated but here looking at the logic of it in French minds. In the columns of the *Moniteur Algérien* of the 15th and 20th of July, 1845, Colonel Pelissier's cause is thus argued:

> The end of June was very near. It was necessary for the subjugation of the Dahra to be completed by that time. The season was advanced; the heat most severe; Colonels Saint-Arnaud and Pelissier had orders to make a simultaneous attack upon the Ouarensenis. Their movements were to be

---

[990] De Montagnac: *Lettres d'un soldat*; Librairie Plon Paris; 1885; p. 431.
[991] Ibid; p. 432.
[992] Ibid; pp. 433 ff.
[993] Ibid; pp. 434-435.

combined. Saint-Arnaud was to attack by the east, and Pelissier by the west. If the Colonel (Pelissier) had gone away, the Arabs would have issued from their caves, and saluted his rear-guard with a sharp fire. The Colonel could not leave the caves, nor lose time in blockading them, for there is a copious stream through the caverns, and they were well supplied with food. Our troops were on the point of failure, and the next day had to be in another direction. To enter the caves and fight the Ouled-Rhia was to destroy them no less unmercifully, and risk the loss of a great many men. The Colonel thought that the burning faggots would drive them out to be caught. He spent five hours in unsuccessful negotiations; they killed the bearer of a flag of truce and several men. He kept up the fire, and the Ouled-Rhia perished by their fatal obstinacy.[994]

Further argument by his supporters, including Bugeaud, stated:

The attack upon such caves is no new thing. Last year General Cavaignac besieged a cave similarly. He lost Captain Louvencourt of the 5th Chasseurs battalion there, and several men. The General placed petards on the rocks, and threw shells inside, we even think he made use of fire. The cave was small, and its defenders few in number; that was the only reason why there were so few victims.[995]

Was Colonel Pelissier to retire before this obstinacy, and give up his task? The consequences of this determination would have been fatal, and caused a great increase of confidence in the caves. Was he to attack by the main force? That was almost impossible, and in any case would have caused great loss. To resign himself to a simple blockade that might last a fortnight, was the loss of precious time for subduing the Dahra, and refusal of the combination with Colonel Saint-Arnaud. After consideration of all these circumstances, he determined to make use of the method that had been recommended him by the Governor-general, in case of extreme urgency.

We would ask whether besieging caverns is more cruel than the bombardment and starvation that we inflict upon the whole population of European cities in war. May there be created in Africa concentrated interests, immovable, such as there are to be found in all the large towns of Europe, and there will be a chance for us to prove that we would not weaken ourselves by running after cattle and people over ravines, mountains, plains, and the desert. . . . But, as in all war, in order to bring it to a conclusion, the interests must be touched, &c., &c. These last words, 'the interests must be touched,' language so often repeated in the speeches and writings of Marshal Bugeaud about the wars in Africa, are equivalent to a signature. It is really the Marshal in person, defending his lieutenant in the official newspaper of the colony. He acted thus with his habitual

---

[994] Count H. Ideville: *Memoirs of Marshal Bugeaud*; op cit; vol 2; p. 166-7.
[995] Ibid; p. 167.

generosity; and was in perfect accord with the feeling of the army, as is plain from the letters written by Colonel Saint- Arnaud at the time of the occurrence.[996]

Not only did the army approve of Colonel Pelissier's conduct, but it must be said 'the whole colony had but one voice in favour of this energetic soldier, who had sacrificed a few victims to the general interest, in order to crush insurrection, strike terror into the Arabs, and prevent bloodshed.'[997]

For Bugeaud, just as for all Frenchmen in charge, or with a degree of influence, whether political, litcrary, or religious, Pelissier's and similar acts had a purpose:

> The population must accept our law before they can be governed, civilised, or made colonial. Thousands of examples show that they only accept it when compelled, and compulsion itself is powerless, when it has not reached their persons and interests. By strict philanthropy the war in Africa would be prolonged for ever, as well as the spirit of rebellion, and so the aim of philanthropy would not be attained.[998]

Sixteen years afterwards, in 1861, Colonel Pelissier, who had by now become Marshal of France, Duke de Malakoff, Governor-general of Algeria, was entertained by the colonists at Mascara:

> The notables did the honours of a club that bore his name, in memory of the struggles of other days. There, in the neighbourhood of the Dahra, in the midst of this crowd of Algerians, he remembered the abuse showered upon him by the French press, and the politicians of the time. It is well known no one could speak with more originality or fire than this soldier with his rough rind. Under the excitement of the occasion, he recalled this terrible deed of war with the eloquence arising from the conviction of having done his duty, painful though it were. And on that day he received fresh proof of the warm gratitude of the colonists.[999]

The Englishman, Dawson Borrer, who was fighting with the French in Kabylia, on more than one instance, came across as a humane and decent being, who felt sorry for the plight of the Algerians, saved many of their lives, saved even a copy of a burning manuscript of the Qur'an. Despite sympathy for both faith and faithful, here, we have a few extracts from him which explain why he had to do what he did, and why he approves with what was being done to the Algerians:

> The abominable vices and debaucheries of the Kabyle race, the inhuman barbarities they are continually guilty of towards such as may be cast by tempest or other misfortune upon their rugged shores, the atrocious cruelties and refined tortures they, in common with the Arab, delight in exercising upon any such enemies as may be so unhappy as to fall alive into

---

[996] Ibid.
[997] Ibid; p. 168.
[998] Ibid; p. 169.
[999] Ibid.

their hands, must render the hearts of those acquainted with this people perfectly callous as to what misfortunes may befall them or their country; and many may be led to think that, as far as the advancement of civilization is concerned, the wiping off of the Kabyle and Arab races of Northern Africa from the face of the earth would be the greatest boon to humanity.[1000]

The same Dawson Borrer:

War is always more or less repulsive with horrors, according to the object desired, and the character of the people engaged in the struggle. In the present case, the army of a civilised nation is in conflict with a people of the most barbarous character. Now the ranks of the French army in Africa are composed, in great measure, of the very scum of France, intermingled with allies of the same blood, religion, and ferocity as those with whom they are struggling. The difficulties of restraining such troops may account for many atrocities committed by them, as offensive to the chivalrous officers often found in command of them, as to the world at large. There are certainly instances where the officers in command are as brutal as the soldiery, from whose ranks they have risen and it is to be lamented: in other cases, policy and even humanity have required energetic and repulsive proceedings, — cruel, barbarous, and apparently unnecessary to the unobservant mind, — but proceedings which tended to prevent a more protracted struggle, and a consequently greater sacrifice of victims.

The only sort of excuse, for the horrors committed by the soldiery in Algeria, is their untamed passions, and the fire added to their natural ferocity, by the atrocious cruelties so often committed by the Arabs upon their comrades in arms, who have been so unhappy as to fall into their power. A thirst for revenge is a passion natural to the human breast, and one of the most difficult to assuage. As the French-African soldier rushes on to overwhelm a tribe, he thinks of the many of his comrades who have been roasted alive before blazing Arab fires, — of others who have been mutilated and tortured in the most horrible manner, and their mangled bodies defiled with insults even after death; he thinks of his own sufferings during the expedition, — of his own fate if the chances of war are against him; and every drop of Arab blood is a salve to his feelings. As he bayonets an infant, he regards it as the mere crushing of a devil's brood; nor, unhappily, are such feelings, betrayed by deeds of equal atrocity, unparalleled amongst the soldiery of other European nations, in their combats with those whom they regard as barbarians.[1001]

And another justification for pitilessness:

The wily Kabyle often conceals his arms at hand in the brushwood, and, taking up his reaping-hook, or entering into conversation with the passing

---

[1000] Dawson Borrer: *Narrative of a campaign against the Kabailes of Algeria;* Spottiswoode and Shaw, London, 1848; p. 10.
[1001] Ibid; pp. 129-31.

enemy, appears the very type of innocence and simplicity: but as soon as the rear-guard passes on he hastily resumes his weapons; and if no decided attack is made in union with his brothers in arms, why he will at all events yield himself the satisfaction to throw in, from behind the brushwood or rocks, a few parting bullets, laughing in his sleeve at those who, their "eyes blinded by Allah," did not take advantage of his presence and affability to cut off his head. And then again he smiles, as, rushing out upon the foot-sore and weary straggler from the column, he passes his hideous knife along his victim's throat, and with a solemn measured step regains his gourbie, joyful at heart for has he not assuredly gained an extra houri in Paradise by slaying another "Roumi dog?"[1002]

Now the Intellectual Justifications of the Colonial Narrative Past and Present:

This point demands focus in analysis (without over elaborating as we might digress away from our main subject: early colonial Algeria). So remaining simple, brief and direct, let's declare:

The way (with the rarest of exceptions) Islam has been depicted for centuries, as a source of darkness, has always justified Western robust action towards Islamic societies. The same views that legitimised the crusades in the medieval period condoned colonisation in the modern times, and legitimise the intrusion (including via military coups) in today's Muslim life. In the medieval period war on Islam was for the purpose of defeating paganism, in the colonial period or today, the purpose is 'to enlighten societies made backward/barbaric by Islam.'

We will avoid here getting entangled in the issue relating to the faith (Islam) and its role in the rise of Islamic civilisation, or its role in the decline of such a civilisation (according to the foes of Islam.) This author has examined this issue in so many of his works, and anyone is capable of tracing such works, available free and easily. Here, we will deal specifically with some aspects of the colonial argument as it stood in the past and as it stands today and that justifies Western meddling in Muslim affairs.

Let us see how Western intellectuals dissected Muslim society and found logic in the French colonisation of Algeria (as in the colonisation of everybody else for that matter). Let's here consider the thoughts of March Philips as we have seen those of the French a plenty in chapter one in relation to the civilising Mission. March Phillips is also fascinating to read thanks to his great sense of observation, and because he remarkably captures the essence of the colonial argument of the past and that of today. He says:

> TWO hills look at each other by the bay of Algiers. One is crusted over with white and yellow houses, sunbleached, roofless, and so close packed, and probed by passages and tunnels so narrow and intricate, that they look like

---

[1002] Ibid; pp. 150.

a piece of honeycomb, or bit of old ivory carved into illegible design by the ingenuity of some Indian artist. Figures in white gowns pass in and out of the mouths of passages, or flit like white moths across the open space by the sea. The white domes of a mosque swell up at its base; the walls of an antique fortress crumble at its summit.

The other is laid out in beautiful gardens, with rose-covered villas at frequent intervals, a comfortable club, and many luxurious hotels. Paths run under shady avenues, and groves of pines and blossoming shrubs vary the view and scent the air. Smart carriages and electric trams roll up and down the smooth roads, and men and women in summer clothes, with straw hats on and parasols up, saunter under the trees or pause to admire the view over the sea far below. Of these two hills, the first is the old Arab town, the second the modern French suburb.[1003]

To pass into this crumbling mass of masonry is to pass into all the intricacies of Arab life. Winding, tortuous alleys meander aimlessly in all directions, drilled along their bases with deep holes, out of which protrude piles of merchandise, richly coloured, making deep blots of purple and crimson in the shadowed way.[1004]

Like all Oriental towns, Old Algiers leaves on the memory an impression of a haunt of animals or insects rather than of men, a mass of crumbling masonry, honeycombed, corroded, and eaten through and into, as by ants or bees, in a network of minute passages and tunnels.[1005]

It is impossible to deny an attractive flavour to the life of such a place. Behind us the electric trams run smoothly down the hill, carrying prosperous-looking occupants to business or pleasure in the town below. On the slopes, among dark evergreens and trees, comfortable villas stand in their well-ordered gardens. Most of them are built in Moorish style, with deep verandahs, fantastic arcades, and ogive windows. Their snowy architecture gleams, like marble sculpture, through glossy leaves and evergreens. The gardens glow with a profusion of flowers; arches and verandahs are half smothered under a surprising display of roses, and the great bougainvillea creeper bursts in purple surf on frequent walls and balconies.[1006]

He also says:

And all this is as true of the Arab as of the sand. He is a social solvent as the sand is a natural one. Fickle and unstable, a creature of impulse and blown about by every whim, he is consistent in nothing but his profound dislike of law and order, of fixed duties and responsibilities, and all that goes to build up a coherent society.[1007]

[1003] L. March Phillips: *In the Desert, the Hinterlands of Algiers*; op cit; pp. 1-2.
[1004] Ibid; p. 4.
[1005] Ibid; p. 5.
[1006] Ibid; p. 35.
[1007] Ibid; pp. 111-12.

I confess I do not see myself how in this matter the line can logically be drawn between any of these North African states. They are all out of the same egg. All are inhabited by the same race and wedded to the same lawlessness. It seems to me that if the French were justified in interfering with Algiers, they were justified in interfering with Tunis, and will be justified in interfering with Morocco. All these states, left to themselves, make any system of law and order impossible, not only within their own borders, but also in their neighbourhood. The Bedouin and Touareg nomads are the pirates of the Sahara. They deal with the Sudan caravan trade just as the Algerine fleet dealt with the commerce of Europe. Lawlessness knows no frontiers, and it is difficult to see how any settlement of the country can take place, until the nation whose interests are paramount in this part of the world assumes responsible control. What the claims of other nations may be to influence France's action is, of course, another matter. But so far as the main question of interference is concerned, that is not a question of France versus Algeria, or France versus Tunisia, or France versus Morocco, but of order versus anarchy in North Africa.[1008]

Then he adds:

The anarchy that possesses Moslem society is generally the most remarkable thing about it, and in these days it is, too, the most practically important thing about it. That Moslem races cannot provide anything of value in the domains of thought, literature, and art, is a matter which chiefly concerns themselves. But that society with them means chaos is a matter which is bound more and more to concern other people as well. I have pointed out how, as social coherence and the ideas of law and order spread through the West, the Arab sphere of influence dwindled and diminished. It is now practically extinct.

But the Moslem problem does not end with the Arab. All its elements appear in the Turkish Empire. More virile and stubborn than the Arab, the Turk displays the same well-known Moslem traits; the same sterility of mind, the same reliance on physical force, the same indifference to the idea of social order and stable government. What is intolerable to the sense of Europe in Constantinople to-day is just what was intolerable in Algiers three-quarters of a century ago. Though we have shifted the ground of difference from religion to politics, the political difference is only the outcome of the religious difference. When we say that Turkish or Arab ideas of law and order, Turkish or Arab ideas of government, are incompatible with European ideas, we really mean that a state of society which is the outcome of Mohammedanism is incompatible with a state of society which is the outcome of Christianity.[1009]

[1008] Ibid; pp. 17-18.
[1009] Ibid; pp. 275-276.

This argument is common amongst scholarship as amongst colonialists, as amongst those who sought to erase Turkey off the map (as this author has shown in his books on that country,) as it is common amongst those who preach the Westernisation of Muslim society (an impossibility for it is like trying to turn a bird into a cat.) But it is a fascinating argument. It had a considerable impact, and even today it shapes opinion not just in respect to colonisation, but also in respect to the whole matter of civilisation and modernity. It is very easy to accept this argument in view of the decayed nature of Muslim society today as we will be obliged to sum in a paragraph or two. It is all the more a convincing argument today in a world of poor Muslim intellect, where hardly anybody reads let alone can argue at a high level, and where rules a culture of institutionalised cretinism fed by cretin entertainment, idiotic media, and mediocre education especially at the higher levels where excellence is unknown. Muslims are incapable of addressing any intellectual challenge thrown at them by the West, which can even accuse them of cannibalism if it wished. Islamic elites are so poor intellectually, without any vision in regard to economic, social, environmental, or whatever matters, to be able to provide any alternative in regard to civilisation or modernity, or to challenge the onslaught on their faith. Only he or she who is armed with knowledge of what Islam stands for in matters of civilisation, knowledge, or love for nature, harmony and order, and their promotion by the faith, and what early Muslim society accomplished, whether the Arabs or the Ottoman Turks, understands that the colonial argument is utterly false. Only he or she knows and is confident enough in expressing themselves can tell you or explain to you that what Islam preaches and what its faithful do today, even those in power, have nothing to do with each other. Only those with vast intellect, some knowledge of the Islamic faith, and above all vast erudition in history can tell you that all vile manifestations of Muslim society: chaos, overconsumption, waste, dirt, noise, destruction of nature, and its hate towards all that is refined (books, reading, arts, intellect, excellence, gardening, walking, silence, thinking,) have nothing to do with Islam, quite the contrary. But these people with such an intellect and honest directness hardly exist in the mucky Muslim societies of today; the few around are hounded into extinction.

Nonetheless, March Phillips's and similar arguments are of interest to us in two fundamental respects:
-They feed the colonial argument, whether past or present.
-They help to a very large measure understand why many Muslim elites today accept the colonial argument and the concept of Western superiority, and even long for Western interference direct and indirect in their countries, which is one of the sources of the misery of the Muslim world. Here, and we won't dwell on this too much, both such Muslim elites and Western colonial theorists of today ignore the central fact that early Muslim society was the very extreme of the society that we have today in 2017-18. All early travellers to the Muslim world

used to be struck by the beauty of Muslim towns and cities, their cleanliness, love of order, serenity, verdure, love of flowers and gardens, whilst libraries, book sellers, and intellectual salons and exchanges thrived. Early Arab, Muslim, Turkish societies made you love Islam, and unfortunately about them little is known or is disappeared from knowledge. Modern Muslim societies of today, which feed the supporters of the colonial argument shatter you with what we mentioned above. In fact, were it not for Islam that still maintains them just about functioning, hell on earth would be the lot of the dwellers of such societies.

March Phillips and his likes, without any exception, insist that Muslims hate what is refined and superior, and only seem to thrive in the ugly and inferior. We won't say much here, except that true: any person meandering or struggling through modern Muslim society and without knowledge of history but aware of the colonial argument would indeed admit the latter's logic or essence. Early Muslim society thrilled the visitors, Muslim society since it came in contact with Western colonisation, and a certain aspect of Western culture today, is at the other extreme. Since their submission to the West Muslim societies have managed the extraordinary feat of mixing the worst of backward societies (described two paragraphs above: death of excellence, love of chaos, war on nature, etc... and not forgetting high procreation rates,) with the smuttiest and most debased that you can import from the West. Muslim society of modern times, as we noted, without enlightened elites or vision, is guided or led by its own backwardness, and the modernisation of colonial gin shops and brothels, and the lewdness of modern Western culture, and rabid consumerism. That's what legitimises the colonial argument of the past and the imposition of more Western filth on, and intrusion in the lives of, such societies.

March Phillips also raises another interesting point:

> Had the solid qualities of slowness and sureness, which are the basis of social and national existence, been inherent in Arab character, Europe would not have been treated to such a spectacle as the decline and fall of Algiers.[1010]

The Prophet Mohammed took twenty years 610-630 of patient preaching of the faith and was happy with a few close Companions, Abu Bakr, most particularly, never compromising to please, or be followed, or even be liked. Rushing his mission or rushing to accomplish the Islamic/Muslim state was never his preoccupation. He delivered the message aware that what he would leave would do the work. Here we have digressed and preached a little. For good reason, for the aim was to show, however briefly, that the point raised by March Phillips and countless observers of Muslim society in recent times is completely at odds with the tradition of the faith. Indeed, Muslims of recent times, and of today, in particular, do, indeed, lack the quality of early Muslims and that Westerners have: calm, and slow sureness. Muslim life from top to bottom today is indeed a sum of

---

[1010] Ibid; p. 16.

rushed, exhausting exertions. Everything is urgent and quick reaction to events, situations, or whatever. Muslims have neither elites with calm and vision, nor do they see their importance, which is even worse. Furthermore Muslims neither dig into the past, that is history, for they know it not, nor are they interested in it. Nor do they dig into the immensity of the future, for as a nation that does not read, and some countries utterly illiterate in any Western language, they have no power to conceptualise an abstract world, that can yet be made real. Gardening, walking in nature, and sitting in silence, being surrounded by a harmonious landscape are all utterly absent in Muslim society today, and hence Muslims are deprived of the elements that can force them to think. The ravenous culture of consumption and waste, and easy access to goods and wealth have made Muslims utterly and intellectually impotent, incapable of delivering anything creative in any field. The gadgets of modernity finish off any space that could have stimulated the brains, and the generalised culture of smut and mediocrity kills off the last cells of intelligence. So, all Muslim actions, as deciders and populations, are just piles of whatever, which just cram their landscape and their lives, illusions of progress, just illusions that can be swept away by an earthquake, a brief war, or just by their successors. So, indeed, if you don't know history, and if you live today, and you see what you see, you do agree with the colonial argument.

Finally, where one profoundly disagrees with March Phillips just as the hundreds who make the similar claim, and which stands at the core of the French colonising act:

> There is a particular interest here in Algiers in noting this haunting deficiency in the Arab character and civilisation, for it is on this that the French claim to the right of interference is really based. Two principles confront each other in North Africa today: the principle of anarchy which is going out, and the principle of order which is coming in. What European civilisation stands for, before all, is just that coherence and continuity which the Arab is destitute of, and for want of which he has been brought to such melancholy shipwreck. It is because these things are absolutely essential to any kind of advance, or social stability even, and because France can supply, and has the best right to supply them, that she is justified in intervening.[1011]

The following chapter will amply show that, rather than civilising, France did everything but that.

[1011] Ibid; p. 17.

Seven

THE DESTRUCTION OF ALGERIAN SOCIETY

The price of peace, which was no peace, rankled. Christian blood, still visible to the imaginative globe-trotter on the colossal walls of the Darse, cried for vengeance. So, fan or no fan, the optimism of Hussein-Dey struck the deathblow of El-Djezair and all the lawless plunder, and the white, shrouded beauty for which it stood. El-Djezair! Oh, the music of it in an Arab mouth — a song with a dagger-thrust at the end! El-Djezair, who scoffed at Charles V and Louis XIV; El-Djezair, who imprisoned Cervantes, is as dead as the sea-wolves of Barbary. Here and there a pallid remnant of her past survives in French Alger — a library that was sometime a palace, a group of twisted tamarisks on the shore where once a garden bloomed — and on the western edge of the town a cluster of huddled houses tinted like caramels, known to the tourists as the Arab quarter of the Kasbah. More than Boa'bdill's mountain in the Sierra Nevada, the Arab quarter merits to be called *el ultimo sospiro del Moro* (the last sigh of the Moor) for any day some Gallic iconoclast may build a boulevard across the Rue des Sarrasins. Already the modern town surrounds it on three sides like the waves of an encroaching sea, and one wonders how long it will continue to offer to the aggressor the passive resistance of its inertia.[1012]

With these lines, Devereux seeks to capture the final moments of Muslim Algeria, reminiscent of the final moments of Muslim Spain; a defeated nation, which had brought its woes on itself through piracy and the Dey's striking the Consul, Deval, with the fly whisk. Just as Boabdill emitted his last sigh as he departed from Grenada surrendering it to the Spaniards in 1492, Algeria, now, defeated, is being devoured from every side by Francification, only the last vestiges of once a pre-colonial land being visible: a palace made into a library, twisted tamarisk..., all soon to join with the sea wolves, gone long ago.

The turning of Algeria into a new France followed on three lines:
1. The destruction of the nation's heritage: natural, cultural and other.
2. The removal of the natives through impoverishment and induced mass starvation.
3. The imposing of a new culture and a new faith.

These themes are examined in turn.

[1012] R. Devereux: *Aspects of Algeria*; London; J.M. Dent and Sons; 1912; p. 5.

1. The Destruction of the Nation's Heritage

> Then the French came, bringing knowledge to take the place of beauty, of
> which supersession, if we are to believe Nietzsche, tragedy is born.[1013]
> One has, however, only to glance at the old prints in the museums to
> realize the extent of that vandalism which seems to be an inevitable
> accompaniment of war. There are men still living who remember the
> mosques, the palaces decorated with faience and carving of El-Djezair,
> which were wantonly destroyed on the morrow of the conquest.[1014]

The French descended on Algeria with a frenzy of destruction, perhaps equalled
nowhere else in the world. When one reads through the accounts of those days
one is shocked not so much by the scale of destruction but by its wantonness in
the first place, and also by the realisation of how beautiful Algeria was prior to
the French arrival. The German, Clemens Lamping, is one of the best sources, a
mind and a pair of eyes that captured much of the beauty, and that saw it being
ravaged. He describes the stunning villas and dwellings he and the army came
across in the vicinity of Algiers.[1015] Now they had been lost by their Algerian
owners, apparently purchased by Frenchmen and Spaniards; villas with very
beautiful gardens, watered by numerous springs, water conducted through
earthen pipes, which creep below the surface of the earth, conveying a fresh and
plentiful supply of water.[1016]
His sight turns onto Blida, west of Algiers, which the Arabs justly called the
Paradise of Africa. The town lies at the very foot of the Atlas, and for miles
westward there extended a beautiful orange grove, 'the largest I ever saw, not
even excepting that of Seville.' The slopes of the mountains were covered with fig
and olive trees, interspersed with cedars 'which rival those of Mount Lebanon.'
Plentiful streams of water 'gush out of a ravine,' to be conducted by numerous
channels through the streets of the town.[1017]
When he reaches Medea, he sees the same, a town surrounded by the most
splendid fruit gardens; a Roman aqueduct still in good preservation, conveying
water to it from a neighbouring mountain.[1018]
And then the same Clemens Lamping laments the following:

> The soldiers proceeded to cut down the orange and almond trees for fuel,
> although there were plenty of large olive trees in the neighbourhood; but
> destruction is the proper element of the soldier.[1019]

[1013] Ibid; p. 20.
[1014] Ibid; p. 13.
[1015] Clemens Lamping: *The French in Algiers. Soldiers of the Foreign Legion; Prisoners of Abd el Kader;* tr. from German
and French by Lady Duff Gordon, London; 1855; p. 18.
[1016] Ibid. p. 19.
[1017] Ibid; p. 44.
[1018] Ibid; p. 48.
[1019] Ibid.

Deeds of similar nature he laments constantly. But what he saw and lamented was generalised and lasted decade after decade. In the end, all green belts once surrounding every town and city were cut down, millions of trees cut down, hundreds of villages and hamlets encircled by green, as in the picture of Laghouat in the previous chapter, turned into barren lands, with burnt out dwellings, with maybe new homes trying to rise amidst scorched earth.

One has lived in Algeria in the final years of colonisation. During the War of Independence, 1954-1962, the sky and the ground used to be covered with thick clouds of falling burnt out leaves, millions, maybe billions of them, their shape still imprinted on their ashen form. There were days, this author recalls, when mornings and afternoons were red from fires blazing through the thick vegetation and woods. Those memories and the accounts one reads through, make one realise the world the French found and they destroyed. Studies, too, show and confirm the scale of destruction of that living space that one witnessed as a child. Between 1954 and 1962, more than 70% of forest land in Bou Taleb (Hodna Mountains),[1020] and 220 000 ha in the Aures were destroyed.[1021] Meddour-Sahar et al. estimate that about 645,414 ha of forest were burned down during the War of Independence.[1022] During the period looked at here (1830-1871), besides the wanton destruction by troops: cutting down of olive trees in the north, palm trees in the Sahara and orchards everywhere, the main source of destruction of Algerian wooded area was for timber uses. Randon, in his memoirs, gives us many instances of this, such as a forest, stretching over 40 kilometres which was cut down in order to supply both colons in Algeria, and France, too, with timber for construction, as he put it, 'in abundance.'[1023]

The wildlife that thrived in Algerian wilderness was, again, according to accounts superbly diverse, and the French literally wiped it out. Accounts of the time, again, emphasise both abundance and instances of destruction. Here we have Dawson Borrer:

> The Oued-Hamza, (or Oued-Bouera, as it is sometimes called,) flowing close to our camp, contains an amazing quantity of a fish which the French termed barbeaux. The largest weighed perhaps two pounds, and they proved excellent eating. So numerous were they, that the soldiers caught them in abundance with their shirts, forming bags, of which, by way of tunnel nets, one would hold a sleeve on either side, whilst others beat down towards it; thus driving the fish in. Some of the "Zouaves" might be

---

[1020] Madoui A (2000). Forest fires in Algeria and the case of the domanial forest of Bou-Taleb, Setif. *International Forest Fire News* 22: 9-15.
Madoui A (2002): Les incendies de forêt en Algérie. Historique, bilan et analyse. *Forêt Méditerranéenne* 23 (1): 23-30. [in French]
[1021] Sari D (1976). *L'homme et l'érosion dans l'Ouarsenis (Algérie)*. Editions SNED, Alger, pp. 224.
[1022] Meddour-Sahar O, Meddour R, Derridj A (2008a). Les feux de forêts en Algérie sur le temps long (1876-2007). *Les Notes d'analyse du CIHEAM* 39: 11.
[1023] A. Rastoul: *Le Marechal Randon; D'apres ses Memoirs et Documents Inedits*; Firmin Didot; Paris; 1890; p. 34.

seen catching them in the same manner with their ceintures; whilst those happy enough to have brought fish-hooks from Algiers, fished, in the more orthodox manner, with beetles, grasshoppers.... In one hole alone, one of these disciples of old Isaac took, in little more than an hour, seventy good fish; and I myself was almost equally fortunate; so that extensive frying went on in camp, and sumptuous were the dinners.[1024]

Another type of wildlife, birds, and here the account by Clemens Lamping:

As we left Blida rather late, we were forced to pass the night on this side of the Col de Mussaia, in an olive grove at the foot of the mountain. In all my life I never saw so many small birds as in this grove; it was positively alive with them. They twittered and warbled in all tongues; the bullfinciies especially delighted me with a melody so like that which they sing in my own country, that I fancied I recognised some old acquaintances among them. The soldiers contrived to catch a number of young birds, who, dreaming of no danger had ventured out of their nests, and to cook them for supper.[1025]

Dawson Borrer again:

Onward we marched, trampling beneath our feet vast extents of corn almost ready for the sickle: smiling fertility before us, — devastation in our rear. Every blade and every head of corn was crushed to earth. The march of eight thousand men, accompanied by hundreds of wild Arab cavaliers, dashing here and there, some playing the fantasia, others chasing at full speed the startled hare, or riding down red-legged partridges, leaves ugly tracks in a narrow cultivated valley. Game abounded here. Quails rose on all sides beneath our feet, followed by their lately hatched young. Many, in their fright and confusion, fell amongst the troops, who captured them alive, or knocked them down with sticks. The same fate often befell the hares. Partridges whirred from their nests, as the crushing host came on.[1026]

It was little and large beasts which were wiped out in equal measure. Colonel Montagnac speaks of large beasts that came every night to feed on the remains of dead animals near his camp. One night, ambushed soldiers shot a large lion, which was purchased by the local commander who distributed its meat to friends and relatives, who appreciated the flesh. Around his camp abounded many such lions.[1027]

I don't recognize Africa [says Saint Arnaud]: I have never seen as many obnoxious and ferocious beasts in huge numbers as this year. People are only talking of victims of lions and panthers. It is snowfall and hunger that drove them down the mountains. As I toured I saw one lion and two

---

[1024] Dawson Borrer: *Narrative of a campaign against the Kabailes of Algeria;* Spottiswoode and Shaw, London, 1848; p. 54.
[1025] Clemens Lamping: *The French in Algiers. Soldiers of the Foreign Legion*; op cit; p. 64.
[1026] Dawson Borrer: *Narrative of a campaign against the Kabailes of Algeria*; op cit; p. 79.
[1027] De Montagnac: *Lettres d'un soldat*; Librairie Plon Paris; 1885; p. 19.

panthers. One passed by only twenty paces off me.[1028] Marshal Bugeaud has put a price on all ferocious animals: 50 francs for a lion, 25 for a panther. We kill so many, but there are always victims.[1029]

By the time the French left in 1962, there were no lions in Algeria, no panthers; hardly any gazelles left; definitely far fewer birds and no longer the swarms Lamping and Borrer describe; and the rivers of Algeria had been literally dried of every sort of wildlife, maybe just water snakes in some of them, whilst the rest were fast turning into sewers.

Besides this, what is even more damaging, France transformed the former Islamic vision and attitude towards nature, whereby humans are only trustees to care for the creation of God into the French belief that nature was for use and misuse according to necessity. Modern day French care for the environment is only a new manifestation that benefits France. French old inimical attitude to nature is still part of its legacies to Algeria, where, because of fast population growth, and the loathing for everything naturally beautiful (common to most in Muslim societies today) is fast turning into a desert. Gone, and for good, indeed, is the Algerian paradise.

There was another side to the Algerian heritage the French devastated in equal measure. Moritz Wagner was another German who marched with the French in their expeditions against Constantine in 1836 and 1837. Here are some extracts of what he saw.

> The centre of the valley is occupied by the camp of Ghelma (North Eastern Algeria), on the slope of the mountain range of Mauna. It is built out of the ruins of ancient Calama, which cover an extent of three miles in circumference. This large Roman city was destroyed by an earth-quake. The French camp is of solid structure, the building materials being at hand. It was founded during the disastrous retreat of Marshal Clauzel, first as a kind of hospital, and as a safe retreat for all the invalids and stragglers, who, overcome by fatigue, were unable to follow the army; they found here an asylum and resting-place. It is the same spot, where, nearly two thousand years back, the legions of Aulus Postumius Albinus were cut to pieces by Jugurtha. Marshal Clauzel left Colonel Duvivier with one battalion among the ruins, and this talented energetic officer willingly undertook the task, to erect here in the wilderness a place impregnable to Arabs, with a handful of soldiers, weakened and dispirited by sickness and reverses, without resources, without tents for shelter against the rain, or any sufficient supply of food. An elongated quadrangular wall was still standing amidst the ruins, evidently heaped up from the scattered remains of the destroyed city, by some new invader, the Numidian or the Arab, as a means

---

[1028] St Arnaud: Lettres de St Arnaud; 2 vols; Michel Levy; Paris; 1855; vol 1; p. 516.
[1029] Ibid; p. 517.

of defence. Colonel Duvivier quartered his troops inside this wall; he had it repaired and raised to double the height; and constructed rough barracks from the ruins. The hungry troops were soon provided with victuals from Bona; in a few weeks, a regular communication was established between the two places, and every fortnight a convoy was sent with provisions to the garrison. Soon after, many speculators, French and Maltese, settled here, and constructed coffee-houses, shops, and taverns. Broken columns and pillars of porphyry supported smoky public-houses, enframed by temple-ruins. There we saw the sign-board of the wine- shop — "Ici on donne a boire et a manger," close to a mutilated Latin inscription, fitted into the wall, which was the sepulchral record of a Roman proconsul. Such a desecration of the relics of the great conquerors, is revolting in a nation which talks so much about civilization and respect for science. But we find in the French people, and especially in the French armies and its camp-followers, a wanton destructiveness, which can hardly be controlled by the orders of enlightened generals, or by the endeavours of educated officers. In Algiers, fine orange-trees were felled for fire-wood in 1830. In Tlemsan, the beams of elegant Moorish houses were cut out for similar purposes, and this proceeding subsequently led to the ruin of entire streets. The gardens of the Dey, the palace of Abd-el-Kader in Mascara, and the Moorish villas on Mount Bujarea, were recklessly sacked. So too the ruins of Calama, which had been respected by Arab indolence, were wantonly destroyed by French soldiers and settlers. Columns were thrown down, because they stood in the way of a wine-cellar, and funeral inscriptions were broken to pave a tavern. Pages of history which told us what Calama had been, and who had ruled and lived here, the eloquent monuments of a great past, were reduced by a few strokes of the hammer, into dumb stones. It was not fanaticism, like that of the early Arabs, which prompted the French to such Vandalism; it was the most petty and miserable love of lucre, the old monuments being more handy for building material than the stones. I often met with soldiers occupied in breaking inscriptions, or hammering away bas-reliefs, in order to fit the 'stone easier into a wall, and it was in vain to repeat our complaints to Colonel Duvivier, when we partook of his coffee in the barracks. He complained of the destructiveness of his soldiers, who did not comply with his orders; but he declared that there was no remedy. He said, "an old stone does not require so much time for fitting, as a new one to be brought from the quarry; and whoever is acquainted with the endless toils of the African soldier, will, after all, find it natural, if he has no antiquarian scruples against saving labour to deter him from destroying ancient inscriptions." Duvivier's remarks were quite natural, and he had probably the same feelings as his soldiers. It was no enthusiasm for a new French- African empire, but ambition which prompted him to exert his energies to the utmost, and this ambition was not that of extending civilization into the countries of Barbary, but the desire of becoming general, with the marshal's baton in prospect. When he founded the camp of Ghelma, he did not care for the interest of antiquarians or of scientific societies; but his sole aim was to raise without delay a place of arms which might keep Ahmet Bey in check. Provided that the soldiers raised the necessary fortifications and barracks in the shortest time, they might have destroyed all the seven wonders of antiquity.[1030]

The same Wagner following the capture of Constantine:

My friend Berbrugger was busy buying Arabic manuscripts from the plundering soldiers, for the library of Algiers, of which he was the keeper. Some of them were valuable, especially the collection of the laws of the Kadis, and the "History of the City of Constantine." But many of the manuscripts were lost on the return. The soldiers of the train did not care for scientific treasures, and threw some of the heavy book-chests from the waggon, where they stuck in the mud. I hope they were found by the Arabs, and think that they were more in place in the hermitages of the Marabuts, than in the hall of the Algiers Library. There are but very few books in the Regency of Algiers, and therefore they are real treasures. It is rare that a Moorish family has more than one book, and it is the common property of all the family. With the four or five hundred manuscripts carried to Algiers in order to fill the dusty shelves of the library, at least as many Moorish families were deprived of their instruction and comfort.[1031]

Other sources give us further detail of the plunder. It lasted for three days.[1032] The ranks led the way, the officers followed; and, 'as always, the leaders of the army and the staff officers came away with the largest booty', observed Saint-Arnaud cynically.[1033] The Englishman, Temple, who was trying, with little success, to get some manuscripts (as well as an Arab horse), was fascinated by the 'tact and rapidity' with which the native soldiers ransacked the houses.[1034]

Back to Dawson Borrer in Kabylia:

In some of these villages my attention was attracted by vast coffers of walnut wood, handsomely carved, and richly ornamented. These were in the houses, probably, of "tholbas" (learned men); for they were full of books and bundles of manuscripts. The destructive soldiery fired these remarkable cases, tearing the contents to pieces; the streets being in some parts strewed with the torn fragments. One work alone I saved, from a coffer, which was at the time in flames at one end, but hundreds of curious works were sacrificed. The one which fell to me was in a goat-skin bag, tied with a green silk cord and tassel; — it proved to be a Koran. It would have

[1030] M. Wagner: *The Tricolor on the Atlas*, op cit, pp. 89-91.
[1031] Ibid, pp. 339-44.
[1032] W. Blunt: *Desert Hawk*; op cit, p. 112.
[1033] St Arnaud: *Lettres*; in W. Blunt: *Desert Hawk*; op cit, p. 112.
[1034] W. Blunt: *Desert Hawk*; op cit, p. 112.

been better to have secured some of the loose manuscripts, which might perhaps have been written in that ancient Berber dialect spoken by these mountain-tribes. The Koran which I thus obtained is in Arabic, and a note upon one of the fly-leaves of it, inscribed by an ancient proprietor of this holy book, may not be uninteresting perhaps. The following is from a translation* given me in French by a taleb of the chief mosque at Algiers, who offered me two hundred francs for the book; "For," said he, "I do not like so holy a book to be in the hands of a Christian."

*[Translation] "May God pardon in his mercy the writer of these lines, a sincere believer I Praises to the All High God! Praises let there be to Mahomet.... Salutation!

Witness, the brother el Hadji [the writer had performed the pilgrimage to Mecca, and thus gained the title of Hadji or Pilgrim] the undersigned, Sidi Haboulekadem, son of Mahomet-el-Makdaoui, the owner of this book, after having acquired it by lawful purchase of its owner, has instituted a usufruct in favour of him who will make use of it for reading, of him, of his children, and of their children; upon condition that they preserve it with care; of them who abandon it God will demand account; he will demand of them justice. In doing this, the undersigned considers it as a charitable action, and no more than his duty. Hoping that God in his generosity will assist him to accomplish his purpose, he declares himself also responsible for the others (those who inherit it?). Salutation!

Signed by the writer of these lines with his own mortal hand; Mohammed-el-Said-ben-Mohammed-el-Makdaoui; at the date of the commencement of Djoumad, the second of the year? (Missing). God will teach us his goodness, and will guard us against all evil. Amen."

> Christian reader! [Exclaims Borrer] admire the fervid piety, the holy regard for the sacred writings of his prophet, evinced by this worthy Moslem, Sidi Ha-boulekadem. Little did he dream that the cloud of adversity would lower so darkly over those to whom he bequeathed this precious work! Little did he think that the defiling hand of a Christian would be permitted to tear it from its coffer! Many a bitter lamentation has since been poured forth upon the devastated hills of the Beni-Abbes, mourning the loss of this venerable volume. Weeping mothers have sought, amidst the smouldering ruins of their once tranquil homes, their slaughtered children: with no less bitterness of heart have the holy marabbutts sought for the remnants of their sacred writings; so deep is the veneration of the Moslem for his religion.[1035]

The work of destruction was not over yet. Borrer still:

> A short halt was ordered. The lofty and picturesque towers in the villages and their neighbourhood were mined and blown up. It was a fine but sorrowful sight to behold these peculiar and characteristic structures

---

[1035] Dawson Borrer: *Narrative of a campaign against the Kabailes of Algeria;* op cit; pp. 105-6.

successively leap in the air in one vast mass; then come thundering down, blown into a thousand fragments; the mountains echoing and re-echoing the fearful explosion. The atmosphere was laden with clouds of smoke wafted from the numerous villages now enveloped in flame. From one spot nine of these might be counted furiously burning; and the crashing of falling habitations resounded in our ears.[1036]

2. The Removal of 'the Inferior Natives'

European colons [remarks with anger Marshal Randon, French Minister of War and Governor of Algeria] are furious for not obtaining satisfaction to their unjustifiable and imprudent claims, that we are favouring the natives, but the accusation is unjust. All that the military authority is trying to do is to have the right of the natives protected... Neither would the Arabs or the Kabyles accept to be oppressed, and if we did not give them some rights, and tried to crush them all regardless would have thrown all of them into a merciless war which would have compromised colonisation itself. We are often reminded, in regard to Algeria, of the instance of North America, where the Red Skins had been pushed further and further away. This is impossible to implement here with adversaries who are so many and so brave.[1037]

Indeed, the difference between Algeria and North America was that the Algerians, united by their faith fought till the end and from every direction as amply narrated, and, thus, made it impossible to remove them all. France had to compromise, and had to come to peace with some tribes to divide Algerians and in order to keep the colony, and that allowed Algerians to survive in enough numbers until the next fight. Algeria was not North America, a land where it was possible to just come, slay, loot, turn the people into drunkards and casino gamblers and then settle.[1038] The Natives of North America were brave and did fight admirably, but in their diversity, they lacked the unifying element; the Algerians, also in their diversity had: Islam.

Marshal Randon, again:

We are told on and on that colonisation is faster and more effective in America and in Australia. That's true, but the situation is entirely different here. In America and Australia the process is easy: empty spaces are created, and when the newcomers (settlers) arrive and can't find land, they chase away the Indian with gunshots, or they just buy him a bottle of gin. But this is not the case in this country. Wherever you go, it only takes you

---

[1036] Ibid; p. 107.
[1037] A. Rastoul: *Le Marechal Randon;* op cit; pp. 184-185.
[1038] D.E. Stannard: *American Holocaust; The Conquest of the New World;* Oxford University Press; 1992.
W. Howitt: *Colonisation and Christianity*: Longman; London; 1838.
W. Churchill: *A Little Matter of Genocide*; City Lights Books; San Francisco; 1997.

three hours in any direction, before there springs out from every bush a burnous (Muslim traditional dress) and a gun. In America there are 60 White Men for a Red Skin little to fear; in Algeria, at this hour, in 1870, you have 20 Muslims for a Christian, and on top of that a nation that likes the smell of powder, which loves war, and fights it at great will...[1039]

Indeed, it was not the will or desire for the mass removal of Algerians that was lacking, it was the capacity to do it. From the moment the French set foot on Algerian soil in 1830, all they did (besides mass slaying) was to loot, despoil, and starve Algerians with the sole aim of gaining a land without its people. Each and every act as recorded in history, not as told by the vastly crooked French and their servants today, confirms this.

It began from the very moment the French set foot in Algeria. Immediately after the capture of Algiers, 'a flight of human vultures swooped on the country,' says Ageron, trafficking in real estate in the cities, grabbing land and cutting down the woods.[1040] The Sahel or coastal hills of the promontory on which Algiers stands, had been full of estates and country houses whose owners had been chased away through violence of war, intimidation, or were simply slain; as these properties became vacant they were offered to dubious European purchasers who were joined 'by romantically-minded aristocrats.'[1041] Marshal Clauzel himself, an ardent 'colonist' according to the theories of the day, acquired many large properties at low prices, and set out to make the plain of the Mitidja the 'dump for Europe's beggars.'[1042] Cheap passages brought poor immigrants from Spain, the Balearic Islands, Malta and Italy; Parisian labourers and German and Swiss emigrants were brought in as an official measure.[1043] Muslim farming retreated in the face of the first European settlements, and at that time, the European population numbered 25,000, of whom 11,000 were French.[1044]

The government obtained land for the purpose by appropriating the so-called public *habous* or religious property administered by the Islamic authorities for charitable purposes.[1045] In 1843 the *habus* lands were placed under the control of the Domaine (land department) and a decree of 1 October 1844 ended their unalienable character, thus making their acquisition by the settlers possible.[1046]

The French also obtained land by sequestrating the estates of those who had fled the country, and by confiscating lands belonging to tribes that had fought against them. At the same time the state lands of the Turkish *beylik* (common public land)

[1039] A. Rastoul: *Le Marechal Randon*; op cit; p. 186.

[1040] C.R. Ageron: *Modern Algeria;* op cit; p. 24.

[1041] Ibid, pp. 24-5.

[1042] Ibid, p. 25.

[1043] Ibid.

[1044] Ibid.

[1045] Arabic *hubs, hubus,* from a root meaning to lock away'.

[1046] J.M. Abun-Nasr: *A History of the Maghrib*, op cit, p. 248.

together with all uncultivated land, were declared French state property.[1047] Finally, a policy of systematic expropriation began to confine the tribes to ever smaller areas of their traditional territory.[1048] During the governorship of Randon (December 1851-June 1858) the acquisition of tribal lands was carried out within the framework of the policy of cantonment.[1049] This policy meant that the lands which in the governor's view were not needed for the use of a tribe, usually the most fertile, were taken away for the purposes of colonisation.[1050] The tribes were thus left with only a small fraction of what they previously owned, which in many cases impoverished them, besides leading to their eventual destitution.[1051]

The transfer of wealth to Europeans went on simultaneously. Between 1842 and 1845, thirty-five centres were created and 105,000 hectares were allocated to the settlers or *colons.*[1052] Immigrants rushed in: 46,180 arrived in 1845.[1053] By the time of Bugeaud's departure in 1847, the number of settlers implanted in the countryside had reached about 15,000 out of a total European population of 109,400, of whom 47,274 were French.[1054]

The big settler bonanza came in the 1860s, when 4 million hectares of arable land were appropriated by the so-called Senatus Consultus of 1863, a piece of legislation that individualised tribal lands before these passed from powerless Muslim individuals into European hands.[1055] The large land holding companies besides ordinary European farmers benefitted greatly from this measure. Then, a decade later, the 1873 Warnier Law gave new opportunities for confiscation. From then onwards for the following three decades over 1000 farms changed hands every year from Muslim to European owners.[1056] Just as they lost their farms, Muslim farmers became share-croppers *(khammas)*, cultivating lands owned by the Europeans for a fifth of the produce. Others became agricultural labourers.[1057]

Whilst this on its own would play a decisive role in the collapse of any entity, there was yet another measure that broke Algerian society, and that was the war of devastation inflicted by the French. Here, the tactics was similar to that that had its impact in the mass eradication of Native Americans: the utter and systematic destruction of resources basic to Algerian survival. The following accounts by French officers leading the campaign, picked randomly from

---

[1047] C.R. Ageron: *Modern Algeria*, op cit, p. 25.

[1048] Ibid.

[1049] J.M. Abun-Nasr: *A History of the Maghrib*, op cit, p. 249.

[1050] Ibid.

[1051] Ibid.

[1052] The hectare, abbreviation ha., a unit of measurement 100 metres square, is the basic French unit of land. 100 ha. = 1 square kilometre.

[1053] C.R. Ageron: *Modern Algeria*, op cit, p. 26.

[1054] Ibid.

[1055] For good detail, see D. Sari, *La Dépossession des Fellahs 1830-1962.* Algiers, SNED. 1978.

[1056] M. Morsy: *North Africa*, op cit; p. 285.

[1057] J.M. Abun-Nasr: *A History of the Maghrib*, op cit, p. 258.

hundreds similar ones, plentifully illustrate this policy better than any historical narrative. Bugeaud tells us:

> In a week two thousand five hundred quintal measures of corn, and almost as much straw were stored at Mascara (about 1200 quarters).[1058]

Mostaganem, 30 June, 1841.

> If 4000 to 5000quintals of wheat and (5000 quintals of straw are taken into the fort, you may be well assured it will do more to subdue the country than winning ten battles, and then going back to the coast.[1059]

> To find the silos, a chain of soldiers was formed one or two leagues in length who went forward probing the ground with their ramrods, or the points of their swords, until they met with the stone that covered the mouth of the silo level with the ground. Then every man setting to work with his hand-mill, ground the corn to flour, and the cake was very soon kneaded. The silos furnished the corn, the razzias found the meat, and so provisions were not wanted. The men no doubt did not live so well, but they marched faster, and comforted themselves for their bad meals by beating the Arabs.[1060]

Montagnac constantly speaks of his razias, in their tens, maybe hundreds.

1st February 1841 to his friend, De Leuglay:

> We left at six in the evening, and marched until late the following day, we captured a hundred cattle, 200 sheep, few horses and asses, a lot of other wealth, two 'pretty' women, six men, and children.[1061]

Letter to his uncle on 9 Nov 1841:

> We left at night on 24 October looking for a tribe. Early in the morning we reached it. We took hundreds of cattle, 30 individuals, men, women, children... Rain and cold caught up with us. I never felt this cold in Africa.[1062]

Letter from Mascara begun 19 Dec 1841, completed 2 Feb 1842:

> At 2 pm we reach the spot of land full of silos. Earth opens up, and everywhere we uncover the hidden treasures: here it is barley; there wheat, and every other imaginable food. Everyone is busy filling up the sacs; our mounts are fully loaded... We remain the 5th and 6th to feed ourselves people and horses, then at night we return to Mascara. We unload, then on the 8th we are marching in another direction, then come across more silos, and same scenario. Then, we do the same on the 10th, we empty everything that the Arabs have preciously hidden away. On the 14th, we are again on the road, we fall on more treasures, are hampered temporarily by bad weather, but our load is full. We take some rest. On the 21st we pounce on a tribe, which thought itself safe in the difficult terrain,

---

[1058] Count H. Ideville: *Memoirs of Marshal Bugeaud*; op cit; vol 2; p. 28.
[1059] Ibid; p. 29.
[1060] Ibid; p. 31.
[1061] De Montagnac: *Lettres d'un soldat*; op cit; p. 142.
[1062] Ibid; p. 172.

two hours later we had captured 614 cattle, 684 sheep, and hundreds more beast, besides 18 prisoners, men, women, children... You see providence protects us. This sort of attack is quite bizarre. We attack, everyone runs in every direction in panic. When we reach the tents, the people brusquely awakened rush in chaos with their beasts, men, women, children, we fire at these defenceless wretches, then we capture the survivors, men, women, children, beasts, men; meanwhile our soldiers burst into the tents, and take all that falls in their hands: carpets, chickens, weapons, clothes, precious objects, anything, everything, and then, after that, we set everything on fire. From the 19th of December till 17 January we deprive the enemy of beasts, women, children, wheat, barley, everything. The 13th of this month, January, 1842, we march out with elite battalions, again we fall on the enemy, and we capture a lot, by morning, we have 1000 cattle, 3000 sheep and goats, and many other animals. That's our meat problem resolved.

To Mr leuglay 11 February 1842: 4 February at night another raid, then on the 7th, another night march, and early in the morning we fall on the Banu Hashem, we capture 1500 cattle, 2000 sheep, other animals, and also 200 women and children, besides 100 men. And whilst we are doing this, General Bedeau, a barber of quality, chastises another tribe elsewhere, also capturing women, children, and livestock.[1063]

It was the same technique throughout the country from east to west and north to south, and for decades. Dawson Borrer was fighting alongside the French in Kabylia:

One vast sheet of flame crowned the height, which an hour or two before was ornamented with an extensive and opulent village, crowded with inhabitants. It seemed to have been the very emporium of commerce of the Beni-Abbes; fabrics of gunpowder, of arms, of haiks, burnooses, and different stuff were there. The streets boasted of numerous shops of workers in silver, workers in cord, venders of silks and other stuffs, and articles of French or Tunisian manufacture, brought by their traders from Algiers or Tunis. All that was not borne away by the spoilers was devoured by fire, or buried amidst the crashing ruins; and then the hungry flames, vomited forth from the burning habitations, gained the tall corn growing around these villages, and, running swiftly on, wound about and consumed the scattered olive-trees overshadowing it. Fire covered the face of the country, and the heavens were obscured with smoke. The soldiers pronounced the country "joliment nettoye' (beautifully cleansed); and I heard two ruffians, after the sacking was over, relating, with great gusto, how many young girls had been burnt in one house, after being abused by their brutal comrades and themselves. They pronounced that house

---

[1063] Ibid; pp. 189-96.

"joliment nettoye" also. Indeed it was a very favourite phrase with them.[1064]

Dawson Borrer, again:

How pleasing the landscape overlooked by these Kabyle cities! — the fertile valley dividing them covered with fine crops of corn, the ground clean, and beautifully cultivated. Innumerable and gigantic olive-trees, some isolated, others clumped together, all most scientifically grafted by their owners, and producing the finest fruit, vary the low-lands, and adorn the slopes of the surrounding hills. The swift stream of the Oued-Mansour, meandering in its course to the foot of the bounding heights on either side, bears fertility upon its generous waters equally to all parts of the vale. The whole scene presents a glorious triumph of nature and of industry.[1065]

Glad enough were the troops to find themselves within a hostile territory. The foragers sallied forth armed; each, bearing his sickle and his sack, fell with hearty good-will upon the unripe crop of wheat for the consumption of the camp. Groups of the Beni-Yala gazed from the neighbouring heights, — the fierce blood boiling in their veins;

'Allah! Allah! Vengeance!' swells the cry. And many an eye glares with rage and hatred beneath the covers of the surrounding brush-wood, watching the movements of the detested "Roumis," lading their horses and mules with the fruit of Moslem toil and industry.[1066]

It is impossible to put the exact figure of all the livestock and other farm products looted and destroyed by the French. It is literally all green belts, most orchards, most palm and olive trees, besides all corn fields which were looted and then destroyed by the French. Regarding livestock, the minimum estimates we have is a total of 18 million sheep, 3.5 million cattle, and one million camels killed between 1830 and 1845.[1067] The same figure can be extrapolated for the period 1846-1871.

And as if that was not enough, the spoliation of Algerians went on in a variety of other means especially in the wake of the various uprisings. Algerians were ruined by the various war indemnities and exorbitant taxes. In the wake of the 1870-1 uprising, a war indemnity of 36.5 million Francs was imposed on 298 peasant communities; a fine that ruined them.[1068] It is estimated that seventy per cent of the total capital of the peoples involved in the rising was levied from them in the form of war indemnity or for freeing their lands from sequestration.[1069] Less than one—third of the sixty-three million francs paid by the Muslims in repurchasing their lands went to the French colons supposedly 'victims of the

---

[1064] Dawson Borrer: *Narrative of a campaign against the Kabailes of Algeria;* op cit; pp. 113.
[1065] Ibid; p. 71.
[1066] Ibid; p. 64.
[1067] N. Abdi quoted in Louis Blin: *L'Algerie du Sahara au Sahel*, l'Harmattan, Paris, 1990; p. 68.
[1068] M. Morsy: *North Africa*; op cit; p. 159.
[1069] J.M. Abun Nasr: *Histoire*; op cit; 255.

rebellion,' whilst the rest financed expanding colonisation.[1070] Even Kabyles who were in German prisons caught fighting for France, and those still in French army ranks had to plead their cases to have their olive trees returned. 500,000 ha were taken by the French, and just in order to buy back some of their lands not wanted by Europeans, Algerians had to pay 27 million Francs.[1071]

To further ruin Algerians into starvation, the French took whatever little they had been left with. Apart from the tax on the soil itself, the native paid on the number and nature of his flocks. The Zekkat as this imposition is named, exacted four francs for a camel, three francs for a cow, while sheep and goats contributed twenty and fifteen centimes respectively.[1072] In Kabylia another imposition, called the Lezmay remained in force. This was a kind of poll-tax, which in the south usually fell upon the palm trees instead of upon the owner himself.[1073]

In a series of articles of then, the *Temps* the correspondent held: "it is unjust that a native should be taxed to the extent of fifty or sixty francs on the little field he sows, while the European or Jewish proprietor of hundreds and sometimes thousands of hectares pays nothing whatever. According to our principles, it is unjust that the section of the population which furnishes the greater part of the budget receipts should not obtain an equivalent share in their allocation. And as we do not keep them in their primitive ignorance, the natives are becoming more and more alive to this inequality. For this reason, we repeat, it is useless to educate the native as long as we maintain this reign of oppression. If we continue to do so without mending our fiscal ways, a catastrophe of some sort will be the inevitable end."[1074]

To give an idea, the settlers who pleaded poverty did not pay taxes but still spent in one year 28,508,000 francs on 2,974 automobiles, as the customs returns testify, whilst the land-tax was crushing out of existence Algerian peasants.[1075] What the colonial excessive tax system meant to do was to force Algerians to sell everything they still owned until in the end they had nothing to own, and even worse, nothing to live on.

Resulting from their utter destitution, Algerians starved to death in huge numbers. The early accounts of starvation can be found in the works of the participants in the war such as here Dawson Borrer writing in 1848:

> Many of these blighted beings, who thus descend like vultures to glean what may have been left by the horses of a passing troop of cavalry, were once proprietors, perhaps, of that very soil upon which they now gather the husks with fear and trembling. Many of them are members of tribes that have not only bowed to, but fought for, their invaders, who, in return,

---

[1070] Ibid.
[1071] A. Rambaud: L'Insurrection Algerienne de 1871; *Extraits de la Nouvelle Revue*; Oct-Nov 1891; p. 53.
[1072] R. Devereux: *Aspects of Algeria*; London; J.M. Dent and Sons; 1912; p. 146.
[1073] Ibid.
[1074] Ibid; 145.
[1075] Ibid.

have deprived them of their lands, in many instances without indemnity; reducing them thus to utter starvation, or forcing them to retire to more remote parts, where the arms of the "Christian civilisers of North Africa" do not yet prevail.[1076]

Ravages caused by war, made worse by recurrent epidemics, such as cholera, which decimated great numbers in 1849 and in 1868, caused population to fall considerably. In just three years, 1867-9, half a million Algerians would die, which at the time represented about one sixth of the population.[1077] Add the ravages inflicted in combat and mass killings in the wake of fighting. In the wars of 1839-1847, over ten percent of the population of Muslim Algerians, 300,000 people, died.[1078] Countless more hundreds of thousands died in further clashes and subsequent waves of repression. Some sources make the claim that native Algerian population fell from 10 millions in 1830 to 2.1 millions in 1872.[1079] Whilst this figure is certainly excessive, Algerians continued to die in ever larger numbers such as in the Great famines of 1893 and 1897.[1080] And whilst, indeed, the first figure was certainly too high, there is ample ground to believe that which states that between 8 and 10 millions died following armed conflict, hunger and diseases between 1830 and 1962.[1081] This figure is further substantiated by the following comparison: in 1800, that is thirty years before the French entry, the population of Algeria was estimated at around 4 millions; that of Egypt between 3-4 millions; by 1890, Algeria had 4.1 millions whilst Egypt had 10 millions; in 1920: Algeria's population had risen to 4.9 millions, whilst Egypt in 1927 had 14 millions.[1082] Statistical evidence of Algerian demographic trend up to the late 1880s seemed to show that the Algerians might become extinct.[1083]

As he marched through the country in Kabylia, Clemens Lamping remarked:

> The owners, of course, were nowhere to be found. In former days this tract of country must have been thickly peopled, judging from the cemeteries which we saw from time to time.[1084]

As the Algerians were being wiped out, they were being replaced by 'a better stock of Europeans.' Here is how Montagnac himself describes these better people:

> Has anybody got any idea of the chaos and waste and robberies. Everyone speculates about everything, everyone steals without restraint, the state's funds are stolen, dilapidated, and in France the media speaks about this flourishing colony, vast projects of development, the superb projects, the

---

[1076] Dawson Borrer: *Narrative of a campaign against the Kabailes of Algeria*; op cit; p. 23.
[1077] H. Alleg et al: *La Guerre d'Algerie*; op cit, p. 80.
[1078] R. Danziger: *Abd al Kader*; op cit; p. xi.
[1079] In L. Blin: *l'Algerie du Sahara*; op cit, p. 68.
[1080] J.M. Abun-Nasr: *A History of the Maghrib*, op cit, p. 258.
[1081] M. Lacheraf, in L. Blin: *L'Algerie*; op cit; note 3; p. 112.
[1082] M. Morsy: *North Africa*; op cit; p. 9.
[1083] Ibid; pp. 287-8.
[1084] Clemens Lamping: *The French in Algiers. Soldiers of the Foreign Legion*; p. 50.

claims of a brilliant future, the probity of the military and civilian authorities... None of that. Nothing; nothing other than a crowd of bankrupt men from throughout the world; the freed criminals, the escaped criminals, the merchants of liquor, café owners and other supposed traders speculating about everything; scum of all sorts, exploiting every single avenue that could lend itself to the imagination, a gathering from hell... These are the colons who thrive in this poor Africa.[1085]

It was to these that Algerian wealth passed. They were granted lands that had been expropriated from their native Algerian owners, who had been either slain, or pushed onto poorer or arid and semi arid lands to eke a living.[1086] Houses were built, roads and infrastructure were erected, and many businesses and services were set up, but they all went to these settlers and to a tiny minority of subservient indigenous classes who assisted colonial rule. Whilst these communities thrived, colonialist elites insisted that the remaining Algerians be 'driven into the desert,' their elimination part of a natural law which led to the 'disappearance of backward peoples.'[1087]

The Algerians, unlike the American natives survived for the reasons seen above. But the French work to civilise the country was not entirely done yet. There was still another act.

*****

The 'Civilised' French, and 'Barbarian' Algerians

Whenever we read of the past or the present, we always come across the basic line: civilised Frenchman (or other Westerners,) and barbaric Algerians (or other Muslims). Reality, though, shows us a different picture. We will not talk of medieval Muslim brilliance and Western barbarism, nor would we speak of the Crusades, the Catholic-Protestant wars, the burning of 'heretics,' of Jews, of women, the slave trade, the World Wars, the sponsoring of murderous military coups in Central and South Americas and today in the Muslim world, the Viet Nam war, and many other things which highlight the civilised and humane nature of Western Christianity. Let's stay focused on Algeria, and just a couple of notes.

It was common for men fighting for the French to be gratified with honours in infamous war deeds. One officer presented 500 pairs of `Arab ears' to be rewarded by the government of the King with 50,000 francs and the Legion d'Honneur for services rendered.[1088] Wherever the French decided to bring back peace, order and civilisation, it was the same story; the French just slew en masse and burnt all. When they went on to submit the Saharan oases (Za'atcha in 1849, Nara in 1850, and Ouargla in 1852), palm groves were cut down, and towns and cities were razed to the ground by gun and canon fire; corpses made mounts and filled wells.[1089]

[1085] De Montagnac: *Lettres d'un soldat*; Librairie Plon Paris; 1885; p. 13.
[1086] D. Sari: *La Depossession des Fellahs 1830-1962;* SNED, Algiers; 1978.
[1087] J Abun Nasr: *A History;* op cit; pp. 287-8.
[1088] H. Alleg et al: *La Guerre d'Algerie*, op cit; p. 68.
[1089] Paul Gaffarel: *L'Algerie: Histoire, Conquete et Colonisation*, H. Alleg et al: *La Guerre d'Algerie*, op cit; p. 77.

The 'barbarian' Algerians, however, seemed to have behaved altogether differently. A book by Louis Rinn on the 1870-1 uprising constantly stresses the fact, that even at the height of bitter fighting, when no quarter was given to Algerians, yet the latter, despite some excesses, showed a humanity beyond equal.[1090] Their fighting remained, as Rambaud puts it, untainted by atrocities which 'Islamic morality, just as ours rejects.'[1091] Maybe on the last point Rambaud got it somehow wrong, for French armies burnt and killed without restraint as plentifully highlighted. During that same uprising, from Greater Kabylia, to M'sila, to the Aures, in Batna, to Bordj Bou Arreridj, countless Algerians, whether of high status, or ordinary people, protected Europeans being threatened by more extreme elements, and yet, many of these who protected the French, with a few exceptions, later on faced French wrath.[1092] Rambaud cites the names of sheiks and scholars like al Hadj ben Dahman or Si Mouna, who saved French lives, and were subsequently condemned to death by French courts.[1093]

The French presented their enterprise as a civilising deed, and their killings as measures for pacifying the country and removing fanatical Muslims. The following incident expresses their sentiments:

> When Emir Abd al-Kader freeing his French prisoners said to them: I have nothing to feed you; I cannot kill you, thus I send you back home....' The prisoners full of admiration for the Emir, according to General St Arnaud: 'had their minds diseased, and had been brainwashed.'[1094]

3. Bringing Back the Christian Heritage

From the onset of the colonial onslaught, Mosques and other symbols of Islam were the first targets for removal. Following the French entry, Duc of Rovigo took the decision to turn a Muslim mosque, the beautiful Ketshawa, into a Church.[1095] When the Algerians protested that this was in breach of the conventions signed when Algiers capitulated in 1830, Rovigo declared he would cut off the heads of those who opposed his will and would, if necessary, storm the building.[1096] He further ordered that after the mosque had been occupied, a cross and the French flag were to be hoisted at the top of the minaret and guns were to fire a salute.[1097] Ketshawa was solemnly opened as a Catholic church on Christmas Day 1832.[1098] Many other mosques were likewise turned into churches, including the Ali Bitchin Mosque which became Our Lady of Victory, and the Kasbah Berradji Mosque which became the Church of the Holy Cross.[1099] On 6 January 1839, Marshal Valee and Admiral de Bougainville attended together with the military

---

[1090] L. Rinn: *Histoire de l'Insurrection de 1871 en Algerie;* Alger, Librairie Adolphe Jourdan; 1891.
[1091] A. Rambaud: L'Insurrection Algerienne de 1871; op cit; p. 61.
[1092] Ibid.
[1093] Ibid; p. 60.
[1094] General St Arnaud in a letter of 16 May 1842.
[1095] M. Morsy: *North Africa*; op cit; p. 134.
[1096] Ibid.
[1097] Ibid.
[1098] Ibid.
[1099] Ibid; p. 160.

and civilian dignitaries the installation of Monseignor Antoine Dupuch, named on 9 August, 1838 Bishop of Algiers by Pope Gregory XVI.[1100] Until the arrival of this first prelate in North Africa since St Augustine (354-430), the Church in Algeria was only represented by four priests and few nuns of the Order of St Joseph de l'Apparition.[1101] Monseignor Dupuch could not refrain from shedding tears of joy on his first visit of the Ketchawa, this act symbolising 'the return of Christianity to the land of Algeria.'[1102]

Besides the reduction of the number of mosques throughout the country, the religious elites were placed under French administration, now their appointment, or dismissal, or elevation, even, being carried at the pleasure of the Frenchmen with power over them.[1103]

Many other measures were put in place to promote as many religious divisions within the community as possible. The creation or encouragement of deviant practices of Islam was the norm. In 1884 Louis Rinn, director of the department of native affairs, went to the extent of proposing that the Tijaniyya order should be made something of a national church for Algeria, and its head appointed Sheikh al-Islam of the country in order 'to counter the religious propaganda of the Ottoman Sheikh al-Islam.'[1104]

Louis Rinn, as per his nature, was 'a moderate.' For others, there were more radical solutions. Henry de Sarrauton insisted:

> To assimilate the indigenous population, the influence of the Quran must be uprooted and the people converted to Christianity. However, experience shows that the Muslim never converts from his own free will. For centuries missionaries have wasted their time and efforts trying to convert Muslim countries. Force must be used. Can we imagine then that the tolerant and freethinking French government sets up an inquisition as did King Ferdinand after the conquest of Grenada? Clearly it is impossible. Assimilation is therefore a fantasy. This people must be driven back, step by step, and replaced gradually and systematically by a French population. This is the only way for Algeria to become truly French.[1105]

Muslim education was particularly targeted by French policy. Morsy notes how:

> By an all-encompassing policy affecting the very nature of Algerian personality, just as in neighbouring Tunisia, the Europeans sought to break down the indigenous population's personality by an onslaught on religion,

---

[1100] G. Fleury: *Comment l'Algerie*; op cit; p. 221.
[1101] Ibid.
[1102] Ibid.
[1103] M. Morsy: *North Africa*; op cit; p. 287.
[1104] J.M. Abun-Nasr: *A History of the Maghrib*, op cit, p. 257.
[1105] Henry de Sarrauton: La Question Algerienne; Oran; 1891; cited by J. Borge and N. Viasnoff: *Archives de l'Algerie*; editions Michel Tinckvel; Paris; 1995; p. 21.

through the action of the Catholic Church, and through control of education.[1106]

Out of thirty-six Franco-Arab primary schools operating in Algeria in 1870, only sixteen remained in 1882 to give instruction to Muslim children.[1107] Even then it was to very small numbers. Contacts of the Algerian Muslims with other Muslim countries were also made increasingly harder through restrictions on travel, whilst obstacles were placed in the way of the pilgrimage to Makkah on 'safety grounds'.[1108] Pressure was also put on the administration to close the three madrasas where students were trained in Islamic law.[1109] The rural zawiyas, little in size and in scope, were allowed to maintain a small degree of literacy, a learning that was by its very nature folkloric in most instances. No sooner did any zawiyas break through the cordon of safety, the French reaction was swift, and they were generally closed as they were seen as:

'Hotbeds of fanaticism, local haunts of Carbonaris dressed in ganduras.'[1110]

Everywhere one of the main alternatives to Muslim education was provided by new missionary organisations. Christian religious brotherhoods were authorised in 1858, and soon counted 1400 pupils. The Trinitarian Sisterhood in the Oran region took care of hospitals and also had schools frequented by 2,300 pupils.[1111] The Sisters of Christian Doctrine in the Algiers and Constantine provinces had 4,000 pupils, whilst the Daughters of Charity, established in the hospitals of Algiers and Constantine, gave instruction to 2,500 children.[1112]

Other than the various religious colleges, there were the multiple institutions set up for orphans. The 'Orphelinats' of Ben Aknoun and Boufarik, with between 1000 and 1200 children, were run by Jesuits who were also authorised to open similar institutions in Constantine and Oran provinces. Orphelinats were also set up for young women by the Sisters of the Christian Doctrine in Bone, by the Daughters of Charity of Algiers, and by the Trinitarians in Miserghin in the Oran region. All in all, these organisations numbered over a hundred.[1113]

The French vision was that:

> The Algerians would love their conquerors for their gentleness and their justice... and religion itself would weave a crown for the Monarch who will bring the sacred fire of Christianity with civilisation to the country of Augustine and Cyprian.[1114]

This ultimate aim to bring back Algeria to the fold of Christianity is stated here by Antoine Salles summing up the work of Cardinal Lavigerie:

[1106] M. Morsy: *North Africa*; op cit; pp. 290-1.
[1107] J.M. Abun-Nasr: *A History of the Maghrib*, op cit, p. 257.
[1108] M. Morsy: *North Africa*; op cit; p. 160.
[1109] Ibid. p. 287.
[1110] Ibid.
[1111] A. Rastoul: *Le Marechal Randon*; op cit; p. 197.
[1112] Ibid.
[1113] Ibid; p. 198.
[1114] N. Daniel: *Islam, Europe,* op cit; p. 329.

> He (Cardinal Lavigerie) sought Algeria to escape the yoke of Islam, which for centuries, suffocated its rise and prosperity, but on condition that it placed itself under the protection of France once its freedom was secured. This is a remarkable programme to turn Christian and to turn French this land which was according to the Cardinal an extension of France.[1115]

Cardinal Lavigerie, Archbishop of Algiers in 1867, gave expression to the views which the settlers did not utter in public. He asserted that conversion to Christianity was the only way the Muslims

> Could be converted from barbarism, and was therefore the only humane policy the French government could follow in Algeria.[1116]

He also attacked the military regime which he held responsible for preventing the assimilation and conversion of the Muslims. He arrived when Algeria was hit by cholera and drought, which took their heaviest toll in 1868 when an estimated 300,000 Algerians perished.[1117] The settler community suffered very little from these calamities because they had greater economic reserves than the Muslims.[1118] In this period of distress Lavigerie collected 1753 Muslim orphans in charitable religious foundations with the express purpose of converting them to Christianity, and by rejecting all demands to hand them over to their relatives.[1119] Lavigerie developed his actions with the support of the Vatican, and attempted to establish the Catholic Church on an official North-African-wide basis.[1120] He set up establishments of the White Fathers and Missionary Sisters of Africa, orphanages and dispensaries, particularly in the Kabylie region where a divide-and-rule policy was at work, according to which Arabs and Berbers bore intense hatred for each other.[1121] Lavigerie claimed that:

> The Berbers had been Christians in antiquity, and his mission was to bring them back to the fold.[1122]

[1115] A. Salles: Le Cardinal Lavigerie et l'Influence Francaise en Afrique, Lyon, 1893, cited in N. Daniel, *Islam, Europe*, op cit; p. 332.

[1116] J.M. Abun-Nasr: *A History of the Maghrib*, op cit, p. 253.

[1117] Ibid.

[1118] Ibid.

[1119] Ibid.

[1120] M. Morsy: *North Africa*, op cit; p. 164.

[1121] Ibid; p. 162.

[1122] Ibid.

French female Missionaries feeding starved Algerians. Note the meekness in the French soldiers eyes; the submissiveness of the Arab to the front left; the vicious look on the other Arab back left (how he looks at the child with the loaf of bread), and the most wonderful kindly smile on the missionary to the right.

Westerners, however condescending towards the natives, have never failed to depict some native groups less inferior than others, especially in the midst of colonial wars. Hence in 1847, in Daumas and Fabar's book on *La Grande Kabylie*, the white Kabyles (as opposed to the swarthy Arabs of course), with blue eyes and red hair, 'en partie germain d'origine' (partly German in origin) was an accepted truth, as was 'the implacable hatred between Arabs and Berbers.'[1123] It was believed that if the French respected Kabyle freedom in Algeria they would be welcomed 'as liberators from their Turkish and Arab oppressors.'[1124] Ageron, who discusses this Kabyle myth, describes its elaboration between 1840 and 1857 and considers that it was deliberately reinforced between 1860 and 1870 for political and propaganda purposes and that it was triumphant after 1870.[1125] This pro-Kabyle stand was only transient, aimed for the usual Western strategy: to split the natives they were colonising. In truth, for French colonialists, all natives were the same when standing in the way of the great French scheme of turning Algeria into a second America. Raymond Peyronnet thus held:

> The Berbers are masters among themselves, masters of their future, but they are masters of disorder, in foolishness and incapable of building anything solid and lasting. No administrative ranks, no social protection, no security. Political anarchy is at its apogee.[1126]

For Stephane Gsell:

> France is a country of harmony and equilibrium. It is not the same in Barbary.... (The aim is) to terminate with the blunt political colonial solution for, in their terms, the troublesome Berber population and Berber

---

[1123] See J. Lecas et J.C. Vatin: *l'Algerie des antropologues*; pp. 104 ffwd
[1124] A. Thomson: *Barbary*; op cit; p. 109.
[1125] C.R. Ageron: *Les Algeriens Musulmans et la France*; Paris; 1968; p. 267.
[1126] R. Peyronnet: *Le Problem Nord Africain*; Paris; 1924; in W.E. Kaegi: *Muslim Expansion and Byzantine Collapse in North Africa*; Cambridge University Press; 2010, p. 22.

question: the peaceful and progressive pushing back that the superior races, alone, know how to accomplish by their system of colonization.[1127]

Hain puts it more bluntly, there is:

No difference between Arab and Kabyles, both equally incapable of civilisation and worthy of extermination.[1128]

He states:

It is ridiculous to think of civilising the inhabitants of the conquered territory, for they are incapable of any improvement; they must be cleared off the land to make the way for French colonists.[1129]

For him, Algerians have reached the level (and are promised the fate of) the American Indians.[1130] Bory de Saint Vincent in his report for the War Ministry in 1838, expresses similar contempt for all the inhabitants of Algeria whom he considers without discrimination as savages.[1131] And the French hatred for the Berbers became boundless later on in the 1870-1871 uprising against the French, which saw Berber and Arab fight side by side, including against evangelisation, which led to the colonial view that

The Kabyle, like the Arab, belongs to the race of the jackal, which only appears resigned and can never be tamed.[1132]

The Failure of a Project

According to Dr Bodichon, one of the French theorists of colonisation:

It matters little that France in her political conduct goes beyond the limits of common morality at times; the essential thing is that she establishes a lasting colony and that, later, she brings European civilisation to these barbaric countries. When a project which is to the advantage of all humanity is to be carried out, the shortest path is the best. Now, it is certain that the shortest path is terror. Without violating the laws of morality, or international jurisprudence, we can fight our African enemies by powder and fire, joined by famine, internal division, war between Arabs and Kabyles, between the tribes of the Tell and those of the Sahara, by

---

[1127] S. Gsell: Histoire Ancienne de l'Afrique du Nord, 8 vols, Paris, 1972, reprints of 3rd edition; originally published 1914, 1928, Onnasbruck; 1: 25. "La France est un pays d'harmonie et d'equilibre. Il n'est pas de meme de la Berberie." Gsell 1972: 1: 39-
G. Medina: Le Christianisme dans le Nord de l'Afrique avant l'Islam; RT 8, 1901; pp. 7-19; 156-168; 293-317; 407-427; at 418-25; first quotation on Byzantines: p. 425, second quotation from p. 427, '"le refoulement pacifique et progressif que les races superieures savant, seules, effectuer par leur system de colonization. All in W.E. Kaegi: *Muslim Expansion and Byzantine Collapse*, op cit; p. 20.
[1128] V.A. Hain: *A La Nation. Sur Alger*; Paris; 1832; pp. 28-33.
[1129] Ibid; pp. 78; 94.
[1130] In A. Thomson: *Barbary*; op cit; p. 101.
[1131] *Note sur la commission exploratrice et scientifique d'Algerie*; 16th October 1838; p. 13.
See: Henry Alleg et al: *La Guerre d'Algerie*. C. Ageron: *Modern Algeria*.
[1132] Louis Vignon, la France en Algerie, 1893; in M. Morsy: *North Africa 1800-1900;* op cit; p. 163.

brandy, corruption and disorganisation. That is the easiest thing in the world to do.[1133]

This, as this work has amply shown, was precisely what France did.

However, as Wagner remarks:

> The sober and frugal habits of that people, also an unchanged feature of their ancestors, is a great hindrance in the way of civilization; it makes their improvement as difficult as their expulsion or destruction. The North American red men were defeated and driven from the country of their fathers by the "fire-water;" wherever those savages tasted spirits, they were-enslaved by them, and lost both energy and freedom. But such means are of no avail with the Arabs.... Spirits never become necessities with them, and all the remembrance of the merriment caused by wine is not able to wrest out a boojoo from their pocket. I never saw a drunken Arab during all my stay in Africa. Only milk and water are tasted in the encampments, and yet this people is not inferior to any other, either in bodily strength or mental energy.[1134]

[1133] Cited in C.H. Favrod: *Le FLN et l'Algerie;* Paris; Plon; 1962; p. 31.
[1134] M. Wagner: *The Tricolor on the Atlas*, op cit; pp. 144-5.

CONCLUDING WORDS

This author does not have access to archives and primary sources dealing with the second phase of French colonial history in Algeria (1872-1962). He therefore cannot deal with that phase, for to write on such a phase by relying on secondary sources is not feasible.

Others will have to deal with the second half; they also have the duty to improve this work, for this author, regardless of whatever he has done, cannot be said to have done the perfect job.

The necessity for both tasks is very simple: nations without history have no souls; nations without knowledge of their history cannot build the future.

Grave challenge will come when generations of the future will seek to know and to build. As things stand today, in 2017-18, they will find not a jot except the crooked. On the crooked they will try but will fail to build just as they have failed since 1962.

Until the day Algerians know their history, and feel proud of how great their forefathers fought from 1830 until 1962, and faithful to the memory of such greats they build a great nation, all they will do will be to perform some native dance, gory and pathetic at once, to the tune of Mother France.

SELECT BIBLIOGRAPHY

Abd al-Qadir: *Tuhfat al-Za'ir fi Tarikh al-Jaza'ir wa-al-Amir Abd al-Qadir*, Beirut, 2nd ed., 1964.

J.M. Abun-Nasr: *A History of the Maghrib*, Cambridge University Press, 1971.

C.R. Ageron: *Modern Algeria*, tr., by M. Brett, Hurst and Company, London, 1990.

C.R. Ageron: *Histoire de l'Algerie Contemporaine;* Presses Universitaires de France, Paris, 1964.

H. Alleg; J. de Bonis, H.J. Douzon, J. Freire, P. Haudiquet: *La Guerre d'Algerie;* 3 vols, Temps Actuels; Paris, 1981.

P. Bernard and F Redon: *Histoire, Colonisation, Geographie et Administration de l'Algerie*, Librairie Adolphe Jourdan; Algiers, 1906.

Louis Blin: *l'Algerie du Sahara au Sahel*, L'Harmattan, Paris, 1990.

W. Blunt: *Desert Hawk*; Methuen & Co. Ltd; London; 1947.

Dawson Borrer: *Narrative of a campaign against the Kabailes of Algeria;* Spottiswoode and Shaw, London, 1848.

D. Brahimi: *Opinions et regards des Europeens sur le Maghreb aux 17em et 18em Siecles*; SNED; Algiers; 1978.

General Boyer to Minister of War, Oran, 25 April 1832, no. 2984, AHG: H-13.

Buchanan: *Memoir of the Expediency of an Ecclesiastical Establishment for India;* London; 1805.

C.H. Churchill: *The Life of Abd Al Kader*, Chapman and Hall, London, 1867.

J.A. Clancy Smith: *Rebel and Saint*, University of California Press; 1994.

J.J. Cook: The Maghrib through French Eyes; 1880-1929; in *Through Foreign Eyes;* edited by A.A. Heggoy; University Press of America; 1982; pp. 57-92.

R. Danziger: *Abd Al-Qadir and the Algerians*; Holmes and Meier Publishers; New York; London; 1977.

R. Devereux: *Aspects of Algeria*; London; J.M. Dent and Sons; 1912.

A. Dournon: Constantine sous les Turcs d'Apres Salah al-Antari; in *RSAC*; 1928-29; Constantine, 1930; pp. 61-178.

M. Emerit: les Memoires d'Ahmed Bey de Constantine, *Revue Africaine*, 1er et 2em trimester; 1949; pp. 71-125.

G. Esquer: Correspondence du general Voirol; Voirol au MG., 14 September 1833; Paris, 1924.

G. Esquer: *Correspondence du Duc de Rovigo*, 1831-1833; t1. Algiers, 1914; T2. Algiers, 1920; T3: Algiers, 1921; t.4 Algiers, 1924. T.1; p. 43; 1st January 1832.

F. Fanon: *Les Damnés de la Terre,* Editions ENAG, Alger, 1987.

G. Fisher: *The Barbary Legend;* Oxford; 1957.

G. Fleury: *Comment l'Algerie Devint Francaise*; Perrin, Paris, 2004.

P. Gaffarel: *L'Algerie, Histoire, Conquete et Colonisation*, ed. Firmin Didot, 1883.

P. Gaffarel: *Lectures Geographiques et Historiques sur l'Algerie et les Colonies Francaises*; Garniers Freres; Paris; 1886.

A.A. Heggoy ed., *Through Foreign Eyes;* ed, University Press of America; 1982.

Le Comte d'Herisson: *La Chasse a l'Homme, Guerre d'Algerie*; Paul Ollendorff; Paris; 1891.

W. Howitt: *Colonisation and Christianity*: Longman; London; 1838.

Count H. Ideville: *Memoirs of Marshal Bugeaud from his Private Correspondence and Original Documents*; 2 vols; edited from French by C.M. Yonge; Hurst and Blackett; London, 1884.

C.A. Julien: *History of North Africa;* tr., from French by J. Petrie; Routledge & Kegan Paul; London; 1970.

C. A. Julien: *Histoire de l'Algerie Contemporaine*, 1827-1871; Presses Universitaires de France, 1964.

Y. Lacoste, A. Noushi, and A. Prennant: *L'Algerie: Passe, Present*; Editions Sociales; Paris; 1960.

Clemens Lamping: *The French in Algiers. Soldiers of the Foreign Legion; Prisoners of Abd el Kader;* tr. from German and French by Lady Duff Gordon, London; 1855.

L. March Phillips: *In the Desert, the Hinterlands of Algiers*; Edward Arnold; London; 1909

Colonel L. Francois de Montagnac: *Lettres d'un Soldat*; Paris; 1885.

M. Morsy: *North Africa 1800-1900;* Longman; London; 1984.

M.A. Nettement: *Histoire de la Conquete d'Alger;* Jacques Lecoffre; Paris; 1856.

A. Noushi: *Enquete sur le Niveau de Vie des Populations Rurales Constantinoises de la Conquete jusqu'a 1919*; Tunis, 1961.

A. Rambaud: L'Insurrection Algerienne de 1871; *Extraits de la Nouvelle Revue*; Oct-Nov 1891.

A. Rastoul: *Le Marechal Randon; D'apres ses Memoirs et Documents Inedits*; Firmin Didot; Paris; 1890.

L. Rinn: *Histoire de l'Insurrection de 1871 en Algerie*; Alger, Librairie Adolphe Jourdan; 1891.

C. De Rotalier: *Histoire d'Alger*; Chez Paulin, Paris; 1841.

St Arnaud: Lettres de St Arnaud; 2 vols; Michel Levy; Paris; 1855.

D. Sari: *La Depossession des Fellahs 1830-1962;* Algiers; SNED; 1978.

W. Shaller: *Sketches of Algiers*; Boston; 1826.

E. Siberry: *The New Crusaders*; Ashgate: Aldershot; 2000.

A.G. Slama: *La Guerre d'Algerie*, Decouvertes, Paris, 1996.

B. Stora: *Histoire de la Guerre d'Algerie*, La Decouverte, Paris, 1993.

A. Temimi: *Le Beylik de Constantine et Hadj Ahmed Bey (1830-1837), Revue d'Histoire Maghrebine*, Vol 1, Tunis, 1978.

A. Temimi: Trois letters de Hadj Ahmed Bey de Constantine a la Sublime Porte, in *ROMM*; No 3; Aix, 1968; pp. 132-55.

A. Thomson: *Barbary and Enlightenment:* Brill; Leiden; 1987.

L. Valensi: *Le Maghreb avant la Prise d'Alger;* Paris; 1969.

M. Wagner: *The Tricolor on the Atlas,* London; T. Nelson and Sons, 1854.

Printed in Great Britain
by Amazon